AF560317

Poverty in India

A Great Stumbling Block to Development

Measurement and Strategies for Poverty Eradication

Poverty in India

A Great Stumbling Block to Development Measurement and Strategies for Poverty Eradication

Dr. Tapan Kumar Shandilya
Vice-Chancellor
Nalanda Open University, Patna
(Bihar)

Dr. Samir Kumar
M.A. (Gold Medalist), P.G.D.B.M., Ph.D.
Usha Martin Academy
Jamshedpur (Jharkhand)

Dr. Shakeel Ahmad Khan
M.A., Ph.D.
Assistant Professor of Economics
Oriental College, Patna (Bihar)

REGAL PUBLICATIONS
New Delhi - 110 027

POVERTY IN INDIA
A Great Stumbling Block to Development
Measurement and Strategies for Poverty Eradication

ISBN 978-81-8484-316-3

Typeset by
RAHUL COMPOSERS
New Highway Apartments, Lakshmi Niwas
760, Pocket-D, Lok Nayak Puram, New Delhi - 110 041

Printed in India at
MAYUR ENTERPRISES
WZ Plot No. 3, Gujjar Market, Tihar Village, New Delhi - 110 018

Published by
REGAL PUBLICATIONS
F-159, Rajouri Garden, New Delhi - 110 027
Phone : 45546396, 25435369
E-mail : regalbookspub@yahoo.com, regaldeepbooks@yahoo.com

Contents

India has
predicament
including the
to be a basis
we cannot
and the peo
first time th
nothing div
outcome of
remedied.
amorphous
thus come to
throughout th

Reduc
increment is
poverty. The
a help rather
country. In
as industry
constrained
ownership

The
Poverty Alle
Poverty is n
social probl
will. A soci
certain power

Preface

India has moved a long way from its nineteenth century predicament, as indicated by her remarkable gains in many fields, including the GNP and industrialization. Surely, these could prove to be a basis for hope for the common man for a decent living. But we cannot ignore such facts as the increasing gap between the rich and the poor, despite overall developments in the country. For the first time the realization dawned on the poor people that there was nothing divine about poverty that it was man-made, that it was the outcome of inadequately rewarded efforts and that it could be remedied. This realization has acted like a catalyst fusing the amorphous aspirations of the masses into a definite want. Poverty has thus come to possess the subjective dimension which it lacked throughout the centuries.

Reduction of inequality of income, wealth and unearned increment is, to a certain extent, closely connected with reduction in poverty. The proponents of equality contend that greater equality is a help rather than a hindrance to the pace of growth of a developing country. Increased equality promotes effective demand. Sectors such as industry which are capable of faster rates of growth are at present constrained by lack of effective demand. Greater equality in land ownership among the farmers can boost agricultural production.

The emergence of the Basic Human Needs Approach to Poverty Alleviation has revolutionized the concept of poverty itself: Poverty is no longer an individual household's problem but a broad social problem which public policy, or due to lack of strong political will. A social malady like this has also existed because it has benefited certain powerful sections of society, and being in administration they have wielded maximum power. The gains have snowballed. Social myths have proved to be the greatest energizers of the masses but most of their paraders have turned to be the worst betrayers of the people's cause. The degree of inequality has increased because the growth, process has led to a trickle-up in favour of the top one-sixth of the income pyramid. Poverly has increased as the lower middle class has been gradually marginalised. While poverty-alleviation programme is being managed, the rural-urban dichotomy should be paid due attention and its aggravation countered with a strong hand. The reverse resource transfer from rural to urban areas, a latter-day development, should be halted. The criteria and procedures relating to the supply of inputs and finance to the peasantry class should be simplified, with an eye to inequality reduction. At the same time, the pattern of production and commercial activities has to be restructured and streamlined in favor of those belonging to the low-income brackets.

Poverty-alleviation programmes management has to resolve the conflict between number and quality as well as between physical and pecuniary targets, and strive to improve both the quality of the programmes and the quality of the instruments used. Thanks to the authors of the Eighth Plan Approach Paper who view development as a holistic endeavour of the planner interrelating various dimensions, sectors and disciplines. This make the task of the planner easier. In our country public measures to alleviate poverty, measures to eradicate unemployment, and measures to mitigate inequality overlap. Public expenditure on social services is calculated to reduce poverty and inequality but to the extent that they include construction works they are designed to combat unemployment as well. For our study we have used data compiled from different sources: Government of India, State Governments, Planning Commission, NSSO, Economic Survey State Planning Boards, Reserve Bank of India, Centre for Census, Monitoring of Indian Economy, private institutions and institutes, private persons, etc. In so far as there were discrepancies in the data on certain items they had to be used with due care. Each table gives at its bottom the sources of the data contained in it. In the book the data were taken from their respective sources in two forms—directly and after necessary processing. The data drawn from different sources were based on different conceptualizations and different defamations of the terms used, on different assumptions, on different methods of estimation, with different base years, etc. Comparability of the data and the estimates made was impaired by one or more or all of these factors. The estimates made could be reliable only in the proportions in which the data were based were reliable. Even the Union Government's, more particularly the State Governments', publications of successive years were beset with discrepancies and presented data which contradicted themselves. Nothing but confusion resulted from this. These data had to be distilled and processed before they could be used. They had, however, to be presented despite their limitations because if this was not done, even a rough and ready idea of that aspect of the problems could not have been formed and complete ignorance would have prevailed.

TAPAN KUMAR SHANDILYA
SAMIR KUMAR
SHAKEEL AHMAD KHAN

Chapter 1

Different Views on Definition of Poverty and Poverty Line

Poverty is a multidimensional concept involving economic, social, political and cultural dimensions. If one confines to economic aspects only, say income or wealth, then two types of definitions are available in the literature. Rowntree's (1901) work in Great Britain was perhaps the first systematic attempt to define poverty in absolute terms. According to this definition, a *family* is in poverty if its total earnings are inadequate even to obtain the minimum necessities for the maintenance of normal physical efficiency. The minimum necessities are food, clothing, housing, heating, lighting and utensils for cooking and washing—all purchased at the lowest prices and in quantities necessary for physical subsistence only. Once the subsistence standard is scientifically defined, all that is needed is to update it to take into account the rise in prices of the basic necessities. As this concept of income inadequacy is itself dynamic, as is the case in industrially advanced countries, Rowntree's definition of poverty may not be so useful for long-term comparisons. If such definition can be applied to India, for example, its current poverty line would be many times smaller than the one based on Rowntree's methodology.

However, if standard of living is the main concern, then the most straightforward way to determine the poverty line is to specify a basket of commodities by commodity vector q $(q_1, q_2 \, . \, . \, q_n)$

purchasable at market prices P (P_1, P_2 . . . Pn) and to set the poverty standard as a subsistence standard $(1 + h)pq$, where h is a provision for items not included in the list q. This was in effect the method followed in the United States in the derivation of the official poverty line, where q represents food items and h stands for allowance for spending on other items of consumption. The list q is based on the U.S. Department of Agriculture's "economy food plan" for households of different compositions, and the multiplier allowed for other commodities is 3. This method differs from, but has some relation to, the definition of poverty line as the income at which households spend as specified proportion of their total budget on necessities. The Canadian low-income cut-off is based on the income level at which more than 70 per cent of average is spent on food, clothing, and shelter *(Puduluk,* 1967). When the US official poverty line was introduced, there was considerable disagreement about the subsistence standard, but political judgment played a considerable role in determining the "$3,000 for a family of four" that featured prominently in the speeches launching the war on poverty. Similarly, political considerations guided the European Commission in arriving at a benchmark of 50 per cent of average national income in measuring poverty in Europe. The above analyses serve to illustrate the poverty line based on a norm and adjusted for price changes and often referred to as an "absolute" poverty line, and a "relative" poverty line linked to current levels of living. The European Community defines poverty as follows: "The poor shall be taken to mean persons, families, and groups of persons whose resources (material, cultural, and social) are so limited as to exclude them from the minimum acceptable way of life in the member-state in which they live" *(Council Decision,* December 19, 1984).

Various attempts have been made by social scientists and statisticians to quantify this concept. Poverty is variously described; it is a curse on humanity and its eradication is the greatest challenge for any country infected by mass poverty. Considerable effort has been made all over the world to design and implement public policies to combat it. Despite all this effort, almost 400 million people live in conditions of abject poverty, unable to receive even one US dollar a day. They constitute a third of the world population, according to a World Bank report.

Public policies to eradicate poverty emphasize the need to evolve an optimal mix of strategies like acceleration of growth and through the initiation of direct anti-poverty intervention through employment generation and building safety nets. Rapid growth by itself could contribute to generation of black money, but it is important that the poor also should be empowered to have enough opportunities to reap benefits from growth. It is in this context that one has to examine the relevance of the 'trickle-down" hypothesis as applicable to the developing countries like India, that have adopted the World Bank-IMF-sponsored economic reforms in recent years.

The man in poverty reconciles himself to his poverty. His rich neighbor may show all sympathy he can but feels that nothing can be done to relieve him of his poverty, because he believes that he is condemned to poverty by his previous *karma*. In the past, therefore, the Indian society had learnt to live with poverty and there, the matter ended. But times have changed. Philanthropists like Dadabhai Naoroji took up the case of the poor. The socialistic preaching awakened the Indian masses that no longer sweat by the thesis that the poor must remain poor. Indira Gandhi's election slogan "Garibi Hatao" caught the imagination of the masses, though they are at present dejected and disillusioned and may think that this slogan was a cruel joke. The world community is compelled to acknowledge the ancient truth that only equitable distribution of wealth and reduction of mass poverty could lead to all round development.

According to Adam Smith, *"No society can surely be flourishing and happy,* of *which by far the greater part* of *the number are poor and miserable"*. Poverty is a multidimensional concept and depends upon several social and economic factors. It can be defined as a social phenomenon in which a section of the society is unable to fulfill even its basic necessities of life. When a substantial segment of a society is deprived of the minimum level of living and continues at a bare subsistence level, the society is said to be plagued with mass poverty. The subject of sustainable development and poverty has engaged the attention of scholars for centuries. In September 1994, the program of action at the Cairo International Conference on Population and Development asserted: "Despite decades of development efforts both the gap between rich and poor nations and inequalities within nations have widened. Widespread poverty remains the major challenge to development efforts." This view was echoed again and again at the United Nations World Summit for Social Development held in Copenhagen in March 1995 and attended by more than 134 heads of states. Despite significant improvements over the past half-century, extreme poverty remains widespread in the developing world. More than 1.2 billion people, almost half the world's population, live on less than US $2 a day. These impoverished people often suffer from under-nutrition and poor health, have little or no literacy, live in environmentally degraded areas, have little political voice, and attempt to earn a meager living on small and marginal farms or in dilapidated urban slums. The World Bank has recommended certain new suggestions for poverty reduction along with enhanced rates of growth, and several developing countries like India are experimenting with the Bank-IMF prescriptions for poverty eradication.

THE INDIAN APPROACHES TO MEASURE POVERTY IN THE COUNTRY

CSO Approach

The Task Force (1979) set-up by the Planning Commission defined poverty line as the per capita expenditure level of households at which the calorie norms of 2400K and 2100K cals were set as the basis of the all-India consumption basket for rural and urban households at 1973-74 prices. The poverty line so defined came to Rs. 49.09 and Rs. 56.64 for the rural and urban poor, respectively. For subsequent years, these poverty lines were updated initially by wholesale price deflators and later on by the implicit private consumption deflators available in the National Accounts Statistics (NAS). On the recommendations of a Study Group set-up by the Planning Commission *(Perspective Planning Division,* November 1984) in order to arrive at the estimates of population in poverty, the Planning Commission used a device to adjust the NSS data, so that the aggregate private consumption expenditure as given in the NSS is exactly equal to the aggregate private consumption expenditure estimated as a residual in the NAS. In other words, the NAS estimate of the consumption aggregate is distributed into selected household's per capita expenditure categories using the population estimates of NSS as weights. The old NAS statistics were used for deriving the adjustment factor for estimates earlier to 1983, and thereafter, the new NAS series were used. The population in poverty was estimated by applying the updated poverty line to the corresponding NSS distribution of households.

The NSS Approach

This approach was used by Minhas and others (1991) in which the base period consumption basket was retained as before, that is, when the poverty line was defined as Rs. 49.09 and Rs. 56.64 for rural and urban distributions. Then, at the all-India level, two alternative approaches were made to estimate poverty: one that used an all-India poverty line and the associated all-India distribution of per capita total consumption in value terms, and the other, combining the poverty ratios of the state distributions using the State populations as weights. The price adjustments for poverty line updating involved the consumer price index for industrial workers and for non-manual employees for urban areas. This method is almost similar to the one recommended by the Lakdawala Committee.

The other approaches to measure poverty are also very significant in economic literature. Here some of them has been discussed.

A BAYESIAN APPROACH TO POVERTY MEASUREMENT

As already noted, poverty is a multivariate concept involving several dimensions. In a purely economic sense it may be regarded as the state or condition in which some goods and services essential to maintain an acceptable minimum standard of living are lacking. However, a precise definition of poverty will have to differ from society to society, as the concepts of subsistence, deprivation and income adequacy vary across the regions within a country and between different countries. In India, for example, poverty is understood and interpreted as the lack of the very basic energy required for subsistence. The underlying assumption here is that the consumption pattern of households will ensure that when the food intake reaches the desired level, other essentials like clothing, housing and health would also be available. Initially, protein was considered crucial for ensuring nutritional adequacy, but later on it was established that calorie intake is the most important criterion to be considered for purposes of measuring poverty *(Gopalan, et. al.,* 1971; *Gopalan,* 1983; and *Sukhatme,* 1977, 1982). For Indian conditions, an ideal requirement of 2400K cals for the average sedentary male adult has been prescribed *(Gopalan and Rao,* 1968; *Indian Council of Medical Research,* 1980).

Calorie norms for other categories of people were linked to this average. Calorie intake is not directly and easily available, and further, there may be inter and intra-individual variations in calorie consumption within a household, quite unrelated to the poverty level. Hence, it becomes necessary to translate the calorie norm into a more readily observable economic indicator such as the household per capita monthly consumption in money terms. The Planning Commission in India first desired a minimum per capita calorie norm and then took as the poverty line a central measure like the mean, mode, or the median of the per capita total expenditure class for which the mean calorie intake exactly matched the fixed norm. Using this procedure, the Planning Commission (1979) estimated the poverty lines for 1973-74 as Rs. 49.09 per month for the rural calorie norm of 2400K cals daily and Rs. 56.60 for the urban calorie norm of 2100K cals per day. A subsequent Sub-Group of the Planning Commission made estimates of similar poverty lines for later years for different States of India.

There are obvious limitations to this procedure. Firstly, the area covered is too large for either calorie norm or the poverty line to serve any practical purpose. Secondly, for this large area, a rather general occupational profile was considered, which is necessarily inaccurate and probably unrepresentative. Consequently, applying these poverty lines in a specific region for identification of the poor becomes an exercise fraught with dangers of misclassification. This possibility is clearly brought out in Iyengar and Gopalakrishna (1985).

Iyengar, Joshi and Gopalakrishna (1992), in their Karnataka study, used a novel approach based on Bayesian methodology, which departed from other traditional methods where conditional measures were used to estimate the consumption threshold and formulated the poverty line as follows: If y is the per capita consumption of a household in rupees and x is the corresponding per capita calorie intake per day, the poverty line is defined as the minimal y^* which guarantees the availability of the predetermined minimum calorie intake level of x^* cals with probability arbitrarily close to one. They assumed a familiar log-linear relationship between y and x, and adopted the Bayesian approach for estimating the poverty cut-off so defined. Extensive computations using the available official statistics for the Indian state of Karnataka revealed that poverty was considerably *underestimated* by traditional methods employed by official agencies. (Iyengar NS 2010)

Emphazing on poverty and mass deprivation. Amartya Sen says, everyone who is poor should be given entitlement without exception for "sustainable prosperity, even the poorest should be properly educated, their health well protected and that everyone (including the rich) should have a safety net, in case something goes wrong.

To him, the problem of poverty, inequality and deprivation *are* rampant in Europe and America. In a democracy, political leadership can hardly allow a famine to be ignored. Western Europe can afford to ignore a double-digit unemployment figure. No American Government can afford to survive a day with the extent of jobless. Similarly, America can put up with half the people without health insurance, a situation that would not be tolerated even for a single day in any of the West European Countries. In India, the high rate of illiteracy does not seem to have any impact on the political fortunes of the ruling party. In sub-Saharan Africa, the governments are able to go on even in the face of very high, rate of morbidity. It is Sen's work which explains why Indians in certain regard are more malnourished than even those in the infamous sub-Saharan Africa. Sen's best known work in this area is his book (1981): "Poverty and famine: An Essay on Entitlement and Deprivation". Here, he challenges the common view that a shortage of food is the most important (some times the only) explanation for famine; on the basis of a careful study of a number of such catastrophies in India, Bangladesh and Saharan countries from the 1940s onwards, he found more explanatory factors. He argues that several observed phenomena cannot in fact be explained by a shortage of food alone. Famines have occurred even when the supply of food was not significantly lower than during previous years (without famines), or that famines, as a set of social and economic circumstances that deprive people of purchasing power. Among these circumstance are deprivation of elementary human capabilities that ability of the poor to take advantage of economic opportunities. Education, health and access to market mechanisms are all parts of capabilities that individuals must have, so as to be able to avail opportunities. He says, famines are caused not simply by the shortage of food but the inability of people to have access to that food. Without education and awareness of alternative, human capabilities are reduced *to* their lowest levels and thus people are rendered incapable of taking advantage of economic opportunities.

Thus, Sen shows that a profound understanding of famine requires a thorough analysis of how various social and economic factors influence different groups in society and determine their actual opportunities. For example, part of his explanation for the Bangladesh famine of 1974, is that flooding throughout the country that year significantly raised food prices, while work opportunities for agricultural workers declined drastically as the crops could not be harvested. Due to these factors, i.e. the real income of agricultural workers declined so much that this group was disproportionately stricken by starvation. Later works by Sen (in book of 1989 with Jean Dreze), discuss—in a similar spirit—how to prevent famine, or how to limit the effects of famine once it has occurred. Even though a few critics have questioned, the validity of some empirical results on poverty and famines, the book is undoubtedly a key contribution to development economics.

Sen Poverty Measurement Approach

Nobel Prize Laureate Economist Prof. A.K. Sen challenged the methods of poverty measurement devised by those who had visited interest in showing lower/higher poverty incidence. His axiomatic approach was simple yet elegant. Most countries use calorie norms to measure food poverty. India measures it in terms of 2100 calories per day needed for the urban family consisting of equivalent to five adults and 2400 calories per day needed for a rural family of equivalent to five adults. Suppose Rs. 12000 per year are needed at the current prices for this then one rupee more the family is above the poverty line and one rupee less the family is below the poverty line. This is headcount method of food poverty only. The depth/distance/ intensity poverty are not measured. Headcount method would underplay poverty. Then there was that augmented poverty ratio which included in the direct per capita income earned by a family a sum equivalent to per capita government expenditure on development programmes. This would being millions of families above the poverty line and would still more underplay the incidence of poverty. Sen corrected these incorrect approaches.

Sen consider H and I in the first instance. If headcount method income is Rs. 12000 and one family is getting Rs. 6000 per year and another Rs. 3000 per month, the depth of poverty is 50% slippage the first and 75% slippage for the second. At Rs. 12000, it is 'poor family'; at Rs. 9000-12000, it is poor at 6000-9000, it is "very poor"; at Rs. 3000-6000, it is "very very (sic) poor" and at less than Rs. 3000 it is the family of destitute or ultra poor. Sen would like the poverty gap of depth of the poverty to be measured and wanted that three axioms be used for the real measurement of poverty.

They are:

The focus axiom, it is highly desirable that there should be stratified per capita income data. Inclusion of the income of the very rich unnecessarily increases the incomes of very poor. Only after the inclusion of i.e., the depth of poverty can give us the per capita income of the poor. There can be increase in the incomes of the non-poor only but this will increase (quite illegitimately) the incomes of the poor who may be experiencing no change at all.

The monotonicity axiom of Sen highlights the need for taking into account the accretions in the incomes of the poor only. If there is increase in the national income which bypasses the poor, the H (headcount income) remains the same as the value of I is not reduced, There are inequalities not amongst the rich and the poor but amongst the poor themselves which should be bridged. This axiom is based on the concept of Unto the Last of Carlyle and Ruskin which Gandhiji translated as "Sarvodaya" and Vinobaji and Jaiprakashji as Antodaya, This enjoins us to concentrate our attention on the poorest of the poor, The sensitised transfer axiom enjoins us that there should be transferences from the rich to the poor and not from the poor the rich. This accords with the neo-classical Land Pigovian concept that the marginal utility of money with different classes of persons should be more of less the same: though this is difficult to achieve. The human deprivation index is to be minimized and human development index is to be maximized. Transfer axiom is to be sensitized i.e., activated i.e., transfers from the rich and spend more for the benefit of the poor. This spend it well satisfy Sen's poverty measurement axioms:

P = H[+(1 – I) G]
H = headcount income
1 = measure of inequality
G = Gini's coefficient

I is the average rise in income needed for a poor person to reach the poverty line H income. Gini coefficient is well known to the statisticians.

Sen, along with Mahabubul Haq (and many others) devised HDI for the benefit of those who wanted to concentrate on the economics of studying and eradicating poverty. Sen wanted to prove the "Impossibility Theorem" of Arrow that poverty in the poor countries cannot be eradicated. He argued that this possible if there is the will. Sen does not see the poverty eradication. He has vehemently argued that famines take place where democratic governments are absent. Famines are not due to lack of food but due to lack of purchasing power which in turn is due to the poor person not having access to natural resources or being well-employed.

Poverty is hunger, loneliness, loss of dignity, loss of self-respect: and it means ill health, Illiteracy, lack of settlement and deprivation. These are the issues to which the Human Development Reports addressed themselves at the behest of economists like Sen. Sen and other drew attention to the poorest of the poor of the world. Economists like Sen drew attention to the sub-Saharan economies. Sen pointed out that here is the "real world". It is necessary that LPG model (Liberalisation, Privatization and Globalisation) should ensure that the market paradigm is poor friendly. This is not possible without the intervention of the government.

Sen and others addressed themselves to the measurement of the Human Development/Deprivation (reciprocal of each other) indices. Human poverty index HPI and Human Deprivation Index are the same. Human Development Index will be the reciprocal of the value of Deprivation Index. (It becomes necessary, therefore, to define HDI i.e., whether is "development" or "deprivation". The calculation is simple :

$$\frac{\text{Maximum} - \text{Actual}}{\text{Maximum} - \text{Minimum}} \quad \textit{or} \quad \frac{\text{Maximum} - \text{Actual}}{\text{Maximum} - \text{Minimum}}$$

It is necessary that the maximum and the minimum should be chosen with care. If the minimum literacy percentage is 90 and the actual is 50 for a district and the minimum anywhere else is 30 then 40/60=0.66 is deprivation and 0.34 is the development index.

Human deprivation/development indices are unweighted average of three variables:

> Literacy which is the proxy of the tradeable skills and employment ability, Longevity which is the proxy for the all facilities relating to nutrition, health care and living and per capita income adjusted to the purchasing power for a representative basket of goods and services.

The value of each percentage of increase in literacy will be equal to 1:60, i.e., 1.67 and thus if literacy percentage increases by 5 the achievement will be 5 × 1.67 = 8.33 percentage terms. From these three variables a composite index can be prepared. It was on this basis that India's development value was 0.439 and deprivation value 1-0.439=0.561 and India's position 139th in the world. Sen was responsible for development of empowerment economics along with many other economists of UNDP. This empowerment economics tells us that economic development if it is not engendered it will be endangered. Women, inter alia, must have the equal rights to education, nutrition and Medicare; equal rights in spouse selection); equal rights in employment and enjoying the income; equal rights in owning property and their bodies should not be mutilated for the denial of their sex pleasure. Then there should be no practice of amniocentesis. The "people" as a whole will be empowered if they have; rights over the natural resources, if they can imbibe tradable skills; if they have equal opportunities in getting employment; if they own properties and if they are not discriminated against. If minimum in a district is 60% literacy and the state HDI is prepared of the maximum of the State (suppose 80) then the HDI will be 80-60-80-60, i.e. I or no development.

According to Sen, the problem of gender inequality is not just a theoretical one. It has some serious practical consequences. India suffer from two of such major concerns. One, concerns gender inequality, the disparity between man and woman. The advantages of women are not of course unique to India and there is much evidence of extensive gender-based inequality even in the elementary matters of health care and nutrition in many regions across the world, for example, West Asia to China. But a fairly detailed comparison of mortality rates, morbidity rates, hospital care, nutrition, etc. have been made in India despite variations between region within India. They clearly conform to a fairy decisive picture of women being substantially deprived of opportunities in much of the country especially in rural India.

It has been pointed out plausibly enough that rural Indian women typically do not suffer from every of the position of men, do not see their situation as one of the painfull inequality and do not pine for reform, it would be hard to claim that, there is at this moment, widespread dissatisfaction with gender inequality a strong desire for radiation change among rural Indian women. In objective sense, women in rural India are indeed less free to do various things than men are and there is nothing in the history of the world indicate that women will not value more freedom when they actually come to experience it. The absence of present discontent cannot wipe out the moral significance of this inequality of individual freedom including the freedom to assess this situation and the possibilities of changing it—it accepted as a major value.

The second example concern illiteracy in India. Since Independence in 1947, India has made considerable progress in higher education, but remarkably little in elementary education. In the last census, 1981, 41% of adult population was found to be illiteracy, while the proportion of illiteracy among women was only 28%. In fact, elementary education has never received importance that other social objectives have enjoyed in Indian public policy. There are factors for this policy failure. But, Sen argues that Indian illiterate is not actually unhappy about being illiterate and seeking education is not one of the intense desires of the deprived Indian.

Sen's joint work with Jen Dreze extends the "doctrine of empowerment" to the role of the education in poverty alleviation and human development indices. They show that despite, the low GDP in states like Kerala, the higher education levels have ensured that poverty is far lower than those in relatively richer states. It is also these higher education levels that have resulted in lower birth rate and lesser inequality.

The study of development economics has come a long way since the 1940s. Sen has highlighted the central role of development economics in the field of economic growth in developing countries. Economic growth can only be an instrument for development and not an end in itself. To Sen, the concept of H.D. is an alternative objective of state policy. The combined effort of public action with economic growth is hound to achieve rapid human development.

Consumers in Europe and the U.S., spend $ 17 billion ever; year on pet foods. Yet the world can't find the additional $ 13 billion 'that is needed every year to provide basic health services to all the U.S. annually spend $ 12 billion on perfumes. This is the additional amount needed to meet the basic reproductive health needs of the women in the developing countries. Consumers in Europe spend $ 11 billion every year on buying Ice cream which is more than the extra $ 9 billion required to provide universal access to drinking water and sanitation in the developing countries.

The Pakistani economist, Mahbub-ul-Haq, the architect of HDI, was the one who thought of HDI while the concept of HD and its measurement can be traced to many aspects of Sen's work. A fundamental question is often raised, what is Development? A question that Philosophy rather than Economics is better capable of answering. Sen has consistently argued that the goal of development is the expansion of human capabilities that will give people the freedom to do the things that they will value. It is the commodities that they can acquire which is of intrinsic importance. If human development is seen as enlarging people choices, then there are three basic and essential elements for the level of development, (i) for people to lead a long and healthy life, (ii) to acquire knowledge, and (iii) to have access to resources needed for a descent standard of living.

A new form of debate on anti-poverty measures will ensue, demanding a closer examination of the various concepts and techniques of measurement. Critics of the official approach, in very recent years, have raised the issue of "thin" *vs.* "full" sample. The relevant question then will be: If poverty ratio declined during the crucial period 1991-93, as revealed by NSS data, could it be attributed to the economic reforms which were initiated in mid-July 1991. Before attempting a formal answer to this question, one has to begin with a careful analysis of the observed changes in the poverty ratios, which are only *estimates.* In such analyses, sampling errors become crucial for all pair-wise comparisons, over time or space, as the information contained in a sample is both incomplete and inaccurate because of large non-sampling errors, both conceptual and statistical. It is only after the significance of the difference between the two estimates is established by standard tests of significance, then only the question of explanation of why inter-temporal or inter-spatial differences occurred. One can perhaps look for the underlying causes for the observed changes.

If the number of households in a sample is larger than 30 and the variability in the population is not large, the sample is to be considered as large enough to carry out a large sample test for the poverty ratios, which uses the familiar normal distribution. For small samples, a t-test can be used under standard assumptions. However, there are many economists and statisticians who believe that standard methods of hypothesis testing that are generally applicable to random samples, may not strictly apply to the NSS-type situations in which a multistage probability design is employed, which is more complicated than simple random sampling, particularly when it comes to the question of calculating the standard errors. It is perhaps for this reason that Mahalanobis had to introduce the practice of interpenetrating sub-sampling in NSS, which recognizes the presence of both sampling and non-sampling errors in the estimates of various aggregates, averages, ratios and rates, and also facilitates the computation of margins of error for purposes of inter-temporal and spatial comparisons. The modern methods of Fractile Graphical Analysis was especially designed by Mahalanobis (1960) for comparing economic size distributions, using the generalized concept of distance. However, the sub-sampling aspects of the NSS are ignored in current practice. It is ironical that the nation spends large amounts of its limited intellectual and material resources on gathering of information, while a very little of the information so collected is actually utilized for drawing valid scientific inferences. The main user of NSS data are the economists who demand quick tabulations and convenient results, and the meek statisticians often oblige without cautioning the users about the dangers of loss of reliability and validity of their quick estimates which actually results in confusion and unending debate.

NEW METHODOLOGY

In this connection, the methodology used by Australia may be worth noting According to it, the country takes into account even non-income indicators to estimate poverty and updates its poverty line every quarter. Adopting a liar approach, Mohan Guruswamy and Ronald Joseph Abraham for Policy Alternatives, Delhi in a February 2006 report, "Redefining *verity:* A New Poverty line for a New India" presented a case for fixing the invert line at about Rs. 840 per capita per month after factoring in costs for wtrition (Rs. 573), health (Rs. 30), clothing (Rs. 17), energy consumption and miscellaneous expenditure (Rs. 164). Even this figure of Rs. 840, they fid, would not fully reveal the true state of poverty in India because a person finding more than Rs. 840 a month does not necessarily have access to all fundamental needs of life such education, health, nutritious food, clean, after, clothing, sanitation, transport, housing, and access to national resources.

ENVIRONMENT OF POVERTY

The environment of poverty is conditioned by malnutrition, which increases a person's vulnerability to disease and reduces his learning ability, Malnutrition adversely affects fuller mental development, physical growth, productivity, the span of working years, all of which significantly influence the economic potential of men and women. Lack of education increases ignorance and reduces the scope for self-improvement, and generates ignorance of the means to prevent sickness. It also affects the norms and value system of a society. Illiteracy and fertility are a vicious combination. Poor housing with lack of basic amenities create a physical environment, which results in a high incidence of water-borne and air-borne diseases. On the other hand, a conditioned learning environment *inter alias* develops ignorance about food source, diet, food preparation, storage, etc., poor health reduces one's ability to absorb food. The net result of malnutrition, illiteracy, poor housing and poor health is reduced production of basic goods, low skills, lower productivity and lower incomes. Poverty affects the quality and quantity of the human capital, which is the end and means of economic growth.

The environment of poverty stresses the key importance of participation. Low participation constitutes the fifth segment of the circle, demonstrating how, in addition to institutional factors, unsatisfied needs detract from more active participation: work capacities are reduced by disease, poor nourishment, low skill and even poor housing. Reduced participation in turn capacities to produce basic goods and earn incomes, and feeds back into the circle of deprivation. The involution of the poverty environment is thus complete. The key changes capable of transforming this environment obviously consist in the removal of the obstructive factors at the centre. This symbolic representation of the environment of poverty is thus transformed from a vicious into a virtuous circular arrangement, raising levies of satisfaction of needs conjointly and then becomes a self-generating process.

Rural poor population includes landless agricultural labour households, agricultural labour with small holdings, landless non-agricultural rural labourers including village artisans progressively losing their traditional jobs and small land operators with cultivating holding of less than 2 hectares and particularly less than 1 hectare. (Minhas, Burdhan, Dandekar and Rath). The urban poor, according to Dandekar and Rath, "they belong to the same class as the rural poor".

At least 70% of the population is in agriculture, which engages 60% of the work force. Its contribution to GDP is merely 27% and that too is constantly declining from 31.6% in 1987-88 to 26.8% in

1998-99. Out of the 70% of agricultural population 80% of the farmers are small and marginal farmers and 75% of Indian poor are in rural areas. More than 60% of them live in five states, namely, Bihar, V.P., M.P., Rajasthan and Orissa.

Several attempts have been made to estimate purely or the pre and post reform period Gupta, 1955; Chandrashekhar and Sen, 1966; Jain, 1996; B. OzIer, G. Dutt and M. Ravallion, 1996; Shenggen Fan, Peter Hazell, S.K. Thorat, 2000 and Bhijit Sen, 2000 are some notable estimates. These studies medicate that the rural poverty has constantly reduced during the pre-reform period 1973-74 to 1980-90 and increased significantly during the first two and half years of reform 1991-92, 1992-93 and 1993-94. During this period rural poverty increased by about 2 percentage point while the urban poverty declined by 4 percentage point. Tendulkar's estimates of severity of poverty (FGT-index) show that there was a very mild decline in severity for rural areas while a significant decline is found in urban areas. A lower level of FGT index implies less severity of poverty and a high value signifies more server poverty. Following table shows these levels of severity during pre and post-reform period.

The State-wise estimates reveals that four states, namely, Bihar, M.P., U.P. and Maharashtra, together accounted 55% of the rural poor in 1993. Bihar and U.P. together accounted 18% of the total rural poor. These states had the highest incidence of poverty in 1993 with 42.68% of their rural population falling below the poverty line. On the other hand, A.P., Haryana, Kerala, Punjab and West Bengal had only 25 to 35% of their rural population below the poverty line in 1993. The study also reveals that most of the states experienced an increase in poverty after 1990. In Orissa, for example, the poverty ratio increased from 19% to 25% between 1990-93. (*Shandilya*, 2010)

To Sum up the measurement of poverty involves two distinct problems, namely:

(i) The Specification of "poverty line," and
(ii) Determination of the index of poverty.

In India, most of the studies on poverty regard the proportion of people below the line as the index of poverty. This ratio is called the Head Count Ratio. More specifically,

$$H = \frac{q}{n}$$

H = Poverty Index,
q = The number of people below the poverty line, and
n = The total number of people in the community.

According to Sen (1976), H is obviously a very crude Index. This index is highly insensitive to the extent of the aggregate shorfall of the income from the poverty line as well as to the distribution of income amongst the poor. In spite of these limitations, H is still widely used. In the debate on whether or not rural poverty in India is on the increase, Dandekar and Rath (1971), Ojha (1970) and Bardhan (1971) have used this index.

Another common measure is the so-called "poverty gap" which is the aggregate shortfall of the income of all the poor taken together from the poverty line. That is:

$$I = \frac{\sum_{i=1}^{q} gi}{qz}$$

where gi = Z – Yi'

In the above measure,

z = Poverty line
Yi = Income of the ith

The above ratio gives up the percentage of their mean shortfall from the poverty level. This measure is totally insensitive to the number of living below the poverty line. Thus, while the head-count ratio (H) is completely insensitive to the extent of the poverty shortfall per person, the income-gap ratio (I) completely insensitive to the numbers involved. According to Sen (1976), both should have some role in the index of poverty. But H and I together are not sufficiently informative either, since neither gives adequate information on the exact income distribution among the poor. Sen (1976) has suggested a measure, which is sensitive to the gaps in the incomes of the poor. His measure is:

P – H (I + (1 – 1) G)
where

$$H = \frac{q}{n} + \text{Head-count ratio}$$

$$I = \frac{\sum_{i=1}^{q} gi}{q'}$$ Income gap ratio and G is the Gini coefficient of the income distribution of the poor.

The index lies in between zero and unity. If P - 0, this index shows that every one has as income greater than z, and if P = I, everyone has zero income. In practice of course, P will never taken these two extreme values.

Referring to the problem of poverty, A.K. Sen says that the usual procedure is to identify some level of income, which is required for the recommended balanced diet, and to consider those falling below that level poor. He has added two more criteria.

(i) We should be concerned not merely with the number of people living below the poverty line but also with the amount by which to incomes of the poor fall short of the specified poverty level, and.

(ii) The bigger the shortfall from the poverty measure.

On this basis, Sen develops his P measure of poverty as:

$$p = \frac{2}{(q+1)xy} \sum_{i=1}^{q} Y - Y_1 (q+1-i)$$

where

N is the population size,

Y is the income of ith individual arranged in the ascending order of magnitude,

Y is the minimum acceptable level of income or the poverty line, and

q is the number of people at or below the poverty line.

The basic idea behind the concept of poverty is the criterion whereby we identify the poor. Evolution of this criterion culminates in establishing a poverty line' does only the part of the job. Though it is correct that the poor are those whose income lies below poverty line. However, Sen observes that, generally, poverty line does only part of the job. The concept of absolute poverty is based on absolute norms for living (measured in terms of consumption expenditure), laid down according to specific minimum standard and all such individuals or groups whose consumption expenditure is below this standard, are classified as poor. The proportion of such individuals and groups in the population indicates the extent of poverty. Under the relative concept of poverty, a family (or an individual) is deemed to be poor if its level of income/consumption expenditure falls below the predetermined level. Then the income distribution of the population in different fractile groups is estimated and a comparison is made between the level of living of people at bottom layer and at the top layers of population to assess the relative levels of poverty. The relative concept is more suitable for developed countries while the absolute concept is more relevant for the developing countries. In developing countries, for the purpose of measurement of poverty, consumption expenditure maybe considered more appropriate than income. In addition, the concepts of poverty has two connotations, namely, individual poverty and collective poverty. By individualized poverty is meant those individuals who are not able to incur even the minimum expenditure on the most essential items for survival viz. food, clothing and housing. This can also be eliminated by the government through suitably increasing expenditure on human welfare needs such as education, health, etc., and also by discouraging expenditure on various social customs.

After defining the different concepts of poverty, the factors responsible for poverty may be grouped into four heads, viz. economic, demographic, sociological and other:

1. The economic factors include:
   (i) Land;
   (ii) Irrigation facility;
   (iii) Employment Potential;
   (iv) Availability of loan;
   (v) Saving capacity; and
   (vi) Investment potential.
2. Demographic factors include:
   (i) Size of family,
   (ii) Age-composition of family members, and
   (iii) Level of Literacy.
3. Sociological factors include:
   (i) Caste;
   (ii) Joint family; and
   (iii) Rigidity of social systems.
4. Other factors are:
   (i) Awareness about developmental programmes;

(ii) Level of participation in village politics; and
(iii) Ability to provide local leadership.

A country's GNP per capita is not a good measure of poverty for it takes no account of distribution and ignores other dimensions of poverty. The most common income poverty measures is the head-count, i.e. the percentage of the population falling below the poverty line.

This measure takes, in fact, no account of how far people are below the poverty line so that a rise in the income of the poor which leaves them in poverty appears to have no effect. Hence, another measure, the poverty gap, is often used which can be interpreted as the product of head-count and the average distance of the poor below the poverty line (expressed as the percentage of the poverty line) and the benefit of targeting.

The poverty severity index is a similar measure which puts together weights on those furthest below the poverty line. These three measures-then head-count, the poverty gap and the poverty severity index-are known collectively as the Foster-Greer-Thorbecke poverty measure. For a non-negative living standard indicator (say, consumption) y is distributed with density f(y) and with a poverty line z, the poverty measure P is given by.

$$p =) \; (\underline{z: y}). \, f(y) \, dy, \; a > 0$$

When a is 0, P is the same as the head-count measure, and when a is 1, P is known as the poverty gap index. As a increases, P becomes increasingly sensitive to the living standard indicator of the poorest people. Thus, this measure is sensitive to differences in the depth of poverty or to inequality among the poor.

Over the years a number of composite measures of development have been proposed. A previous measure, the Physical Quality of Life Index (PQLI) has been superseded in recent years by the UNDP's Human Development Index (HDI); the latter being a composite of GDP per capita, life expectancy and measure of educational attainment. It is noteworthy that it is the UNDP which has done the most to address poverty in all its dimensions not least within the annual 'Human Development Report'. For example, one calculation made by UNDP is that the cost of eradicating poverty across the world is relatively small compared to global income—not more than 0.3% of world GDP—and that political commitment, not financial resources, is the real obstacle to poverty eradication.

Just as income per capita takes no account of distribution neither does the HDI. However, UNDP has also proposed a Human Poverty Index (HPI) which focuses on deprivation-specially the deprivation in living standards. This HPI is based on three main indices: the percentage of the population not expected to survive beyond the age of 40, the adult literacy rate, and a deprivation index based on an average of three variables—the percent age of the population without access to safe water, the percentage of population without access to health services, and the percentage of children under the age of 5 years who are underweight through malnourishment.

Though HDI is widely used, there are several criticisms labelled against it, such as which variables are to put in the index, the arbitrary choice of weight in constructing the average and that information lost by combining three or four pieces of data into a single number. The technical appendix to the 1996 Human Development Report already has highlighted this. Thus, it may be preferable to report a small range of social indicators rather than attempting to combine these to an overall poverty index. (*Karmaker*, 2010)

The World Economic Review (Vol. 5, May 1991) contains several papers which examine the nature and magnitude of poverty in Eastern Europe and China, besides OECD countries, USA, Canada, and Australia, particularly in the wake of worldwide reforms after the fall of socialism. Some of these papers are of high methodological value and others are substantive, dealing with case studies in the developed as well as in some of the developing countries. Studies comparing poverty across countries usually contain an evaluation of their past policies for reducing poverty. If comparisons are to be a valid foundation for such assessments and, in particular, if they are to serve as a guide to effective allocation of public funds, the underlying concepts must be thoroughly examined. Atkinson (1991) lists four important issues that are critical in this respect, the choice of poverty indicator, the determination of poverty line, the unit of analysis and the choice of equivalence scale. He provides stimulating examples from the case studies, on poverty in the OECD countries—France, Spain, Italy, United Kingdom, Germany, Portugal, Greece, Ireland, Netherlands, Belgium, and Denmark. He also makes reference to practices in other industrially advanced countries like USA, Australia, Canada, Norway, and Sweden. Ravalli on and Huppi (1991) describe a number of tools available for empirical analysis which allow researchers not only to test the sensitivity of poverty assessments measurement assumptions but also to decompose observed changes in aggregate poverty in terms of the underlying changes in the regional and demographic variables. These authors, like Indian scholars, base their poverty measures on the distribution of household consumption per person, after adjusting for inflation using the consumer price index, though modifying the expenditure weights to accord most closely with the spending patterns of the poor. Poverty comparisons have been made in terms of income in France, Britain and Germany by taking the poverty standard as 50 per cent of the national average income. One of the two studies for UK uses households below average income as poor. According to a study by UK Department of Social Security (1990), in 1984-85, 9.2 per cent of households lived with incomes below 50 per cent of the mean. In France, in 1984-85, 10.9 per cent of households had incomes below 50 per cent of the median. In Germany, in 1983, 7.0 per cent of the population lived in households with income below 50 per cent of the mean.

MEASUREMENT OF POVERTY IN INDIA

In India, the approach based on the minimum requirement of food, clothing and shelter which reflects purchasing power is generally used for measurement of poverty. The Planning Commission obtaining the data from the National Sample Survey and the recommendations of the Task Force on projection of Minimum Needs and Effective Consumption Demand (1979), defined the poverty line on the basis of caloric norms of 2400 per capita per day in rural areas and 2100 per capita per day in urban areas in the base year 1973-74. The poverty line was so defined was Rs. 49.10 for rural areas and Rs. 56.60 for urban areas.

From the following Tables, we can see the population below the poverty line determined by Planning Commission and The Expert Group Methodology.

The Tables 1 and 2 shows a lot of difference in the number of population below poverty line and percentage of poverty ratio between the Planning Commission, GOI and Expert Group. In 1983-84 as per there were 271.0 million people (percentage of Poverty ratio is 37.4) below the poverty line as per Planning Commission whereas according to Expert Group methodology 322.9 million people below

TABLE 1
Population Below the Poverty Line
(As per the Planning Commission, GOI)

(*Population in Millions*)

Sector	*1983-84*	*1984-85*	*1987-88*	*1989-90*	*1993-94*
Rural	221.5	222.2	196.0	168.6	141.1
Urban	49.5	50.5	41.7	42.2	27.1
Total	271.0	272.7	237.7	210.8	168.2
Poverty Ratio (%)					
Rural	40.4	39.9	33.4	28.4	21.7
Urban	28.1	27.7	20.1	19.3	11.6
Total	37.4	36.9	29.9	25.3	16.9

Source : CSO, Press Report.

TABLE 2
Population Below the Poverty Line
(As per the Expert Group Methodology)

(*Population in Millions*)

Sl. No.	*Sector*	*1973-74*	*1983-84*	*1987-88*	*1993-94*	*1999-2000*
1.	Rural	261.3	252.0	231.9	244.0	193.2
2.	Urban	60.0	70.9	75.2	76.3	67.0
	Total	321.3	322.9	307.1	320.3	260.2
Poverty Ratio (%)						
1.	Rural	56.4	45.7	39.1	37.3	27.1
2.	Urban	49.0	40.8	38.2	32.4	23.6
	Total	54.9	44.5	38.9	36.0	26.1

Source : Planning Commission, Ninth Five Year Plan, 1997-2002, Volume 1, "Number and Percentage of Population Below Poverty Line by States", *The Hindu*, 26 Feb. 2001.

the poverty line and percentage of poverty ratio is 44.5. In the same way we can see that in 1993-94 as per Planning Commission 166.2 million people were below the poverty line whereas according to

Expert Group methodology it was 320.3 millions people. Projection of National poverty ratios in percentage are given in Table 3. It is seen that projected national poverty ratio is less than 5 per cent in the year 2011-12 which is quite satisfactory for a populous developing country.

TABLE 3

Projection of National Poverty Ratios

(*in percentage*)

Region	*1996-97*	*2001-02*	*2006-07*	*2011-12*
Rural	30.55	18.61	9.64	4.31
Urban	25.58	1.6.46	9.28	4.49
Total	29.18	17.98	9.53	4.37

Source : Planning Commission, Ninth Five Year Plan, 1997-2002, Vol. 1.

The following Table 4 shows the number and percentage of population below poverty.

The total number and the percentage of population below poverty line have been shown in the Table 6 and 6A for 1983-84, 1993-94 and 1999-2000 respectively. We see that the total number of people below poverty line has decreased in rural areas from 2529.6 lakhs in 1983-84 to 1932.43 lakhs in 1999-2000. The combined (taking both rural and urban areas) number and percentage of people below poverty line is also decreases sharply from 3221.0 lakhs in 1983-84 to 2602.50 lakhs in 1999-2000 and from 37.6 per cent to 26.10 per cent respectively..

Distribution of households by availability of two square meals a day in India is shown in the above table. It is revealed that according to 55th Round 1999-2000, 96.2 per cent members of the households getting two square meals a day in rural areas whereas it is 98.6 per cent in 1999-2000. In case of the percentage of members of households getting two square meals a day in only some months of the year and not even some months is very less in comparison to earlier category. (Brobora & Mahanta, 2010)

Poverty is defined by the head count ratio which is expressed as the percentage of the people living below the poverty line. In India, there are different methods to measure poverty: (i) Official estimates by the CSO, (ii) NSS estimates by the NSSO, (iii) Expert Group estimates by the Planning Commission. These methods are quite different. Official estimates are made after certain adjustments in

TABLE 4

State-wise Rural-Urban Number and Percentage of Population Below Poverty Line

Sl. No.	States/UTs	1883-84 Rural		1883-84 Urban		1883-84 Combined		1993-94 Rural		1993-94 Urban		1993-94 Combined	
		No. of Persons (lakhs)	No. of Persons	No. of Persons (lakhs)	No. of Persons	No. of Persons (lakhs)	No. of Persons	No. of Persons (lakhs)	No. of Persons	No. of Persons (lakhs)	No. of Persons	No. of Persons (lakhs)	No. of Persons
	(1)	(2)	(3)	(4)	(5)	(6)	(7)	(8)	(9)	(10)	(11)	(12)	(13)
1.	Andhra Pradesh	112.2	26.0	57.1	40.8	168.2	29.7	79.41	15.92	74.47	38.33	153.97	22.19
2.	Arunachal P.	—	—	—	—	—	—	3.62	45.01	0.11	7.73	3.73	39.35
3.	Assam	57.1	29.9	6.0	26.3	63.1	29.5	94.33	45.01	2.03	7.73	96.36	40.86
4.	Bihar	405.2	62.7	51.0	51.3	465.2	61.2	450.86	58.21	42.49	34.50	493.35	54.96
5.	Goa	—	—	—	—	—	—	0.38	5.34	1.53	27.03	1.19	14.92
6.	Gujarat	50.0	20.3	36.5	31.4	86.5	23.8	62.13	22.18	43.02	27.59	105.19	24.14
7.	Haryana	19.1	17.8	9.9	30.1	29.0	20.6	36.56	28.02	7.31	16.38	43.88	25.05
8.	Himachal Pradesh	5.9	14.2	0.5	13.3	6.4	14.1	15.40	30.34	0.46	9.18	15.86	28.44
9.	J & K	110	22.1	5.1	36.7	16.2	25.3	19.05	30.34	1.86	9.18	20.92	25.17
10.	Karnataka	103.6	37.5	54.3	45.1	157.9	39.8	95.99	29.88	60.46	40.14	156.46	33.16
11.	Kerala	73.3	33.9	24.9	47.2	98.1	36.5	55.95	25.76	20.46	24.55	76.41	25.43
12.	Madhya Pradesh	237.2	54.31	61.8	51.3	299.0	53.7	216.19	40.64	82.33	48.38	298.52	42.52
13.	Maharashtra	175.0	41.0	83.6	34.4	258.6	38.6	193.33	37.93	111.90	35.15	305.22	36.86

(Contd.)

TABLE 4 (*Contd.*)

(1)	(2)	(3)	(4)	(5)	(6)	(7)	(8)	(9)	(10)	(11)	(12)	(13)
14. Manipur	1.8	16.2	0.8	18.8	2.6	16.9	6.33	45.01	0.47	7.73	6.80	33.78
15. Meghalaya	—	—	—	—	—	—	7.09	45.01	0.29	7.73	7.38	37.92
16. Mizoram	—	—	—	—	—	—	1.64	45.01	0.30	7.73	1.94	25.66
17. Nagaland	—	—	—	—	—	—	4.85	45.01	0.20	7.73	5.05	37.92
18. Orissa	167.3	69.1	15.7	43.2	183.0	65.7	140.90	49.72	19.70	41.64	160.60	48.56
19. Punjab	13.7	10.8	15.0	29.0	28.7	16.1	17.76	11.95	7.35	11.35	25.11	11.77
20. Rajasthan	91.1	31.5	32.2	39.0	123.2	33.1	94.68	26.46	33.82	30.49	128.50	27.41
21. Sikkim	—	—	—	—	—	—	1.81	45.01	0.03	7.73	1.84	41.43
22. Tamil Nadu	162.8	48.3	81.6	47.5	244.1	48.1	21.70	32.48	80.40	39.77	202.10	35.03
23. Tripura	—	—	—	—	—	—	11.41	45.01	0.38	7.73	11.79	39.01
24. Uttar Pradesh	487.8	51.2	126.3	55.3	614.1	52.0	496.17	42.28	108.28	35.39	604.46	40.85
25. West Bengal	215.5	51.0	62.3	39.8	277.8	47.9	209.90	40.80	44.66	22.41	254.56	35.66
26. Delhi	0.3	6.2	10.2	15.5	0.5	4.9	0.19	1.90	15.32	16.03	15.51	14.69
UTs												
27. A & N Islands	—	—	—	—	—	—	0.73	32.48	0.08	39.77	1.06	34.47
28. Chandigarh	—	—	—	—	—	—	0.07	11.35	2.38	11.35	0.80	11.35
29. D & N Haveli	—	—	—	—	—	—	0.72	51.95	0.06	39.93	0.77	50.84
30. Lakshadweep	—	—	—	—	—	—	0.06	25.76	0.08	24.55	0.14	25.04
31. Pondicherry	—	—	—	—	—	—	0.93	32.48	2.38	39.77	3.31	37.40

Source : Central Statistical Organisation (CSO), Selected Socio-economic Statistics India, 1993 and 1996-97.

TABLE 5

Number and Percentage of People Below Poverty Line by States

States/UTs	1999-2000 Rural		1999-2000 Urban		1999-2000 Combined	
	No. of Persons (Lakhs)	% of Persons	No. of Persons (Lakhs)	% of Persons	No. of Persons (Lakhs)	% of Persons
(1)	(2)	(3)	(4)	(5)	(6)	(7)
Andhra Pradesh	58.13	11.05	60.88	26.63	119.0	15.77
Arunachal Pradesh	3.80	40.04	0.18	.47	3.98	3.4
Assam	92.17	0.04	2.38	7.47	4.55	-36.09
Bihar	376.51	4.30	9.13	2.91	425.64	42.60
Goa	0.11	1.35	0.59	7.52	0.70	4.40
Gujarat	39.80	13.17	28.09	15.59	67.89	14.07
Haryana	11.94	8.27	5.39	9.99	8.74	
Himanchal Pradesh	4.89	7094	0.29	4.63	5.12	7.63
Jammu & Kashmir	2.97	3.97	0.49	1.98	3.46	3.48
Kamataka	59.91	17.38	44.49	25.25	104.40	20.04
Kerala	20.97	9.38	20.07	27	41.04	12.72
Maharashtra	125.12	23.72	102.87	26.81	227.99	25.02
Manipur	6.53	40.04	0.66	7.47	7.19	28.54
Meghalaya	.89	0.04	34	47	8.23	33.87

(Contd.)

TABLE 5 (*Contd.*)

(1)	(2)	(3)	(4)	(5)	(6)	(7)
Mizoram	1.40	0.04	.45	.47	85	-19.47
Nagaland	15.21	40.04	0.28	7.47	5.49	32.67
Orissa	143.69	11.40	42.83	169.09	17.15	
Punjab	10.20	6.35	4.29	5.75	14.49	6.16
Rajasthan	55.06	3.74	26.78	19.85	81.83	15.28
Sikkim	2.00	40.04	0.04	7.47	2.05	36.55
Tamil Nadu	80.51	20.55	49.97	22.11	130.48	21.22
Tripura	12.53	40.04	0.49	7.47	13.02	34.44
Uttar Pradesh	412.01	31.22	117.88	30.89	529.89	31.15
West Bengal	180.11	31.85	33.38	14.86	213.49	27.02
Delhi	0.07	.40	11.42	.42	1.49	8.23
A&N Islands	0.58	20.55	0.24	22.11	0.82	20.99
Chandigarh	0.06	5.75	0.45	.5.75	0.51	5.75
D&N Haveli	.30	17.57	0.03	13.52	0.33	17.14
Lakshadweep	0.03	9.38	0.08	20.27	20.27	15.60
Pondicherry	0.64	W.55	1.77	22.11	2.41	21.67
Daman & Diu	0.01	1.35	0.05	7.52	0.06	4.44
All India	1932.43	27.09	670.07	23.62	2602.50	26.10

Source : Number and Percentage of Population below poverty line by States, *The Hindu*, Feb. 2001.

different. Official estimates are made after certain adjustments in aggregate private household consumption expenditure as estimated by the NAS and the distribution of households by consumption expenditure levels provided by the NSS. The NSS estimates of Poverty seem appropriate since the NSS provides household expenditure data (as opposed to private expenditure data provided by the NAS) as well as commodity composition, not only for expenditure class groups but also for all states and for rural and urban areas separately. On the other hand, Expert Group constituted by the Planning Commission in 1993 has estimated alternative poverty head counts based on the NSS consumer expenditure distributions and with modifications incorporating the state-level price differentials. The expert did not adjust for the discrepancy in the NAS and INSS figures on consumer expenditure.

The levels of poverty have been and relative declines sharper in the official estimates compared to the expert group estimates. Estimates reveal that, while the official estimates have shown a dramatic decline in poverty in urban areas, the expert group has presented a more sustained picture of decline in rural poverty relative to urban, i.e., urban poverty is not declining drastically as given the official estimates (UNFPA, 1997). Let us now discuss the measurement of poverty in India by the Expert group method.

The Planning Commission in India has estimated the incidence of poverty on the basis of the Task Force Method. The Task Force was constituted under the chairmanship of Dr. Y.K. Alagh since the early 1970s. As a measure of poverty, head-count ratio measured by the percentage of people below the poverty line was taken. The Task Force has formulated a quantitative index of poverty by taking the basic minimum needs of the poorer people and the effective consumption demand of the non-poor people. Then it has defined the poverty line as monthly per capital consumption expenditure level, which meets the average per capita daily caloric requirement of 2400 kcl in rural areas and 2100 kcl in urban areas with the associated quantum of non-food expenditure. Using the 28th Round (1973-74) NSS data on household consumer expenditure both in quantitative and value terms the poverty line is defined as monthly per capita consumption expenditure of Rs. 49.09 in rural areas and Rs. 56.64 in urban areas. In later years the poverty lines were estimated by updating the 1973-74 poverty line initially by Wholesale Price Index (WPI). But the use of WPI was controversial because consumers buy goods at retail and not at wholesale prices.

In 1989 the Planning Commission has constituted the Expert Group on Estimation of Proportion and Number of Poor under the chairmanship of Prof. D.T. Lakdawala. The method is known as the Expert Group Method. The Expert Group has recommended that the Task Force poverty line is adopted as the base line. It has disaggregated national poverty line to state-specific lines. The national rural poverty line is disaggregated into state-specific poverty lines by using state-specific price indices of 1973-74 and interstate price differential. The state-specific price indices are constructed by averaging the state-specific food and non-food price indices of Consumer Price Index of Agricultural Labourers, while the inter-state price differential is done by using Fisher's Index. These state-specific rural poverty lines are updated in later years by state-specific price indices, which are constructed as weighed average of food, fuel and light, clothing and footwear, and miscellaneous of CPIAL.

Like the national rural poverty line, the national urban poverty line is disaggregated into state-specific poverty lines by using state-specific price indices of 1973-74 and interstate differential. The state-specific price indices are obtained from the Consumer Price Index (CPI) of industrial workers and the inter-state price differential is estimated by using Fisher's Index. The state- specific of CPI of industrial workers are done by averaging the CPI of food, fuel and light, housing, clothing, bedding and footwear and miscellaneous with their respective weights in the consumption basket of the poor. Later on, this Expert Group Method is modified by the Planning Commission by dropping the Consumer Price Index of Urban Non-Manual Employees and the method is known as "Modified Expert Group Method". This is *because* of the fact the rate of increase of the Consumer Price Index of Urban Non-Manual Employees has been faster which in turn causes a rise in the money value of the poverty line and hence the incidence of urban poverty.

The Expert Group has estimated state-specific poverty lines and hence the poverty rations, but not specifically the national level poverty lines. The national poverty lines are worked out as an interpolated value from the national level expenditure distribution obtained from the NSS data on consumer expenditure. The national level poverty ratio is estimated as an average of state-wise poverty ratios. Based on availability of state level prices the Expert Group has estimated the poverty lines and poverty ratios in rural and urban areas of 18 states and UTs. These are: Andhra Pradesh, Assam, Bihar, Gujarat, Haryana, H.P., J&K, Karnataka, Kerala, M.P., Maharashtra,

Orissa, Punjab, Rajasthan, T.N., U.P., W.B. and Delhi. Unsung neighboring state's poverty line, the poverty ratios for other states and UTs are estimated (*Pal, P.K.*, 2010).

Different Views on Definition of Poverty and Poverty Line

Although poverty also exit even in the developed countries of Europe and America. The term 'Poverty' has been defined in different Societies in a different way but all of them are conditioned by the version or minimum of good life to be obtained in society. For instance, the concept of poverty in USA would be significantly different from that in India because the ability to afford a higher living standard is much higher in the United States.

Two types of standards are common in economic literature: (i) the absolute, and (ii) the relative, in the absolute standard, minimum physical quantities of cereals, pulses, milk and utter, etc. are determined for a subsistence level and then the price quotations convert into monetary terms the physical quantities. Aggregating all the quantities included, a figure expressing per capita consumer expenditure is determined. The population whose level of income (or expenditure) is below the figure, is considered to be below the poverty line. According to the relative standard, income distribution of the population in different fractile groups is estimated and a comparison of the levels of living of the top 5 to 10 percent with the bottom 5 percent of the population reflects the relative standards of poverty. The defect if the latter approach is that it indicates the relative position of different segment of the population in the income hierarchy. Even in affluent societies, such pockets of poverty exist. But for underdevelopment countries, it is the existence of mass poverty that is the cause for concern.

The identification process of persons below the poverty line has been put to a controversy for the last few years. Planning Commission adopted the Survey of NSSO as a basis for defining poverty line and determining the number of persons below it. On the basis of this criteria Planning Commission estimated 18.96% of total population below the poverty line for the year 1993-94. The Expert Group under the chairmanship of Prof. D.T. Lakadawala (appointed by Planning Commission which submitted its report in July 1993 found earlier estimates of poverty unreliable and suggested and alternate approach for identifying poor in which different poverty line was determined for different states on the basis of price level of that particular state.

Lakadawala Expert Group suggested that it will be most suitable to rely on the disaggregated commodity indices for consumer Price Index for Agricultural Labourers (CPIAL) to update the rural poverty line and a simple average of suitably weighted commodity indices of Consumer Price Index for Industrial Workers (CPIIW) for updating urban poverty line. 32 different poverty line has been suggested by the expert group for different states to adopt this approach.

Tendulkar Poverty Line

It is not surprising that the Planning Commission, mandated by the National Development Council to steer the poverty line issues, has reserved its judgement on the Tendulkar poverty line. However, the Finance Ministry is already quoting it (GOI, 2010, p. 24). Adventurously taking-off from Tendulkar, who recommended that the present official urban poverty line be used as the national poverty line, the Urban Development Ministry has suggested that the average level of household expenditure in the urban areas be used as a poverty line cut-off, notwithstanding the fact that their number of Rs. 6,000 per household per month is roughly double of Tendulkar's cut-off point. The issues involved, therefore, are of some importance.

THE OFFICIAL POVERTY LINE

A set of scholars argued that India's official poverty line was not based on the demand and welfare theory, and was therefore analytically deficient. The argument goes back to scholars like C.H. Shah, who argued that poverty line baskets were ignoring the 'taste' patterns of poor people, and that if this fact were taken into account, the cut-off points would be higher. This kind of argument has been advanced many times, including in World Bank studies (*Datta*, 2006). In one of the better laid out arguments of this genre, S. Subramanian (2005), has computed some interesting numbers, assuming that the underlying consumer behaviour pattern is a Utility function of a Cobb Douglas type, and that there are two goods—Food and Non-food, and a budget line. Employing the usual elementary textbook manipulations, he shows that a calorifically fixed basket of goods would not be consistent with consumer optimization as both prices and income change. Alternately the income required to meet the consumption of the fixed calorie norm 'optimally' would be higher than the poverty line. Leaving aside trivial objections such as that the Cobb Douglas type of demand functions are, over some ranges, inconsistent with well-behaved demand surfaces (*World and Jureen,'*

1953, pp. 5-8) or the puzzling nature of statements like the *optimality* or *fixed norms,* (emphasis added), some of the critics, World Bank studies, and others miss out the essential point that the official poverty line in India was identified (in a strict econometric sense) in well-behaved demand and welfare theory terms.

The critics are right in terms of many of the issues they raise, but not in stating that the poverty line was originally developed outside a foundation of theory. While this has been recognized in some influential quantitative and policy studies outside India, since the original paper is seldom referred to in Indian studies and those originating from the Brettonwoods institutions, it would be useful to lay down the detail, so that the debate is at least fact-based. This is particularly so since strong language ('conceptual muddle', 'fundamentally flawed', to cite two examples) on the past work of the Indian Planning Commission, on the grounds of both non-native and on behavioural demand theory is becoming fashionably acceptable. A reference to the original work may perhaps uplift the debate.

The Task Force stated that to "allow for differentials in calorie needs of the population, the Nutrition Expert Group distinguished fourteen relatively homogeneous person categories... on the basis of age... men/women workers three each for men and women engaged in heavy moderate and sedentary work respectively. To these fourteen, another two, one each for non-working men and women were added to account for the whole of the population. In constructing the weighting diagrams for these 16 mutually exclusive and exhaustive person categories, the estimated age-sex structure of the population for 1982-83, derived from the population estimates (III projection) of the Expert Committee on Population (1977), coupled with the 1972 Census on occupational structure and participation rates based on usual activity status gleaned from the NSS employment data contained in the 27th Round (1972-73), is used. The age, sex, and occupation-specific distribution of the rural and urban population assumed in deriving the nutrition-based poverty norms for the base year and the terminal year of the Plan have been included in a separate paper prepared by the Perspective Planning Division.

Following are the main assumptions for its applicability:

(i) Calorie requirements for workers aged 15 but less than 19 years is the same to men/women workers. Accordingly, the worker's weight in the weighting diagram relates to adult workers, that is, those aged 15 years or more. Similar remarks apply to adult non-workers also.

(ii) Heavy *workers* include persons engaged in cultivation, agricultural labour, mining and quarrying, and construction.

(iii) Moderate workers include persons engaged in livestock, forestry, fishing, hunting, lantations, orchards and allied activities, manufacturing, servicing and repairing (both household and non-household).

(iv) Sedentary workers include persons engaged in trade and commerce, transport, storage, communication and other allied services.

(v) Calorie requirements for adult non-workers are the same as those for sedentary *workers.* In terms of rupees, the poverty line was the mid point of the expenditure class (in 1973-74 consumer expenditure data) in which the calorie needs *were* satisfied (Planning Commission, 1979).

As regards the lack of demand behaviour, for developing the official poverty line, an effective demand analysis was undertaken in the framework of linear expenditure systems. Since these *were* not taken into account at all in recent critiques of India's poverty line, it is again useful to put them down as specified then so that scholars decide to take a holistic perspective on their comments on the work of the Planning Commission, may refer to the original (Planning Commission, 1979, pp. 10-11).

MODELS

Those who are now stating that there is no theoretical base to the Planning Commission's demand and redistribution work may need to look at the following counterfactuals:

> "Effective demand has been considered in two stages. In the first stage, commodities and services have been grouped into 13 categories and the demand each of these 13 groups has been estimated by considering the Linear Expenditure System (LES). In the second stage, Engel/Demand curves have been considered estimating the demand for different commodities and services included in each of 13 LES groups. Within each LES groups, the total demand of various items in group is adjusted to equal the LES estimate of the group demand. These LES Engel curve/ Demand functions have been separately developed for people

below poverty line and above the poverty line, also in rural and urban areas separate (Planning Commission, p. 11). The formal systems on this count were as follows:

Linear Expenditure System (LES)

The Linear Expenditure System is a complete demand system, which is derived from the additive utility function for commodities, $q_i \ldots q_n$ given by

$$U(q_i \ldots q_u) = \sum_{i=1}^{n} b_i \log (q_i - a_i) \quad (1)$$

where

$$\sum_{i=1}^{n} b_i = 1 \text{ and } (q_i > a_i)$$

Maximizing (1) subject to the budget constraint given by

$$\sum_{i=1}^{n} p_i q_i = c \quad (2)$$

we obtain the complete demand system (3)

$$c_i = p_i q_i = a_i p_i + b_i \left(c - \sum_{i=1}^{n} a_i p_i\right) \quad (3)$$

The fulfillment of the second order conditions of equilibrium requires that $b_i > 0$ (that is, non-inferior n commodities or groups) and $c > \sum a_i p_i$ where $d_i = 1$ is the monthly per capita expenditure incurred on the *ith* commodity and p_i is the price of the *ith* commodity or equivalently index number for the *ith* commodity group as the case may be, and c-monthly per capita total expenditure incurred on various commodities (or commodity groups), $a_i p_i$ represents some sort of committed expenditure, while b_i is the proportion of the *ith* group in the remaining aggregate consumption.

The LES parameters are estimated by applying the Newton-Raphson method (Technical Appendix I) to the time series of cross-section data obtained from the 17th through the 28th Rounds of the NSS (excluding the 18th, 26th, and 27th Rounds) on household consumption expenditure, first for sixteen broad commodity groups at 1976-77 prices. The LES parameters for these groups are set out in Appendices 5.2, and 5.3. In order to be made compatible with 89 sector input-output classifications, these 16 LES groups had to be collapsed into thirteen groups. The parameter estimates for these groups are set out in Appendix 6.1 through (Planning Commission, 1979, p. 11).

Actually instead of ignoring the demand studies, the 1979 Task Force was based one of the more detailed demand and income distribution studies, and developed the income and price response of both poor and rich households separately in the rural and urban areas. This work started a tradition of econometric investigation of some policy significance, which has continued since then. Its use in plan models has been referred to above (*Parikh*, 2010).

DUAL PRICING AND EMPOWERMENT

Income supplementation and public distribution policies working through pricing and dual markets (an open market and a rationing system) could be integrated (quantitatively into the commodity market and parastatal policies that are specifically aimed at households below the poverty line. The late D.T. Lakadawala (1977) and the present author (*Alagh*, 1994) have written about this in detail. The price elasticities of rich and poor Indians in rural and urban areas attracted Lakadawala immensely as price theory, common sense, and a concern for the poor were his forte up to the very last day of his life. Price elasticities of the kind shown in Table 1 were estimated from the work of the 1979 Task Force and used for policy analysis. Therefore, "It would be desirable to adopt a system of dual pricing in respect of selected goods of mass consumption. The rationale of such a policy is derived from the fact that price elasticity in respect of essential commodities—cereals, pulses, edible oils—is relatively higher for persons below the poverty line both in urban and rural areas." (Planning Commission, 1980, p. 129). The recent review of plan models by K.S. Parikh, *et al.*, 2010, specifies in detail the use of these LES models and the poverty sub-blocks in the Sixth to Ninth Plan models as noted above (*Parikh*, 2010). We note in passing that these elasticities are complete demand system variants of the partial demand curve estimates used by S. Subramanian (2005, p. 60) to argue that the Indian poverty literature is theory-deficient.

There was considerable global recognition of this work. (See the well-known feschtrift to Jan Tinbergen edited by Cohen, Comillise, Teekens, and Thorbeckc, 1984, and the paper by Y.K. Alagh, *et al.*, contained in it; also see the appreciation by Lance Taylor, 1991, of their use in policy reform in transitional regimes.) In a fairly widely

TABLE 6
Own Price Elasticities of Agro-products in India

Sl. No.	*Commodity*	*1970s*	*1970s*	*1990s*	*1990s*
		Rural Poor	*Urban Non-poor*	*Rural Poor*	*Urban Non-poor*
1.	Cereals	-0.73	-0.04	-0.53	-0.10
2.	Pulses	-0.83	-0.19	-2.57	-0.86
3.	Edible Oil	-0.63	-0.19	-0.79	-0.42
4.	Sugar	-0.84	-0.33	-0.94	-0.29

Source : Planning Commission, 1979.

quoted paper, Taylor described a Multi-faceted Price System (MPS) as a "transition from an administered towards a market regime" (Taylor, MIT, 1993, p. 7). Citing Polish and Indian examples, he pointed out that "its homely virtues are perhaps becoming more evident" (*Ibid.*, p. 7), and the Indians working for policy systems in transitional regimes are "developing effective multi-tiered pricing systems for their nationalized firms and even in agriculture." (*Alagh*, 1994).

EXPERT GROUP

The critics of the poverty line are correct in stating that the 1979 poverty line cannot be taken as a *Lakshman Rekha* (final incontestable one) that cannot he re-examined, and it was never seen as being so in the technical work. The original 1979 Task Force was very clear on this and was also very sensitive to price corrections. It realized that price approximations can ravage poverty numbers and thus refused to give state level correction factors. The non-native official poverty line was conceptual well-founded and the behavioural demand work was intended for policy analysis. (*Y.K. Alagh*, 2010). The normative line needed to be re-evaluated but this was not done. The Lakadawala Expert Group, (*Planning Commission*, 1993), however, did not do the work that it was primarily set-up for.

Getting back to some of the proposals, an often-quoted recent World Bank study sets the agenda and accords respectability to high numbers. Shaohua Chen and Martin Ravallion estimate that while the $1-a-day figure was consistent with the Indian poverty line, the population below the poverty line in India as now estimated is as given in Table 7.

TABLE 7

Estimates of India's Population Below Poverty Lines by Chen and Ravallion

(in million)

Sl. No.	*Year*	*Poverty Norm US $ 2 a day*	*Poverty Norm US $ 2.5 a day*
1.	1990	701.6	766.5
2.	1993	735.0	808.9
3.	1996	757.1	841.1
4.	1999	782.8	875.2
5.	2002	813.1	911.4
6.	2005	827.7	938.0

Source : Chen and Ravallion, 2008, pp. 34-35.

Almost a billion Indians are estimated to be poor. India overtakes Chinese poverty absolute numbers much earlier now as compared to their earlier estimates. It is based on the original Purchasing Power Parity (PPP), Estimates. PPP estimates for any country, even those adjusted for rural/urban price differences, do not capture the consumption pattern of the poor. The work that R. Radhakrishna and A. Sarnla (1975) carried out at the Sardar Patel Institute in the late 1960s, of estimating the price indices separately for the rich and the poor in rural and urban areas in India produced robust results of a kind not seen elsewhere. It imparted a certain quality to the Indian poverty estimates, which other work lacks. In the recent Bank estimates, for some countries, even rural-urban indices are unavailable and for most countries, the indices for the poor are not available. The fact that poverty estimates are highly affected by price adjustments at the state level and not so much by consumption differences has been documented by the data exercise of S. Gangopadhyaya and Amaresh Dube.

Critical Appraisal of Tendulkar Poverty Concept

These controversies have been placed in context by the excellent work of the Tendulkar Committee (*Planning Commission*, 2009), which has finally facilitated the background preparation for a more focused strategy of poverty removal. The Tendulkar Committee report, which is available for discussion, is an appreciable report, the kind that we should have seen in the early 1990s. The work done by R. Radhakrishna and S. Sengupta under the care of Prof. Suresh Tendulkar offers an excellent technical back-up for a larger consultation and policy-focused process. At a more practical level, the N.C. Saxena Committee (*GOI, MORD*, 2009), set-up for identifying beneficiaries through the latest Below Poverty Line Census, has presented a multi-dimensional and many-splendoured menu, which is spiced up with seven comments. (Given the length, technical content and policy perspectives, the question arises as to if they are comments or minutes of dissent.)

The Tendulkar Group has moved over from a calorie-determined poverty line to a food expenditure-determined line. Its constituents are happy with the existing urban poverty ratio or head-count ratio of 25.7 per cent derived from the 1977 Task Force as adapted for price adjustment from time to time. They now suggest that this should he the national poverty line and that the expenditure required to meet this goal should he the poverty line for both rural and, of course, the urban areas. The exercise is fascinating, both for policy and in theory. We are all critical of the official poverty line, but they "found it desirable in the interest of continuity to situate it in some generally acceptable aspect of the present exercise". (GOI, 2009, p. 5). Like Banquo's ghost, the 1977 Alagh Task Force casts its shadow, possibly since both Tendulkar and Radhakrishna were its members. The poverty ratio for urban areas derived from that method now drives the new system. That ratio was derived from caloric norms. Now the argument has been turned on its head and the same ratio, in turn, determines the required food expenditure-determined poverty line basket. That basket is also suggested for rural areas. Viewed in a causal sense, the urban poverty ratio in 1979 came from calorie requirements and the poverty line basket. Now the ratio determined the basket for both the rural and urban areas. In the official poverty line, calorie requirements determine household expenditure requirements, which, in the second equation, determine the poverty line. In the Tendulkar poverty line, the urban expenditure requirements determine the poverty line.

Public policy is not an exercise in logic or causal chain systems, and the Tendulkar report has many advantages. For one thing, it shifts the emphasis from calories to the demand for food. In its logical structure, the 1979 Task Force permitted this through its complete demand systems but the focus then was on grains. That structure of reasoning with separate price elasticities for the rich and the poor led to dual pricing. The Tendulkar Committee framework provides the food purchasing power, and the framework allows the poor to substitute food items.

It works in the framework whereby the State now would not have the full responsibility for overseeing the education and health needs or for that matter the drinking water needs of the poor. Here, the Tendulkar Committee is one-sided in stating that "the earlier poverty lines assumed that the basic social services of health and education would be supplied by the State." It does not clarify that the 1979 Task Force stated that the State must have a Basic Needs Plan and must give it the highest priority, in terms of pro-poor priorities in expenditure (*Y.K. Alagh*).

The Tendulkar Report has a concept of inclusive growth wherein the State does not take on itself such pro-poor responsibilities but provides for a concept of income supplements for private expenditures for them. It shows that with these supplements the new poverty line would correspond to standards that would lead to physical nutrition norms, like nutrition for basic metabolic needs and others being met on an average, in fact being exceeded. Statistically, this part of the report, overlaying averages of nutrition norms with food expenditure is tentative, but it is early days yet, the approach is creative and more can and will be done in this direction. A more serious issue is that if expenditures on education and health are included in the poverty line calculations, how the public expenditures on them would be accounted for these complex questions need to be considered seriously.

The political economy preferences are just below the surface. Tendulkar and Radhakrishna refer many times to the 1979 Task Force, in fact, these are the largest number of references, but with the current allergy to anything that happened before 1992, do not list it in their references. That credit goes to the World Bank. More importantly, will the present standard dividing the poor and the rich, poor and that too on the basis of the 1979 poverty line in urban areas, be acceptable as a norm?

In the sections based on Radhakrishna's presidential address to the Indian Econometric Society, the point has been making that following norms does not require policy to go overboard is underlined by the Tendulkar Committee. The relation between income growth, diversification of food intake away from cereals, calories, and food demand is handled in an extremely competent manner and, in fact, an intake of 1700 calories justified.

SAXENA COMMITTEE DEFINING POVERTY

The Saxena Committee set-up for defining concepts for the next BPL Census goes overboard and comes out with very high numbers. Food security can be achieved at much lower costs than those suggested by Saxena, but he scores in his emphasis on access to social facilities and asset and education opportunities, for which he suggests a system of deprivation points based on many deprivation indicators, including caste, asset positions, educational achievements, and so on.

The Saxena Committee offers interesting proposals for giving deprivation points and weights to different sections of the population in defining poverty. It says that we actually have limited experience in developing deprivation points in an admission. system for the Jawaharlal Nehru University (JNU). When I was its Vice-Chancellor, the University placed resources with the Student's Union for an extensive debate to develop a workable system of deprivation in an appropriate form in a debate for admission reform. In early discussions, it was agreed that the system must actually serve its objectives and not permit cheating or be mere sloganeering. Incidentally, some of the participants included Dr. Thorat, Sarva Shri Yechuri and Karat, both JNU Student Union Presidents in their days. Ultimately, a system of deprivation points was designed. Points were given on the basis of the location of the college of the last degree, with the advantage being given to those who graduate from the poorest quarter of districts in India, based on sex and BPL status. For instance, if you were a girl OBC, graduating from Bastar, and your father was BPL, you got nine deprivation points. A non-BPL GBC boy from Delhi, on the other hand, got three points. In the first year, only five children made it on this count. Real social change is gradual, since 5 out of 1000 is half of one per cent. But those five children made it. But this kind of an argument becomes blurred when applied to the provision of universal social facilities like drinking water and education or health. Saxena, in fact, recognizes that differential entitlement systems will be required for different facilities, a very valid point but becoming virtually a nightmare for the real world if it is all from the State. (*Y.K. Alagh*).

There has to be a matching with scarcities not only of the available resources, but also of the more basic non-renewable kind as well as delivery capabilities otherwise the kind of exercises undertaken by Saxena will remain sporadic acts of activism. The task that the Expert Group was asked to carry out needs to be undertaken today, two decades after the Group was set-up. While current dominant development thinking does not emphasize it, this exercise will have to unequivocally define the rights of sections of the population.

These are not just questions of resource use, but also of governance, and would, in fact, be resource-conserving if they are properly designed and implemented. The systems will demand greater fairness and self-restraint in the use of government power. The demands on transparency and the right to information will be related to this. There will have to be a response to the demand for protecting vulnerable groups, either the historically underprivileged, or the victims of marketization, concerns for human rights and particularly of specific groups such as women, children, the minorities, the *adivasis,* and the mentally and physically challenged as defined by saxena.

References

Alagh, Y.K. (1994). Indian Development Planning and Policy, Vikas, Delhi, Second Edition.

Subramanian, S. (2005). "Unravelling A Conceptual Mnddle; India's Poverty Statistics in the Light of Basic Demand Theory", *Economic and Political Weekly*, January 1, pp. 57-66.

Taylor, L. (1993). The Rocky Road to Reform, WIDER, Helsinki. Wold, H. and L. Jureen (1953). Demond Analysis, North Holland, Amsterdam.

Datta, K.L. (2006). The Debate an the Poverty Estimates 1999-2000. Working Paper No. 188, ICRIER, Delhi.

Lakadawala, D.T. (1977). Presidential Address to the Indian Labour Economics Conference, Tirupati.

Parikh, K.S. (ed.) (2010). Macro-Modelling for the Eleventh Five Year Plan of India. P.P.D., Planning Commission and Academic Foundation, Delhi.

Radhakrishna, R. and A. Sarma (1975). Price Indices by Income Class in Rural and Urban Areas, Sardar Patel Institute of Economic and Social Research, Ahmedabad.

Bardhan, P.K. (1974). "The Pattern of Income Distribution in India—A Review in T.N. Srinivasan and P.K. Bardhan (Ed) Poverty and Income Distribution in India, Statistical Pub. Society, Calcutta.

Iyenger, N.S., Poverty Concepts and Measurement—A Review Poverty and Sustainable Development: Concepts and Measures, pp. 6-7, 2010.

Shandilya, T.K., Poverty, A danger to Prosperity, same book of Iyenger, N.S. (Same) pp. 73-74 (2010).

Karmakar, A.K., Poverty Alleviation in India for Sustainable Future in Iyenger NS book—Poverty and Sustainable Development: Concepts and Measures pp. 220-21 (2010).

Borbora, S. and Mahanta, R., Measurement and Poverty in India, pp. 153-59 (2010). Future in Iyenger, N.S. book—Poverty and Sustainable Development: Concepts and Measures, pp. 220-21 (2010).

Pal, P.K., Dimension of Poverty in India; Measurement Determinates Future in Iyenger, N.S. book—Poverty and sustainable Development: Concepts and Measures, pp. 220-21 (2010), pp. 167-69 (2010).

Gopalan, C., B.V. Rama Sastry, and S.C. Balasubamanyam (1971). Nutritive value of Indian foods, National Institute of Nutrition, Hyderabad.

Iyenger, N.S. and Mallika Gopalakrishna (1985). Appropriate Criteria for the Measurement of Levels of Living", *Indian Economic Review,* XX(2), pp. 191-229.

Iyenger, N.S. and Manjula Nadig (1993). "A test for Expenditure Elasticity Estimates from Survey Data", *Indian Journal of Applied Economics.* I(3 & $) pp. 42-52.

Mahalanobis, P.C. (1960). "A method of Fractile Graphical Analysis," *Economietrica,* 28(2), pp. 325-57.

Minhas, B.S., *et. al.* (1991). Declining Incidence of Poverty", *Economic and Political Weekly,* July.

Podulk, J.K. (1967). Incomes of Condian, Dominican Bureau of Statistics Ottawa.

Rowntree, B.S. (1901). Poverty: A Study of Town Life, p. 117., Macmillan, London.

Sukhatme, P.V. (1977). Poverty and Malnutriuon, Lal Bahadur Shastri Memorial Lecture, New Delhi, ed. (1982) Newer Concepts in Nutrition and their Implications of Policy. Maharashtra association for the Cultivation of Science Research Institute, Pune.

Iyengar, N.S.S.N. Joshi and M. Gopal Krishan (1992). A Bayesian Approach to Measurement of Poverty in India.

P.K. Goel and N.S. Iyengar ed. Bayesian, Analysis in Statistics and Econometrics, New York, Springer-Verlog, pp. 379-87.

Dandekar, V.M. and Rath, N. (1971). Poverty in India, *EPW.,* Jan. 2 & 9 1971-(Special articles) pp. 25-45 and pp. 143-46.

UNFPA for V.N. System in India (1997). India towards Population and Development Goals, OVP, Delhi.

Chapter 2

Poverty, Income, Inequality in India

An Analysis

Normally inequality refers to the uneven distribution of income and wealth as well as status and power. It is a common feature of all economies irrespective of economic development, political system, social and cultural values. Poverty and inequality are closely related phenomena, and their interrelationship can be easily demonstrated analytically by choosing an appropriate model of income distribution. In fact, it turns out that policies designed to reduce inequalities are precisely those which will also serve as instruments to reduce poverty. Exploiting this basic idea it is possible to provide a simple definition of poverty that is almost price invariant. An outline of this new approach to measuring relative poverty is given below.

Let us assume that the relevant indicator, such as per capita total consumption in current prices or income of households, has been selected for classifying the ultimate survey units (households) in an ascending order from poor to rich. Let the distribution of the variable indicator (X) be denoted by its density function, $f(x: e)$, where e is the unknown parameter vector. The mean (cl) and the inequality (L) are functions of the elements of e. One can take for the inequality the co-efficient of variation (c), or the Lorenz ratio (L), which are independent of the monetary units in which x has been expressed. Let us further assume that the poverty line can be defined as a simple fraction of the mean of the distribution, i.e. $x^* = k/l$, where k lies between zero and one. Here, k is arbitrary and may be left to be determined by a parliamentary decision. For example, k may be fixed as 50 per cent, so that whatever be the mean income or consumption the relative poverty line is just one-half of that income or consumption. When rapid development takes place, the policy-makers may fix a higher proportion of income as the poverty cut-off. This way of defining relative poverty has its own merits. It can be easily tried without demanding any additional data from NSS.

Let us assume that the distribution of income or consumption levels of households closely follows the Law of Proportionate Effect. According to this famous Law, like the celebrated Pareto's Law, the income or wealth status of a household is determined by a multiplicity of random influences, including inheritance, windfalls, etc., each contributing an infinitely small share. It implies that households which are already rich have better chances of improving their rich status in a market-driven economic system in the absence of effective state intervention. This Law has been extensively tested and fairly well established for India using published data from NSS (*Iyengar*, 1960, 1964, 1967; *Bhattacharya*, 1978; *Suryanarayana*, 1987; for example).

One implication of the Law of Proportionate Effect is that households' incomes or per capita expenditures when measured in natural logarithms, follow the famous Gaussian or normal law of distribution (*Cramer*, 1954, *Aitchison and Brown*, 1957).

A random variable (x) is said to be log-normally distributed with parameters θ and λ, if $In\ x$ is normally distributed with mean θ and standard deviation λ. The mean of the distribution (μ) and the Lorenz measure of inequality (L) are, respectively

$$\mu = \exp(\theta) + \lambda^2/2); \; L = 2\ \varphi\ (\lambda/2)-1 \qquad (1)$$

where $\varphi\ (u)$ is the cumulative distribution function of the standard normal variable with mean zero and standard deviation one. The cumulative distribution of x is given by:

$$F(x) = \varphi\ (ln\ x - \theta)\ \lambda/2 \qquad (2)$$

If x^* is the poverty line, then the poverty ratio is simply $F(x^*)$.

If we assume that $x^* = k\mu$ and use this definition in equation (2), we obtain the poverty ratio as :

$$F(x^*) = F(\mu/2); \varphi [\lambda/2 + (I/\lambda) \ln k] \qquad (3)$$

Thus, the relative poverty is dependent upon the policy parameter *(k)* and the degree of inequality *(L),* as reflected in A. Incidentally, the co-efficient of variation for the two-parameter log-normal distribution is given by :

$$c = \exp(\lambda^2) - 1 \qquad (4)$$

which also entirely depends on the single parameter λ . It is easy to show that the poverty ratio increases as inequality increases, and *vice versa.* Also, empirically, it is not difficult to estimate the inequality parameter from the available grouped size distribution data published by NSSO using the technique of concentration curves developed by Iyengar (1960). Appropriate standard errors can also be computed for the poverty estimates assuming large samples under realistic assumptions *(Iyengar and Nadig,* 1993).

Studies comparing poverty across countries usually contain an evaluation of their past policies for reducing poverty. If comparisons are to be a valid foundation for such assessments and, in particular, if they are to serve as a guide to effective allocation of public funds, the underlying concepts must be thoroughly examined. Atkinson (1991) lists four important issues that are critical in this respect, the choice of poverty indicator, the determination of poverty line, the unit of analysis and the choice of equivalence scale. He provides stimulating examples from the case studies, on poverty in the OECD countries—France, Spain, Italy, United Kingdom, Germany, Portugal, Greece, Ireland, Netherlands, Belgium, and Denmark. He also makes reference to practices in other industrially advanced countries like USA, Australia, Canada, Norway, and Sweden. Ravallion and Huppi (1991) describe a number of tools available for empirical analysis which allow researchers not only to test the sensitivity of poverty assessments measurement assumptions but also to decompose observed changes in aggregate poverty in terms of the underlying changes in the regional and demographic variables. These authors, like Indian scholars, base their poverty measures on the distribution of household consumption per person, after adjusting for inflation using the consumer price index, though modifying the expenditure weights to accord most closely with the spending patterns of the poor.

Poverty comparisons have been made in terms of income in France, Britain and Germany by taking the poverty standard as 50 per cent of the national average income. One of the two studies for UK uses households below average income as poor. According to a study by UK Department of Social Security (1990), in 1984-85, 9.2 per cent of households lived with incomes below 50 per cent of the mean. In France, in 1984-85, 10.9 per cent of households had incomes below 50 per cent of the median. In Germany, in 1983, 7.0 per cent of the population lived in households with income below 50 per cent of the mean. Of course, these comparisons will have to be qualified, since the methods followed in these countries are not quite the same. (*Iyengar, N.S.*, 2010)

MESURING INEQUALITY

Let *c* be the household monthly consumption in rupees per capita, as defined by the NSSO. It is a measure of the welfare that accrues to the household, and varies from one household to another, depending upon the size and composition, location and region, season, occupation, and several other social demographic factors. It can be treated as a random variable, with a distribution function *F (c)* or a probability mass function *f (c)* which is the first derivative of *F*. The distribution function may be broadly characterized by two parameters which are of economic interest-the mean consumption level *(Me)* and an inequality or dispersion parameter *(Le)*. Changes over time in the value of Me indicate growth or decline, depending on the sign. Similarly, an increase or decrease in Le over time can be interpreted as deterioration or improvement in the distribution of aggregate consumption. For the dispersion parameter, it is preferable to use the Lorenz measure rather than the 'variance or the coefficient of variation. Moreover, these dispersion parameters are comparatively less sensitive to different types of inter-household transfers (*Sen*, 1973) and more affected by grouping of the individual observations (*Prasad and Iyengar*, 1984). The Lorenz Ratio and the Lorenz curve are easily constructed and interpreted for comparing economic size distributions. They are least affected by grouping of observations and appear most appropriate as tools of analysis for the NSS grouped data that are readily available. Among the other important advantages are the decomposability and analytical facility in cases of linear transformation of data.

The Lorenz Curve always lies below the line of equal distribution, and the Lorenz Ratio is twice the area bound by the

Lorenz Curve and the line of equality. This ratio is designed to lie between 0 and 1, and expressed as a percentage independent of the currency in which incomes and consumption are observed. The ranking of income or consumption distributions on the basis of the Lorenz Ratio is not necessarily the same as the ranking based on the coefficient of variation. Interestingly, the Lorenz Ratio has an upper bound. It is possible to compute the Lorenz Ratio for the income distribution on the basis of an observed distribution of consumption using the well-known identity, $y = c + 5$, where y and 5 represent the income and saving of households respectively, and c, the residual, is consumption. Appendix A gives supporting mathematical justification for choosing the Lorenz Ratio in our present analyses. The Lorenz Box diagrams serve as a useful descriptive tool for studying inter-temporal and spatial shifts in size distributions. When these statistical tools are applied to sample survey data, it is customary to attach the margins of error to our conclusions. It is possible to estimate standard errors for all estimated Lorenz Ratios in large samples (*Iyengar*, 1960), based on realistic assumptions.

As already mentioned, the NSS estimates of consumption and its distribution are available in current prices. But changes in consumption valued in current prices do not reveal the real magnitudes, particularly in a context marked by inflation. Also, making judgments about changes in the distribution becomes rather difficult because of differences in consumption patterns between consumption groups and changes in relative prices. This problem is to be overcome by differential price mechanism using separate price indices for each consumption group. For this purpose, we need appropriate price indices for each sector in each State. However, in the absence of reliable retail price indices for all commodity groups at national and State levels, one prefers to use Vaidyanathan's (1974) procedure in preference to that of Iyengar and Jain (1978) in constructing the required price indices. Accordingly, we can use the All-India Wholesale Price Indices with base 1961-62 as 100, in the construction of the consumption-specific price indices. For this purpose, the weighting diagrams are obtained from the respective NSS distributions, for the base year. Given the relevant data, the price deflator for the ith fractile in the tth year is given by

$$d_{it} = \Sigma j\ Pjt\ Wif \qquad \ldots (1)$$

The summation goes from $j = 1$ (cereals and cereal substitutes) to $j = 11$ (other non-food items); for t^{th} round of NSS, Pjt denotes the price index for the pth commodity group and *Wif* is the weight of commodity group in the aggregate price index, assumed fixed on the basis of the 1961-62 survey. For illustrative purposes, we consider the following commodity groups for the construction of differential price deflators:

1. Cereals and cereal substitutes
2. Pulses and pulse products
3. Milk and milk products
4. Fish, egg, and meat
5. Edible oils
6. Sugar
7. Fruits, vegetables, and nuts
8. Other food items
9. Clothing
10. Fuel and light
11. Other non-food items

The relevant wholesale price indices for these groups have been taken from the Reserve Bank of India's annual reports on currency and finance (For details, (*Suryanarayana*, 1980). It may also be noted that we have used linear interpolation to convert the distribution of consumption available in fixed interval form into equal-frequency distributions. *(Iyengar, N.S. 2010)*

The estimates of per capita consumption *(Me)* and the Lorenz Ratio *(Le)* based on current price distributions are given separately for the rural and urban sectors of India for the period from 1961-62 to 1973-74 in Table B-1 in Appendix B. We find a marked difference in levels of living and improvement in their distributions in both the sectors. This may tempt us to conclude that there was indeed a marked increase in welfare levels in either sector.

The 'within inequality' was also estimated using the NSS class intervals 0-8, 8-11, 11-13, 13-15, 15-18, 18-21, 21-24, 24-28, 28-34, 34-43, 43-55, 55-75, 75 and above. The estimates show that grouping bias is generally within 5 per cent of total inequality (*Suryanarayana*, 1984). Table B-1 gives estimates of per capita consumption and the Lorenz Ratio based on current-price distributions: India (rural and urban), 1961-62 to 1973-74. Table B-2 shows estimates based on deflated distributions. A closer look at Tables B-1 and B-2 reveals that the movements in the estimates at current prices are different from those indicated by the price-adjusted estimates. Further, it may be noted that:

(i) During the period 1961-62 to 1973-74 taken as a whole, there was no significant trend in per capita real consumption in either of the two sectors;

(ii) Per capita real consumption generally fell in the early phase of the study period and rose more or less steadily from around 1967-68 in both rural and urban areas;

(iii) Per capita real consumption in the terminal year, 1973-74, was generally no higher than that in the initial year in both the sectors; and

(iv) The Lorenz Ratios also did not show any consistent trend; they fluctuated around a stagnant trend irrespective of the sector.

Thus, on the whole, it appears that with stagnant consumption and inequality levels, there was neither growth nor reduction in inequality in the two sectors at the national level during the period 1961-62 to 1973-74.

Operationally, justice is considered to have been delivered if improvement takes place at least for the "poorest of the poor". Accordingly, we adopt a positive concept of poverty and measure changes in levels of living of 'this poorest household using the three-parameter log-normal framework. (For further details, see *Iyengar* and *Suryanarayana*, 1984). The per capita consumption of the poorest households, denoted by *cp'* measured in 1961-62 rupees, are given in Appendix Table B-3. We also measure the distance between the average household consumption *(Me)* and the consumption level of the poorest household, i.e. *Mc – cpa* The mean poverty ratio may be defined as *(Mc – cp)/Me* or *I* – y, say. The y-parameter shows movements in *cp* in relation to *Mc.* It can be seen that the poorest household's consumption level also deteriorated up-to the mid-sixties and recovered marginally in the late-sixties in both the sectors. The mean poverty gap broadly shows that the poorest experienced relatively faster deterioration (improvement) than the average household during periods of decline (growth) in overall consumption levels. Thus, it appears that the poorest household still continues to be the most vulnerable part of the society. The estimates of the subsistence level and the mean poverty gap are reproduced from Iyengar and Suryanarayana (1984, 1996) and shown in Appendix Table B-4.

The Fifth Five Year Plan (Perspective Planning Division, Planning Commission, Government of India, 1973) had specifically stressed the need for increasing rural consumption levels at a much faster rate than the urban in order to reduce the rural-urban disparity. However, there is no way of verifying how far this target of reducing the inter-sector disparities has been achieved. We are, again constrained by the non-availability of information about the inter-sector price differences. Hence, we have to look at the behavior of inter-sector disparities in nominal per capita consumption, which shows a high degree of fluctuation over time (Appendix Table B-5).

Another way of examining the question of inter-sector equity would be by examining the pattern of movements in their consumption levels. However, we do not find any strict relation in the pattern of fluctuations in real consumption levels in the two sectors. But it appears that the declines in consumption levels have been of a much higher order for the rural sector than for the urban in the initial years.

INCOME INEQUALITIES IN INDIA

The scanty NCAER data on households' income and saving have very limited use for any inter-temporal or inter-state study in real terms. However, a few crude attempts have been made from time to time by Indian scholars, using an indirect approach and combing published aggregate data on consumption and savings with standard macro-economic identities. (*Iyenger*, 1978), for a survey of economic literature on income distributions in India. In what follows, we present a somewhat different approach, based on an early study by Iyengar and Suryanarayana (1996), for estimating the *income* inequality. In this approach there is no need to assume any model of income distribution.

Suppose we have an empirical estimate of the linear consumption function,

$$C = \alpha + \beta y \qquad \text{.... (2)}$$

where the variable c is consumption, as already defined, and y is household's disposable income; c and y *are* household variables. The Greek letters α and β are unknown parameters. The Lorenz-Gini index of income inequality *(Ly)* is given by

$$Ly = [2\ My] - 1 \int^{\infty} o \int^{\infty} o \ \mathrm{I}\ u - v\ \mathrm{I}\ dF(u)\ dF(v) \qquad \text{.... (3)}$$

where *My* is the mean disposable income. From Appendix A it is easy to establish the following property:

$$LcMc = \beta\, LyMy \qquad \text{.... (4)}$$

If one has direct estimates of *My, Me,* and â, then *Ly* could be easily derived. These computations are shown for 11 successive rounds of NSS, which provides the basis for estimating *Me* and *Le.* For *My* the Central Statistical Organization's National Income Statistics were used. A *consistent* estimate of β was obtained by applying Wald's method, rather than the standard least squares, in fitting the straight line, $C = \alpha + \beta y$, since both the variables *c* and *y* are subject to unknown errors of estimation. For basic data, Appendix Table B-7 can be viewed. The main limitations of pour approach may be stated as follows:

> We ought to have estimated the parameters of the consumption function using cross-section data for each year. But, constrained by the non-availability of such information, we have sought an easy way-out by using the time series data. This approach may have two implications: One, the income inequality is always a constant multiple of the consumption inequality, which, on *a priori* grounds, may appear unrealistic. Further, it implies that whatever may be the changes in the structure of income distribution, it is always related to consumption distribution according to a fixed relationship which is time invariant. Two, the estimate of the slope parameter ~(marginal propensity to consume) depends upon the sample size chosen. Hence, for the same consumption inequality, one may get different estimates of income inequality, depending on the number of observations in the sample. However, these limitations appear rather minor in the context of the social importance attached to income inequality estimates when they are not readily available.

For the inter-state analysis, we consider trends in per capita consumption and disparities, in nominal and real terms, and try to compare the 'welfare levels'. For purposes of analyzing state disparities, we consider the following 14 states of the Indian Union: (1) Andhra Pradesh, (2) Assam, (3) Bihar, (4) Gujarat, (5) Karnataka, (6) Kerala, (7) Madhya Pradesh, (8) Maharashtra, (9) Orissa, (10) Punjab-Haryana, (11) Rajasthan, (12) Tamil Nadu, (13) Uttar Pradesh, and (14) West Bengal. The estimates of per capita consumption at current prices for the rural and urban sectors for each of the selected States in Appendix Tables B-5 and B-6. As expected, they show significant improvements in levels of living. However, for analytical purposes, we construct growth indices of consumption in current prices for all the States, by sectors. With 1961-62 as the base, we construct these indices just for two years 1967-68 and 1973-74. This is because of our finding at the national level that consumption in real terms declined up-to 1967-68 and recovered in the later years. Such growth rates are presented in It can be seen that for the rural sector of all the States, consumption grew at a much faster rate during the second period, 1968-69 to 1973-74. The growth has been particularly faster in the rural areas of Andhra Pradesh, Bihar, Kerala, Maharashtra and Rajasthan. We find a similar picture of growth for the urban sector also. The second period analysis shows particularly marked growth in the States of Assam, Bihar, Karnataka, Kerala, and Punjab-Haryana. However, given that prices tend to *move* at a faster rate in the urban areas, the above statements would imply a situation where the rural-urban disparities in consumption have declined at least in the second group of States. The estimated coefficients of variation of per capita consumption are shown for all the States, in Tables Appendix B. They show a tendency for inter-State disparities to widen over time in the rural sector. The per capita consumption estimates (see, Tables B-8 and B-9 in Appendix B), after deflation for price changes, do not show much improvement in levels of living. The all-India pattern of decline in real consumption up to mid-sixties and recovery thereafter, was determined for the rural sector of Andhra Pradesh, Gujarat, Karnataka, Kerala, Madhya Pradesh, and West Bengal. The urban sector of any State does not show such pattern. Rather, it exhibits frequent fluctuations. A comparison of the terminal year results reveals that in most of the States, the real standard of living had remained either stagnant or declined. Coming to inequality in current and fixed prices, we find some improvement in the distributions over time in almost all of the selected States. However, the inter-State disparities do not show any significant trend. The State rankings on the basis of the Lorenz Ratio estimates do show some degree of consistency as judged by their rank correlation. The Lorenz Ratio estimates based on re-constructed consumption distributions in 1961-62 prices are shown in Tables (Appendix B). As expected, they show no improvements in the distributions. In fact, we find significant trend increase in inequality in rural West Bengal and trend decrease in the rural sectors of only four States—Assam, Karnataka, Punjab-Haryana, and Tamil Nadu. On the other hand, we find a declining tendency, though not significant, in urban Punjab-Haryana. We find definite signs of deterioration, particularly in urban Kerala and Tamil Nadu.

We also examined how the distributions behaved *vis-a-vis* per capita consumption over time in each State. The correlation between the two appear significant only in the rural sector of Andhra Pradesh and Assam; it is significant also in the urban sector of Assam and Bihar. The correlation is positive and, hence, implies that whenever there is increase in average per capita, the distribution of total consumption deteriorates and *vice versa.* The coefficient being positive for both rural and urban sectors of Assam, it appears that in the entire State, the benefits did not percolate to the poorest sections to the same extent as to the rich in periods of growth. Significantly enough, it would also imply that during years of hardship the poorer sections suffer less compared to the better-off. The coefficients are found to be negative though not significant for a few other State sectors. That only indicates a mild tendency for distributions to improve during periods of growth in consumption and *vice versa. (Iyengar, N.S.,* 2010*).*

GROWTH-POVERTY-INEQUALITY SYNDROME

The impact of growth on poverty and income distribution is viewed differently by, different studies. (Table 1). The earlier work of Simon Kuznets out a negative relationship between the extent of inequality (wide gap of rich and poor) and the level of growth in the name of growth-inequality syndrome. Some of the recent empirical works in India point out reductions in poverty consequent on higher level growth and certain other studies point out increase in poverty, particularly after 1991 despite greater level of growth. These became reduction in the rural poverty during the post-reform period (*Mahendra Dev,* 2000). At the same time there became increasing inter-state inequalities measured in terms of per capita SDR. On the other hand, NSS data reveals the fact that the rank concordance index across states does not usually show convergence (*Raghvendra Jha,* 2000). A worrisome development is that there is greater dispersion in rural poverty across the states, though also the convergence of inequality, poverty, and mean consumption in selected states. The concerned table presents the trend in the magnitude of the rural and urban poverty measured in terms of head-count ratio by different sources. It is found that at All India level; percentage of poor below poverty line (BPL) was nearly 53.07% as in as in 1977-78 and declined round 39% in 1990-91. However, these same quickly shot up to 45% in 1998. The studies of World Bank as well IGIDR Indira Gandhi Institute of

TABLE 1

Poverty Estimates in All-India (Head Count Ratio)

Year	*PC*	*WB*	*IGIDR*	*PCWB*	*IGIDR*	*All India*	
1977-78	53.07	50.6	50.64	45.24	40.5	40.5	51.32
1983-84	45.65	45.31	45.31	40.79	86.65	36.65	44.48
1987-88	39.09	39.23	39.52	38	W.2	35.6	39
1990-91	NA	36.43	36.4	NA	—	—	—
1992-93	NA	43.47	43.47	NA	NA	NA	NA
1993-94	37.27	36.66	38.71	32.36	30.51	30.09	35.97
1997-98	38.5	35.78	34.22	NA	NA	NA	NA
1998	45.2	NA	NA	34.6	NA	NA	NA
1999-2000	NA	NA	NA	NA	NA	NA	26.1

Source : PC = Planning Commission (1997) Estimate based on Expert Committee Estimates, WB = World Bank Reported in Datt (1995). IGIDR = Indira Gandhi Institute of Development Research, estimates Reported in Jha (1999).
Estimated quoted in Deepak Lal etc. at *EPW*, March 24, 2001 (pp. 10-19).

Development. Research) bring out a falling and an urban context too. The magnitude of inequality seems to have widened measured by gini-coefficient, particularly during the decade of reform measures. The gini-coefficient for rural India according to the study of IGI was estimated at 33.74 as in 1957-58 and at 35.90 for urban India. During 1990s the gini-coefficient increased to 30.11 and 36.12 for rural and urban India respectively, measured as in 1997-98. This finding was further supported by MISH as well as W. Bank and Tendulkar estimates, though there are statistical variations in estimates *(EPW*, March 24, 2001). This is the short analysis of growth, poverty and inequality (in equality between poor and rich, between rural and urban between inter-states, between forward class and dalits, backwards, etc.)

The data is not related with each other due to methodological different of the sources. The problem of poverty must be analysed by taking rural division into account. Then only one can understand the impact of growth the reduction (or increase) of poverty at all India level or at different regions or areas. The average size of rural poverty is higher in all sources than urban poverty. So there is rural-urban divide in the process of growth in the economy. The inverse relationship between growth and poverty lies the certain coefficient between per capita income and the level of poverty there in. The provisions of globalization and liberalization also are going in favour of rich states (as it is going in favour of developed nations only. The trend of privatization is on the peak. It is increasing unemployment inequality and poverty every day. The future is very dark. The government factories and industries are being closed. The industrial progress of all the BIMARU states (except Rajasthan) has remained negative. There has heavy downfall in the establishment of industrial units in Andhra Pradesh, Bihar, and M.P. Although there is slight progress in the condition of Uttar Pradesh. In the first ten years of liberalization only 17% increase took place in the total number of industrial units. Under the Factories Act following change took place during 1991-92 and 1999-2000 in the number of industrial units in the country (states-wise) as we see in the table below:

TABLE 2

Industrial Units in India, (States-wise)

Sl. No.	*States*	*1991-92*	*1999-2000*	*Increase or Decrease (%)*
1.	Bihar	3,671	1.570	-57.23
2.	M.P.	4,163	.4	
3.	Andhra Pradesh	15,972	164	
4.	Karnataka	5,850	52	
5.	Kerala	3,702	+30.87	
6.	Tamil Nadu	15,502	20,249	+30.6
	All India	1,12,286	1, 1,557	+17

TABLE 3

Industrial Sickness

Satisfactory Condition	*Very Satisfactory Condition*
Northern States	Western States
Delhi, U.P., Haryana, H.P., J&K and Nagar Haweli	Gujarat, Goa, Maharashtra and Dadar, Rajasthan

Industrial development is the most important factor for eliminating poverty. But during the last thirteen years (which remained the period of liberalization and Economic Reform) no progress took place according to expectation in the manufacturing sector due to the effects of liberalization policy. During this period (1991-92 to 1999-2000) of economic reform or liberalization, Bihar has suffered the most. There became 57% decrease in the number of industrial units in the stipulated period, in southern state Andhra Pradesh, though it has made progress in information technology sector has been proved its worst in the case of industrial units. The so-called progress made by liberalization has made no impact on the condition of economically backward and so-called BIMARU States. Really their condition has been worsened during past thirteen years due to the LPG Policy (Liberalization, Privatization and Globalization). (*Thakur, R.N.*, 2010)

The scene of internal economic disparity among the states is visible with some facts such as Bangalore now has more in common with the Bay Area in San Francisco, US, than with Bihar. Life on the fields of eastern U.P. resembles that in certain parts of East Africa more closely than in Western U.R. itself. At the sprawling shopping pulls in Delhi's Southern or eastern outskirts a branded polo shirt costs of $ 100, whereas other parts of Delhi is infested of vast expanses of slums. Although most Indians seem to be better-off today than a decade ago, some regions have improved their lot much more than others. Goa, Delhi, Gujarat, and Maharashtra notched up the fastest growth in the 1990s, whereas growth rates in the half of the 15 biggest of its actually declined. On a per head basis, the difference is even starker. Some states where growth is slower, including the two biggest Uttar Pradesh and Bihar, also have fast growing populations. The yarning gaps are only growing (Table 4). For every new 'hotspot' emerging as a symbol of modern India, there are at least a

TABLE 4

Prosperous States	*Striving Middling States*	*Poor States*
Gujarat, Maharashtra, Haryana, Punjab, Delhi, Goa, Meghalaya	Andhra Pradesh, Karnataka, Tamil Nadu, Kerala, Pondicherry, Sikkim, Arunachal Pradesh, Chhattisgarh, Orissa, Nagaland, Manipur, Mizoram Jammu and Kashmir	Uttaranchal, Uttar Pradesh, Bihar Jharkhand, Madhya Pradesh, Assam

It is indicative, not definitive categorization.
Source : *India Today*, May 19, 2003.

dozen 'rot spots' serving as reminders of decay. The question is no longer whether India's economic fragmentation will happen. The question is, why has it happened and what can be done about it?

Till the mid-1980s there was slow growth rate. Consequently inequalities did not increase rapidly. The impoverishment of rural economy during most of the 1990s, the declining share of agriculture in India's GDP, the urge in, services economy and above all the infusion of competition and market, forces have begun to deepen the divide. Competition promotes efficiency, not equality. It rewards good performers generously and punishes laggards, often harshly. The increasing flow of money and people largely from the rust belt of the east to the Pockets of west, south, and north will only perpetuate the divergence. Some optimist sees hopes of convergence too. They argue that the winners of the free will demonstrate to the losers the price of non-performance. Especially those winners who have come on their own in the competitive environment. For instance, Andhra Pradesh and H.P. one has made strides in economic performance and the other in social development. But right now, such case studies are too few to be hopeful of a large scale convergence.

India still has some time to set things right. Compared to many other poor and developing countries—including China—its inequalities are less severe. The first task is to rise the spending on health and education in the long neglected Hindi-belt and some eastern states. U.P. spends just Rs. 55 a year on the health care of each person in the state, compared with Rs. 382 in Goa. Kerala brings high position in health care (equal to U.S.A.) by spending only Rs. 28 per person.

The laggards states have to doggedly pursue reforms, in governance and in business. It is not as improbable as it sounds. Any way, the most governments can do is to ensure that different regions grow to their potential, even if they still grow unequally.

In the recent ranking survey made by "India Today" group if small Indian states have piped the bigger ones to the post—the top five states (Goa, Delhi, Punjab, Kerala and H.P.) accounts for less than 8% of India's population—it is not because they had suddenly turned into the country's growth engines and became able to make their states most prosperous. These facts have been indicated in the tables ahead.

TABLE 5(A)
Poverty Level

Sl. No.	*Best Three States*	*% Population Below Poverty Line*	*Sl. No.*	*Worst Three States*	*% Population Below Poverty Line*
1.	Goa	4.40	1.	Orissa	47.15
2.	Punjab	6.16	2.	Bihar	42.60
3.	H.P.	7.63	3.	M.P.	37.43

TABLE 5(B)
Literacy

Sl. No.	*Best Three States*	*% of Illiterate Population*	*Sl. No.*	*Worst Three States*	*% of Illiterate Population*
1.	Kerela	9.08	1.	Bihar	50.83
2.	Goa	17.68	2.	J & K	45.54
3.	Delhi	18.18	3.	U.P.	41.89

TABLE 5(C)
Health Care Spending

Sl. No.	*Best Three State*	*Rupees per person a year**	*Sl. No.*	*Worst Three State*	*Rupees per person a year**
1.	Goa	382	1.	U.P.	48
2.	H.P.	251	2.	Bihar	61
3.	J & K	245	3.	M.P.	75

*State government spending.
Source : *India Today*, May 19, 2003.

TABLE 5(D)

Ranking in Highly Population States*

Sl. No.	State	Population (in Crores)	Ranking
1.	T.N.	6.21	1
2.	Gujarat	5.05	2
3.	Maharashtra	9.67	3
4.	Karnataka	5.27	4
5.	Andhra Pradesh	7.57	5
6.	Rajasthan	5.65	6
7.	West Bengal	8.02	7
8.	M.P.	8.12	8
9.	U.P.	17.45	9
10.	Bihar	10.90	10

*Accounts for 84% of India's population.

TABLE 6

Different Sectors and some Major States

Sl. No.	*Prosperity & Budget*	*Law & order*	*Education*	*Health*	*Infra-structure e*	*Invest-ment Scenario*	*Con-sumption Market*	*Agriculture*	
(1)	*(2)*	*(3)*	*(4)*	*(5)*	*(6)*	*(7)*	*(8)*	*(9)*	*(10)*
1.	Delhi	1+1	5+3	3+4	2+2	2+2	6+2	1+1	2+9
2.	Goa	2+2	2+9	1+1	1+1	1+1	1+1	2+2	5+6
3.	Punjab	3+3	17+14	7+7	5+6	4+4	4+5	3+3	1+1
4.	Gujarat	4+4	8+6	8+11	8+9	6+9	3+4	8+9	10+5
5.	Haryana	10+5	12+12	9+12	11+13	8+7	5+3	4+4	3+2
6.	Maharashtra	6+6	9+10	5+6	9+10	7+8	8+7	6+5	17+11
7.	T.N.	8+7	3+2	6+5	7+7	10+6	13+9	11+10	6+3
8.	Karnataka	5+8	4+7	11+8	10+8	9+11	10+8	10+11	17+7
9	H.P	14+9	6+4	4+2	3+4	3+3	7+6	6+6	15+17
10.	Andhra Pradesh	7+10	13+11	15+13	12+11	12+12	12+10	17+14	8+4
11.	J&K	9+11	16+15	13+9	6+3	5+10	2+12	5+8	9+14
12.	Kerala	11+12	1+1	2+3	4+5	11+5	17+14	9+7	13+15
13.	Rajasthan	12+13	7+5	18+17	14+14	14+13	9+13	12+13	18+12
14.	West Bengal	15+14	14+16	12+14	13+12	16+15	18+17	13+12	11+10
15.	M.P.	13+15	10+8	16+16	17+15	13+14	14+16	14+17	4+13
16.	U.P.	16+16	18+17	17+18	19+19	17+16	15+15	15+16	7+8
17.	Assam	17+17	15+18	10+10	18+17	18+18	11+11	16+15	19+19
18.	Bihar	19+18	19+19	19+19	15+16	19+19	19+19	19+19	16+16
19.	Orissa	18+19	11+13	14+15	16+18	15+17	16+18	18+18	14+18
Fastest mover in the 1990s		Himachal Pradesh	Punjab	Rajasthan	M.P	Assam & T.N.	Delhi	Andhra Pradesh	Rajasthan

References

Atkinson, A.B. (1991), "Comparing on Poverty rates Internationally lesson from recent studies in developed countries, *World Bank Review*, 5. I, p. 3.

Bhattacharya, N. (1978), "Studies on Level of Living in India." 'A survey of Research in Economic (eds.) Iyenger, N.S. and N. Bhattacharya, Vol. 7, *Econometrics*, Bombay, Allied Publishers, pp. 231-51.

Sen, A.K. (1973), On Economic Inequality, Oxford University Press, Bombay.

Iyenger, N.S. (1978), Size distribution of consumption and income ICSSR; a surver of research in economic, Vol. Vll allied pub Bombay, pp. 277-316.

Suryanarayan, M.H. and N.S. Iyenger (1984), On Poverty Indicators, *Economic and Political Weekly*, XIX 897-902.

Iyenger, N.S., On Nutrition and Poverty in the book—Poverty and Sustainable Development : Concepts and Measures, pp. 10-11, Deep and Deep Publications (P) Ltd., New Delhi, 2010.

Iyenger, N.S., Poverty, Income Inequality and Growth: An Analysis with Illustrations from Indian data ed. book (same) pp. 25-27-30-31 (2010).

Iyenger, N.S., On Nutrition and Poverty, ed. Book same as above, pp. 10-11 (2010).

Iyenger, N.S., Poverty, Income Inequality and Growth: An Analysis with Illustrations from Indian data ed. book (same) pp. 25-27-30-31 (2010).

Thankur, R.N., Poverty-Progeny of Progress ed. book Iyenger, N.S., Poverty and Sustainable Development: Concepts and Measures, pp. 220-21 (2010), pp. 093-95 (2010).

Iyengar, N.S. (1960), "On a Method of Computing the Engel Elasticities from Concentration Curves", *Econometrica*, 28(4), pp. 882-91.

Iyenger, N.S. (1964), "As consistent Method of Estimating the Engel Curve from Grouped Survey Data", *Econometrica*, 32 (4), pp. 591-618.

Rovallion, M. and Monica Huppi (1991), "Measuring changes in poverty a ethodological case study of Indonesia during an adjustment period the World Economic Review, 5(1), pp. 57-82.

Suryanarayan, M.H. (1987), "The Problem of Distribution in India s Development: An empirical analysis doctoral thesis, India Statistical Institute, Calcutta.

APPENDIX B

TABLE B1

Estimated per capita Consumption and Inequality in Current (Constant) Prices: Rural and Urban India: 1961-62 to 1973-74

Year	*Per capita consumption (Rs. Per month)*		*Inequality (Lorenz ratio)*	
	Rural	*Urban*	*Rural*	*Urban*
1961-62	21.73 (21.73)	30.86 (30.86)	0.3130 (0.3100)	0.3566 (0.3566)
1963-64	22.37 (20.31)	32.96 (30.24)	0.2974 (0.3000)	0.3596 (0.3630)
1964-65	26.44 (20.88)	36.03 (29.51)	0.2936 (0.3080)	0.3492 (0.3640)
1965-66	28.40 (20.84)	36.65 (27.90)	0.2972 (0.3090)	0.3385 (0.3540)
1966-67	30.90 (19.78)	41.54 (27.94)	0.2934 (0.3120)	0.3368 (0.3620)
1967-68	33.40 (18.80)	44.82 (27.19)	0.2908 (0.3150)	0.3324 (0.3650)
1968-69	33.29 (19.49)	46.04 (28.58)	0.3051 (0.3260)	0.3292 (0.3550)
1969-70	34.70 (19.45)	50.39 (29.75)	0.2928 (0.3140)	0.3403 (0.3640)
1970-71	35.31 (19.30)	52.85 (30.14)	0.2831 (0.3010)	0.3265 (0.3490)
1972-73	44.17 (20.58)	63.33 (32.96)	0.2993 (0.3220)	0.3410 (0.3710)
1973-74	53.01 (21.51)	70.77 (30.60)	0.2758 (0.2990)	0.3013 (0.3460)

Source : Suryanarayana (1984).

TABLE B2

Estimates of "Total" Inequality of Consumption, Subsistence Level, and Mean Poverty Gap: 1961-62 to 1973-74

(in content prices of 1961-62)

Year	*Inequality*		*Subsistence level*		*Mean poverty gap*	
	Rural	*Urban*	*Rural*	*Urban*	*Rural*	*Urban*
1961-62	0.3160	0.3621	3.84	8.64	0.8235	0.7200
1963-64	0.3019	0.3685	4.78	6.61	0.7646	0.7814
1964-65	0.3085	0.3707	3.72	6.82	0.8218	0.7689
1965-66	0.3117	0.3616	2.27	7.44	0.8911	0.7333
1966-67	0.3143	0.3707	0.92	5.54	0.9535	0.8017
1967-68	0.3204	0.3796	1.28	6.81	0.9319	0.7495
1968-69	0.3285	0.3663	1.64	8.23	0.9159	0.7120
1969-70	0.3178	0.3852	4.21	7.97	0.7835	0.7321
1970-71	0.4043	0.3732	5.71	5.44	0.7041	0.8195
1972-73	0.3243	0.3780	6.44	7.60	0.6871	0.7694
1973-74	0.3046	0.3443	3.33	3.85	0.8452	0.8742

Source : Iyengar and Suryanarayana (1984).

TABLE B3
Estimates of Inequality in Distributions of Income and Consumption: All-India, 1961-62 to 1973-74 in Current Prices

Year	*Full and partial inequality as measured by the Gini-Lorenz ratio**			
	Consumption Inequality		*Income Inequality*	
	Partial	*Full*	*Partial*	*Full*
1961-62	0.3315	0.3347	0.4069	0.4108
1963-64	0.3216	0.3248	0.3948	0.3987
1964-65	0.3069	0.3115	0.3767	0.3824
1965-66	0.3107	0.3149	0.3814	0.3865
1966-67	0.3094	0.3146	0.3798	0.3862
1967-68	0.3042	0.3104	0.3734	0.3810
1968-69	0.3201	0.3267	0.3929	0.4010
1969-70	0.3137	0.3213	0.3851	0.3944
1970-71	0.3063	0.3144	0.3760	0.3858
1972-73	0.3116	0.3166	0.3825	0.3886
1973-74	0.2898	0.2965	0.3557	0.3639

* The full Gini-Lorenz ratio is normally computed from grouped size distribution data, using the group weights and group means. Usually, the trapezoidal rule of numerical integration is employed to compute the area of concentration. This ratio captures only the inter-group variations in the group means, but cannot reflect the intra-group inequality. The latter cannot be ignored, since it introduces a negative bias in inequality estimation to some extent.

TABLE B4
Estimates of Rural per capita Consumption by State (in Current Prices)*

(In Rs.)

State	Year										
	1961-62	1963-64	1964-65	1965-66	1966-67	1967-68	1968-69	1969-70	1970-71	1972-73	1973-74
(1)	(2)	(3)	(4)	(5)	(6)	(7)	(8)	(9)	(10)	(11)	(12)
Andhra Pradesh	20.11	20.76	26.45	27.66	29.14	30.46	31.47	34.54	34.35	39.79	50.57
Assam	22.23	26.43	29.30	30.66	36.83	41.53	37.57	37.69	40.37	41.67	52.03
Bihar	19.00	21.31	26.60	30.31	29.02	33.36	29.78	33.65	33.15	41.20	56.01
Gujarat	22.58	22.69	26.98	26.57	28.99	31.35	34.53	34.38	36.64	51.70	54.49
Karnataka	25.33	20.43	25.23	26.42	29.29	31.93	31.21	31.08	35.89	44.53	52.32
Kerala	21.07	20.36	22.30	21.80	24.56	28.54	36.18	31.07	36.12	42.19	55.35
Madhya Pradesh	21.46	23.37	26.30	28.07	29.57	31.77	31.15	33.68	32.88	40.72	50.39
Maharashtra	19.91	21.72	25.16	27.74	28.33	30.66	32.04	33.22	36.39	41.55	52.27
Orissa	17.40	19.35	20.61	21.50	26.20	30.24	28.24	28.70	28.86	34.96	42.66
Punjab-Haryana	32.76	28.66	37.52	37.05	44.82	45.01	52.36	53.93	53.97	72.62	74.16
Rajashtan	23.48	23.13	30.55	32.98	37.14	38.42	41.06	41.26	35.39	51.98	64.01
Tamil Nadu	22.53	23.39	24.55	24.57	28.59	29.61	30.02	32.08	29.98	37.70	47.74
Uttar Pradesh	22.73	21.51	27.09	29.46	33.15	35.14	35.09	34.00	29.98	37.70	47.74
West Bengal	20.83	21.69	23.18	26.71	28.98	32.63	29.85	32.86	33.32	38.46	47.50
**Coefficient of Variation (%)	16.25	11.10	15.38	13.88	17.04	14.34	18.42	17.58	16.54	21.17	14.27

* At present, India has more than 14 States. The new States are (15) Haryana, (16) Jammu & Kashmir, (17) Tripura, (18) Jharkhand, (19) Chatisgarh, (20) North-Eastern States, and (21) Group of Union Territories. The NSSO 56th Round Report (2002) gives detailed data for the year 2000-01. See, Government of India (2002).

** The variation is across the States and may be taken as a measure of regional inequality.

Table B5
Estimates of Urban Monthly per capita Consumption by States in Current Prices

(In Rs.)

State	Year										
	1961-62	1963-64	1964-65	1965-66	1966-67	1967-68	1968-69	1969-70	1970-71	1972-73	1973-74
(1)	(2)	(3)	(4)	(5)	(6)	(7)	(8)	(9)	(10)	(11)	(12)
Andhra Pradesh	25.19	28.16	31.78	34.65	37.34	40.49	44.44	47.68	49.27	56.32	65.30
Assam	39.20	46.64	42.66	42.23	60.44	58.70	55.93	60.52	64.24	60.75	72.78
Bihar	34.96	29.89	32.41	33.86	38.95	44.23	44.14	47.15	51.02	59.91	68.36
Gujarat	31.73	33.03	31.19	33.59	38.35	42.42	40.21	44.24	48.83	57.78	66.76
Karnataka	27.21	25.88	32.44	33.84	34.25	38.33	42.90	45.60	50.71	57.89	66.50
Kerala	25.82	27.29	30.11	24.93	35.45	34.81	38.39	44.11	47.63	58.27	68.93
Madhya Pradesh	26.70	29.93	34.44	32.86	40.08	40.20	44.35	45.77	50.37	61.88	65.50
Maharashtra	36.66	37.24	44.48	46.87	49.46	50.34	52.06	62.20	63.60	74.34	79.78
Orissa	33.71	31.92	31.79	34.35	41.98	47.21	48.26	54.66	52.75	62.35	70.09
Punjab-Haryana	29.27	34.33	36.95	36.48	44.12	47.35	51.69	55.30	62.02	75.00	79.58
Rajasthan	28.92	32.53	34.21	34.37	39.93	44.60	46.49	46.72	54.13	63.87	68.76
Tamil Nadu	29.74	31.47	34.34	34.11	35.31	41.22	40.68	43.70	44.69	54.02	64.78
Uttar Pradesh	25.40	29.17	30.05	31.97	38/87	42.67	41.08	42.55	45.17	53.55	60.81
West Bengal	38.42	41.66	41.13	42.77	48.31	51.94	53.52	59.32	60.69	68.23	80.76
Coefficient of Variation (%)	15.83	17.42	13.50	16.63	16.96	13.78	11.92	13.83	12.65	10.98	8.81

TABLE B6

Rural Monthly per capita Consumption by States in Constant Rupees of 1961-62

(In Rs.)

State	Year										
	1961-62	1963-64	1964-65	1965-66	1966-67	1967-68	1968-69	1969-70	1970-71	1972-73	1973-74
(1)	(2)	(3)	(4)	(5)	(6)	(7)	(8)	(9)	(10)	(11)	(12)
Andhra Pradesh	20.11	18.85	20.98	20.28	18.62	17.22	18.45	19.35	18,82	19.55	20.80
Assam	27.23	23.74	22.74	22.04	23.04	22.42	21.61	20.84	21.60	19.71	19.90
Bihar	19.00	19.96	23.93	25.85	21.75	24.41	20.71	18.62	17.67	24.22	26.85
Gujarat	22.58	20.68	21.39	19.57	18.66	17.74	20.17	19.33	19.75	25.06	21.57
Karnataka	25.33	13.57	20.01	19.60	18.98	18.26	19.20	17.52	19.77	21.67	21.05
Kerala	21.07	18.60	18.05	16.47	16.26	16.97	22.29	18.05	20.42	21.70	23.77
Madhya Pradesh	21.46	21.21	20.70	21.95	18.87	17.85	18.29	18.91	18.01	19.20	19.84
Maharashtra	19.91	19.73	19.95	20.53	18.47	17.48	19.12	18.78	19.97	20.53	21.42
Orissa	17.40	17.49	16.04	16.97	16.39	16.63	16.23	15.89	15.69	16.69	16.71
Punjab-Haryana	32.76	26.32	30.72	28.11	30.14	26.91	31.50	31.15	30.11	36.76	31.53
Rajasthan	23.47	21.19	24.58	24.53	24.34	22.28	24.46	23.42	19.47	25.61	25.57
Tamil Nadu	21.72	21.21	19.47	18.12	18.36	16.82	17.70	18.01	16.44	18.57	19.57
Uttar Pradesh	22.72	19.35	21.41	21.68	21.35	19.84	19.61	19.28	19.40	19.94	20.59
West Bengal	20.83	21.47	18/17	19.43	18.32	18.15	17.27	18.34	18.15	18.71	19.14

Source : Suryanarayana (1984).

TABLE B7

Urban Monthly per capita Consumption by States in Constant Rupees of 1961-62

(In Rs.)

State	Year										
	1961-62	1963-64	1964-65	1965-66	1966-67	1967-68	1968-69	1969-70	1970-71	1972-73	1973-74
(1)	(2)	(3)	(4)	(5)	(6)	(7)	(8)	(9)	(10)	(11)	(12)
Andhra Pradesh	25.19	25.70	25.68	25.98	24.59	23.97	26.97	27.51	27.58	28.59	27.52
Assam	39.20	42.45	34.64	35.39	40.11	35.31	34.43	35.81	36.48	30.94	30.36
Bihar	.34.96	26.94	26.94	27.60	29,65	29.91	27.83	29.88	32.24	28.67	31.45
Gujarat	31.75	30.38	25.45	25.51	25.65	25.50	24.72	25.82	27.49	29.76	28.52
Karnataka	27.21	23.61	26.33	25.67	22.88	22.85	25.99	26.32	28.42	29.73	28.53
Kerala	25.82	25.00	24.81	19.16	24.13	21.33	23.93	25.92	27.08	30.92	30.99
Madhya Pradesh	26.70	27.44	28.06	24.91	26.85	24.12	27.33	26.89	28.60	31.83	28.11
Maharashtra	36.66	34.30	36;93	36.19	33.93	31.43	33.08	37.63	37.05	39.99	35.46
Orissa	33.71	29.21	25.87	26.45	28.13	28.47	30.01	32.66	30.47	32.61	30.45
Punjab-Haryana	29.27	31.73	30.35	27.88	29;73	28.72	31.56	32.22	34.75	38.44	.34.03
Rajasthan	28.92	29.87	27.85	25.94	26.54	26.51	28:07	26.90	30.14	32.44	29.06
Tamil Nadu	29.74	28.65	27.90	25.86	25.57	24.66	24.90	25.39	25.15	27.83	27.75
Uttar Pradesh	25.40	26.75	24.46	24.24	26.00	25.54	25.23	24.93	25.61	27.58	26.13
West Bengal	38.42	38.24	33.85	32.16	32.59	31,86	33.45	35.41	34.99	35.90	35.04

Source : The estimates for Kerala, Punjab-Haryana, and Tamil Nadu are from Suryanarayana (1980) and those for Karnataka are from Suryanarayana (1984).

Chapter 3

Different Dimensions of Poverty in India

Poverty is a multi-dimensional concept. The main dimensions are: (i) lack of income and assets to attain basic necessities, food, shelter, clothing, and acceptable levels of health and education, (ii) sense of voicelessness and powerlessness in the institutions of state and society, (iii) vulnerability to adverse shocks, linked to an inability to cope with them.

It is much acute in developing economies than developed economies. We now examine the incidence of poverty in developing economies.

In this chapter an attempt has been made to examine the different dimensions of poverty in India—the changing scenario of international incidence of poverty, the measurement of poverty in India changing scenario of inter-state differentials (rural-urban differentials) of poverty in India. The determining factors (causes) of poverty.

Developing economies have different regions. East Asia and Pacific, Europe and Central Asia, Latin America and the Caribbean, Middle East and North Africa, South Africa and sub-Saharan Africa. In developing economies the incidence of poverty has varied over time across the regions. Estimates reveal (Table 1) that the share of the population in developing economies living on less than $ 1 a day has declined from 28% in 1987 to 24% in 1998. There are large

TABLE 1

Poverty by Region : 1987-98

Region	*People living on less than $ 1 a day (millions)*					*Percentage of population living on less than $ 1 a day*				
	1987	*1990*	*1993*	*1996*	*1998*	*1987*	*1990*	*1993*	*1996*	*1998*
(1)	*(2)*	*(3)*	*(4)*	*(5)*	*(6)*	*(7)*	*(8)*	*(9)*	*(10)*	*(11)*
East Asia and Pacific	417.3	452.4	413.9	265.1	278.3	26.6	27.6	25.2	14.9	15.3
Europe and Central Asia	1.1	7.1	18.9	23.8	24.0	0.2	1.6	4.0	3.1	5.1
Latin America and the Caribbean	63.7	73.8	70.8	76.0	78.2	15.3	16.8	15.3	15.6	15.6
Middle East and North Africa	9.3	5.7	5.0	5.0	5.5	4.3	2.4	1.9	1.8	1.9
South Asia	474.4	495.1	505.1	513.7	522.0	44.9	44.0	42.4	42.3	40.0
Sub-Saharan Africa	217.2	242.3	273.3	289.0	290.9	46.6	47.7	49.7	48.5	46.3
All	1183.2	1276.4	1304.3	1190.0	1198.9	28.3	29.0	28.1	24.5	24.0

Source : World Development Report, 2000/2001, p. 23.

regional variations in the incidence of poverty. Declining poverty level is observed in the regions of East Asia (27.6% to 15.3%), Latin America and the Caribbean (16.8% to 15.6%), Middle East and North Africa (2.4% to 1.9%), South Asia (4.4% to 40%) and Sub-Saharan Africa (47.7% to 46.3%). It is observed that though the poverty level has reduced in Latin America, South Asia and Sub-Saharan Africa, the number of people living on less than $1 a day has risen: Latin America (63.7 million to 78.2 million), South Asia (474.4 million to 522 million) and Sub-Saharan Africa (217.2 million to 291 million). In 1998, South Asia and Sub-Saharan Africa have accounted for around 70% of the population living on less than $1 a day, up 19% points from 1987. This is caused by the geographical distribution of poverty. There are equally large variations in poverty performance across countries within each region. In Europe and Central Asia the proportion of the population living on less than $2 a day (at 1966 ppp) ranges from less than 5% in Belarus, Estonia, Hungary, Lithunia, Poland and Ukraine to 19% in Russia, 49% in the Kyrghz Republic and 68% in Tajikistan. Among seven African countries during 1990s four countries namely Burkina Faso, Nigeria, Zambia and Zimbabwe have experienced an increase in poverty while three countries namely, Ghana, Mauritania and Uganda have a declining trend. Available national poverty estimates for Latin America show that between 1989 and 1996 the incidence of poverty has fallen in Brazil, Chile, the Dominican Republic and Honduras, and risen in Mexico and Venezuela.

It is very significant to note here that in East Asia the incidence of poverty in the 1990s has been influenced by the impact of the recent economic crisis. In most of the countries poverty has risen as a result of the financial crisis of the late 1990s. Estimates reveal (Table 2) that in Indonesia poverty has increased from 11.3% in 1996 to 18.9% in 1998 (the year of crisis). Since then it appears to have declined considerably, though it is still substantially higher than precise levels as the economy recovered. In Russia the incidence of poverty has increased from 21.9% in 1996 to 32.7% in 1998 (the year of crisis). In every crisis in Latin America and the Caribbean the incidence of poverty has increased and several years later remained higher than it has been before the crisis.

In South Asia poverty reduction has also varied in the 1990s. In Bangladesh poverty has reduced from 42.7% in 1991-92 to 35.6% in 1995-96 despite the worst flood situation. But Pakistan and Sri Lanka

TABLE 2
Effect of Economic Crises on Incidence of Poverty in Selected Countries

Country and type of crisis	*Before crisis*	*Year of crisis*	*After crisis*
Argentina, hyperinflation and currency	25.2 (1987)	47.3 (1989)	33.7 (1990)
Argentina, contagion	16.8 (1993)	24.8 (1995)	26.0 (1997)
Indonesia, contagion and financial	11.3 (1996)	18.9 (1998)	11.7 (1999)
Jordan, currency and terms of trade	3.0 (1986-87)	(1989)	14.9 (1992)
Mexico, currency and Financial	36.0 (1994)	(1995)	43.0 (1996)
Russian Federation, financial	21.9 (1996)	32.7 (1998)	
Thailand, currency and Financial	11.4 (1996)	12.9 (1998)	

Source : World Development Report, 2000/2001, p. 163.

have made little or no progress in poverty reduction in the 1990s. (*Pal, P.K.*, 2003)

REGIONAL DIMENSIONS OF POVERTY: RURAL AND URBAN INDIA

Expert Group have estimated the poverty lines, in rural and urban areas of 18 states and UTs. Based on the poverty line, poverty level (percentage of people the below poverty line) is estimated in rural, urban and combined (rural and urban) areas at different points of time, 1973-74, 1977-78, 1993-94 and 1999-2000. Instead of 18 states and UTs we have considered 32 states and UTs in India. Estimates reveal that at the all India level, poverty level was as high as 54.88 in 1973-74 which came down 1038.86 in 1987-88 and to just 26.10 in 1999-2000 (Table 3). Thus the extent of poverty has been reduced by more than 50%. The rate of declining of poverty has been increasing: 1.7% during 1973-77, 3.4% during 1983-87 and 5.3% during 1993-99 per year.

Wide variations in the poverty level are observed among the states in India over time. At different points of time, relative rankings of the Indian states have changed. Among the 32 states and UTs in India the top-most ranking was acquired by H.P. (26.39 in 1973-74)/

TABLE 3

Percentage of People Below the Poverty Line: Total

Sl. No.	States/U.Ts.	1973-74	1977-78	1983-84	1987-88	1993-94	1999-2000
1.	Andhra Pradesh	48.86	39.31	28.91	25.86	22.19	15.77
2.	Arunachal Pradesh	51.93	58.32	40.88	36.22	39.35	33.47
3.	Assam	51.21	57.15	40.47	36.21	40.86	36.09
4.	Bihar	61.91	61.55	62.22	52.13	54.96	42.60
5.	Goa	44.26	37.23	18.90	24.52	14.92	4.40
6.	Gujarat	48.15	41.23	32.79	31.54	24.21	14.07
7.	Haryana	35.36	29.55	21.37	16.64	25.05	8.74
8.	Himachal Pradesh	26.39	32.45	16.40	15.45	28.44	7.63
9.	Jammu & Kashmir	40.83	38.97	24.24	23.82	25.17	3.48
10.	Karnataka	54.47	48.78	38.24	37.53	33.16	20.04
11.	Kerala	59.79	52.22	40.42	31.79	25.43	12.72
12.	Madhya Pradesh	61.78	61.78	49.78	43.07	42.52	37.43
13.	Maharashtra	53.24	55.88	43.44	40.41	36.86	35.02
14.	Manipur	49.96	53.72	37.02	31.35	33.78	38.54
15.	Meghalaya	50.20	55.19	38.81	33.92	37.92	33.87
16.	Mizoram	50.32	54.38	36.00	27.52	25.66	19.47
17.	Nagaland	50.81	56.04	39.25	34.43	37.92	32,67
18.	Orissa	66.18	70.07	65.29	55.58	48.56	47.15
19.	Punjab	28.15	19.27	16.18	13.20	11.77	6.16
20.	Rajasthan	46.14	37.42	34.46	35.15	27.41	15.28
21.	Sikkim	50.86	55.89	39.71	36.06	41.43	36.55
22.	Tainil Nadu	54.94	54.79	51.66	43.39	35.03	21.12
23.	Tripura	51.00	56.88	40.03	35.23	39.01	34.42
24.	Uttar Pradesh	57.07	49.05	47.07	41.46	40.85	31.15
25.	West Bengal	63.43	60.52	54.85	44.72	35.66	27,02
26.	Andaman & Nicobar	55.56	55.42	52.13	43.89	34.47	20.99
27.	Chandigarh	27.96	27.32	23.79	44.67	11.35	5.75
28.	Dadra & Nagar Haveli	46.55	37.20	15.67	67.11	50.84	17.14
29.	Daman & Diu	0.00	0.00	0.00	0.00	15.80	4.44
30.	Delhi	49.61	33.23	26.22	12.41	14.69	8.23
31.	Lakshadweep	59.68	52.79	42.36	34.95	25.04	15.60
32.	Pondicherry	53.82	53.25	50.06	41.46	37.40	21.67
	All India	54.88	51.32	44.48	38.86	35.97	26.10

Source : Planning Commission, Government of India.

Punjab (19.27 in 1977-78, 16.18 in 1983-84)/Delhi (12.41 in 1987-88)/ Chandigarh (11.35 in 1993-94) and J &K (3.48 in 1999-2000) while the lowest ranking was acquired by Orissa (66.18 in 1973-74/70-07 in 1977-78/65.29 in 1983-84)/Dadra & Nagar Haveli (67.11 in 1987-88)/ Bihar (54.96 in 1993-94) and Orissa (47.15 in 1999-2000).ThusOrissa and Bihar are the poorest states (i.e., existence of high poverty) while the northern states like H.P./Punjab, Delhi, Chandigarh, etc. are the richest states due to low poverty level.

Poverty level has declined in almost all the states in India with some exceptional cases over time. But the rate of declining has varied among the state over time. Highest declining growth rates are observed in Goa, Haryana, H.P./J&K, Kerala, Punjab, Dadra and Pondicherry. During the reform periods (1993/94-1999/2000)/ poverty has remarkably reduced in the states of Goa, Gujarat, Haryana, H.P., J&K, Karnataka, Kerala, Punjab, Rajasthan, Andaman & Nicobar, Chandigarh, Dadra & Nagar Haveli, Daman & Diu, Delhi, Lashadweep and Pondicherry. Thus, poverty is relatively low in the northern states compared to other states in India due to proper implementation of poverty alleviation programmes.

Rural Poverty

Like total poverty rural poverty has also reduced in India and in its constituent states overtime. Estimates reveal (Table 4) that at the all India level in has reduced from 56.44 in 1973-74 to 1973-74 to 39.09 in 1987-88 and to 27.09 in 1999-2000. Thus poverty has been reduced by more than 50% during the period under study. Declining annual growth rate of poverty has been rising from 1.5% during 1973-77 to 3.9% during 1983-87 and to 5.3% during 1993-2000. So during the reform periods the declining rate is very high due to implementation of rural poverty alleviation programmes for employment generation through non-farm activities.

Disparity in poverty level among the states are also observed over time. That is, at different time periods the relative ranking of the states have changed. Poverty is low in the states of Delhi (24.44 in 1973-74), Punjab (16.37 in 1977-78) and Delhi (7.66 in 1983-84, 1.3 in 1987-88, 1.9 in 1993-94 and 0.4 in 1999-2000) while it is high in the states W.B. (73.16 in 1973-74), Orissa (72.39 in 1977-78 and 67.53 in 1983-84), Dadra & Nagar Haveli (67.11 in 1987-88), Bihar (58.2 in 1993-94) and Orissa (48.01 in 1999-2000). Thus Bihar and Orissa are the poorest states in India.

TABLE 4

Percentage of People Below the Poverty Line : Rural Areas

Sl. No.	States/U.Ts.	1973-74	1977-78	1983-84	1987-88	1993-94	1999-2000
1.	Andhra Pradesh	48.41	38.11	26.53	20.92	15.92	11.05
2.	Arunachal Pradesh	52.68	59.82	42.60	39.35	45.01	40.04
3.	Assam	52.68	59.82	24.60	39.35	45.01	40.04
4.	Bihar	62.99	63.25	64.37	52.63	58.21	44.30
5.	Goa	46.85	37.64	14.82	17.64	5.34	1.35
6.	Gujarat	46.35	41.76	29.80	28.67	22.18	13.17
7.	Haryana	34.23	27.73	20.56	16.22	28.02	8.27
8.	Himachal Pradesh	27.42	33.49	17.00	16.28	30.34	7.94
9.	Jammu & Kashmir	45.51	42.86	26.04	25.70	30.34	3.97
10.	Karnataka	55.14	48.18	36.33	32.82	29.88	17.38
11.	Kerala	59.19	51.48	39.03	29.10	25.76	9.38
12.	Madhya Pradesh	62.66	62.52	48.90	41.92	40.64	37.06
13.	Maharashtra	57.71	62.97	45.23	40.78	37.93	23.72
14.	Manipur	52.67	59.82	42.60	39.35	45.01	40.04
IS.	Meghalaya	52.67	59.82	42.60	39.35	45.01	40.04
16.	Mizoram	52.67	59.82	42.60	39.35	45.01	40.04
17.	Nagaland	52.67	59.82	42.60	39.35	45.01	40.04
18.	Orissa	67.28	72.38	67.53	57.64	49.72	48.01
19.	Punjab	28.21	16.37	13.20	12.60	11.95	6.35
20.	Rajasthan	44.76	35.89	33.50	33.21	26.46	13.74
21.	Sikkim	52.67	59.82	42.60	39.35	45.01	40.04
22.	Tamil Nadu	57.23	57.68	53.99	45.80	32.48	20.55
23.	Tripura	52.67	59.82	42.60	39.35	45.01	40.04
24.	Uttar Pradesh	56.53	47.60	46.45	14.10	42.28	31.22
25.	West Bengal	73.16	68.34	63.05	48.30	40.80	31.85
26.	Andaman & Nicobar	57.43	57.68	53.99	45.80	32.48	20.5
27.	Chandigarh	27.96	27.32	23.79	14.67	11.35	5.75
28.	Dadra & Nagar Haveli	46.85	37.64	14.81	67.11	51.95	17.57
29.	Daman & Diu	0.00	0.00	0.00	0.00	5!34	1.35
30.	Delhi	24.44	30.91	7.66	1.29	1.90	0.40
31.	Lakshadweep	59.19	51.48	39.03	29.10	25.76	9.38
32.	Pondicherry	57.43	57.68	53.99	45.80	32.48	20.55
	All India	56.44	53.07	45.65	39.09	37.27	27.09

Source : Same as Table 3.

Annual trend growth rate of rural poverty has varied across the states in India. In almost all the states there exists a declining trend growth rate. But in some cases the rate is positive during 1970's and 1980's. Positive growth rate is observed in the states of Bihar, Maharashtra, Manipur, Meghalaya, Mizoram, Nagaland, Sikkim, Tripura and Delhi. States like Haryana, J&K, H.P., Manipur, Meghalaya, Mizoram, Nagaland, Sikkim, Tripura, U.P. and Delhi have positive growth rate during 1987-93 but negative growth rate during 1993-99. Thus, compared to other states the northern and north-eastern states have remarkably reduced their rural poverty during the reform period.

Urban Poverty

Like rural poverty level, urban poverty level has also reduced in India and in its constituent states over time. It has reduced from 49.01 to 38.20 in 1987-88 and to 23.62 in 1999-2000 (Table 5). Its annual declining growth rate has increased from 2% during 1973-77 to 2.8% during 1987-93 and to 5.2% during 1993-99. The acceleration in the decline of urban poverty is due to high income growth achieved during the reform periods, which seems to have percolated to the bottom through the trickle down effect.

Wide variations in urban poverty are also observed across the states. The relative ranking of the states have also changed. Poverty level is low in H.P. for the first four points of time, Assam in 1993-94 and J&K in 1999-2000. While it is highest in Kerala in 1973-74, M.P. in 1977-78 and 1983-84, Bihar in 1987-88, M.P. in 1993-94 and Orissa in 1999-2000. During the reform period (1993-94 to 1999-2000) it has been substantially reduced in the states of Goa, Gujarat, Haryana, HP., J&K, Punjab, T.N., W.B., Andaman & Nicobar, Chandigarh, Dadra & Nagar Haveli, Delhi and Pondicherry. But it has marginally increased only in Orissa (41.64 to 42.83) during the reform period in the country.

Rural and urban poverty show that rural poverty is higher than urban one in India and in its constituent states during the period under study. But in 1999-2000 urban poverty is more than rural one in the states of Andhra Pradesh, Goa, Haryana, Karnataka, Kerala, M.P., Maharashtra, Rajasthan, T.N., Andaman & Nicobar, Daman & Diu, Delhi, Lakshadweep and Pondicherry. (*Pal*, 2010)

It thus follows from the above discussion that Indian states have exhibited a divergent level of poverty in rural, urban and combined areas. Poverty level is low in some states while it is relatively high in

TABLE 5

Percentage of People Below the Poverty Line: Urban Areas

Sl. No.	*States/U.Ts.*	*1973-74*	*1977-78*	*1983-84*	*1987-88*	*1993-94*	*1999-2000*
1.	Andhra Pradesh	50.61	43.55	36.30	40.11	38.33	26.63
2.	Arunachal Pradesh	36.92	32.71	21.73	9.94	7.73	7.47
3.	Assam	36.92	32.71	21.73	9.94	7.73	7.47
4.	Bihar	52.96	48.76	47.33	48.73	34.50	32.91
5.	Goa	37.69	36.31	27.00	35.48	27.03	7.52
6.	Gujarat	52.57	40.02	39.14	37.26	27.89	15.59
7.	Haryana	40.18	36.57	24.15	17.99	16.38	9.99
8.	Himachal Pradesh	13.17	19.44	9.43	6.29	9.18	4.63
9.	Jammu & Kashmir	21.32	23.71	17.76	17.47	9.18	1.98
10.	Karnataka	52.53	50.36	42.82	48.42	40.14	25.25
11.	Kerala	62.74	55.36	45.68	40.33	24.55	20.27
12.	Madhya Pradesh	57.65	58.66	53.06	47.09	48.38	38.44
13.	Maharashtra	43.87	40.09	40.26	39.78	35.15	26.81
14.	Manipur	36.92	32.71	21.73	9.94	7.73	7.47
15.	Meghalaya	36.92	32.71	21.73	9.94	7.73	7.47
16.	Mizoram	36.92	32.71	21.73	9.94	7.73	7.47
17.	Nagaland	36.92	32.71	21.73	9.94	7.73	7.47
18.	Orissa	55.62	50.92	49.15	41.63	41.64	42.83
19.	Punjab	27.96	27.32	23.79	14.67	11.35	5.75
20.	Rajasthan	52.13	43.53	37.94	41.92	30.49	19.85
21.	Sikkim	36.92	32.71	21.73	9.94	7.73	7.47
22.	Tamil Nadu	49.40	48.69	46.96	38.64	39.77	22.11
23.	Tripura	36.92	32.71.	21.73	9.94	7.73	7.47
24.	Uttar Pradesh	60.09	56.23	49.82	42.96	35.39	30.89
25.	West Bengal	34.67	38.20	32.32	35.08	22.41	14.86
26.	Andaman & Nicobar	49.40	48.69	46.96	38.64	39.77	22.11
27.	Chandigarh	27.96	27.32	23.79	14.67	11.32	5.75
28.	Dadra & Nagar Haveli	37.69	36.31	27.00	0.00	39.93	13.52
29.	Daman & Diu	0.00	0.00	0.00	0.00	27.03	7.52
30.	Delhi	52.23	33.51	27.89	13.56	16.03	9.42
31.	Lakshadweep	62.74	55.62	45.68	40.33	24.55	20.27
32.	Pondicherry	49.40	48.69	46.96	38.64	39.77	22.11
	All India	49.01	45.24	40.79	38.20	32.36	23.62

Source : Planning Commission of India.

some other states. All this clearly indicates the existence of inter-state disparity in poverty level. Such inter-state disparity in poverty level is clearly revealed by the Poverty Disparity Index (PDI) as :

$$PDI = 100\left[\sum_{i=1}^{n}(pi-p)^2/(n-1)\right]^{1/2} / p$$

where p : Poverty level in the state i, i = 1, . . . n.
P : Poverty level in India as a whole.
n : Number of states and UTs in India.

Estimates reveal that PDI has risen overtime in rural, urban and combined areas. In rural areas the index has increased from 23.19% in 1973-74 to 40.96% in 1987-88 and to 67.93% in 1999-2000. The respective figures are: 27.75%, 55.98% and 67.65% in urban areas; 19.84%, 36.82% and 57.56% in combined areas. This indicates that inter-state disparity has widened more in urban areas than in rural areas during the period under study. That is to say, although the percentage of people below the poverty level has shown a steadily declining trend, yet the rising values of the index shows that instead of convergence, the Indian states have experienced rather a divergence in respect of the incidence of poverty in rural, urban and combined areas.• Thus, the richer states have shown a tendency to become relatively more richer while the poorer ones to become relatively more poorer.

As per UNDP's Human Development Report (1997) there are three dimensions for human well-being: (a) Longevity—the ability to live long and healthy human well-being, (b) Education—the ability to read, write and acquire knowledge, (c) Command over resources—the ability to enjoy a decent standard of living and have a socially life. So there are three of deprivation: (i) Longevity deprivation, (ii) education deprivation, and (iii) economic deprivation. Based on these deprivations, Human Poverty Index (HPI) has been constructed. As per the estimates of the National Human Development Report (2001), the HPI in India has declined from 47.33 in 1981 to 39.36 in 1991. This is also true both in rural (53.28 to 44.81) and urban (27.21 to 22.00) areas. Thus, the HPI in rural areas is significantly higher than that in urban one. Also, the decline in the HPI in rural areas is slightly higher than that in urban one. The rural-urban ratio of the percentage of people below the poverty line has increased from 1.12 in 1983-84 to 1.15 in 1993-94, whereas the rural-urban ratio of HPI is a little more than two both in 1981 and 1991.

Thus, there is a gap for the availability of these amenities which are better in urban areas while these are scarce in rural areas of India. (*Pal*, 2002).

NATURE, TREND AND VARIOUS DIMENSIONS OF POVERTY IN BIHAR

The state being primarily a rural economy and having no industry worth the name, majority of workforce depends on agriculture for their livelihood. In this regards, there has been little structural change since independence. Some major industries, which were established in the state after independence, are now part of the newly created state of Jharkhand. A few industrial centres which remained in the state after its bifurcation, are lying sick and are in no position to contribute to the state's employment or income.

Less than 45% population is literate in rural Bihar which is much lower than the national average. Even it is lower than poorer states like Orissa and Uttar Pradesh. Similar is the case of female literacy in the State. The state also lags far behind in the process of human capital formation. This can be seen clearly in data pertaining to gross enrolment ratio and drop-outs. Nearly 84 percent of the children in the age-group 6-10 years are enrolled in primary schools in Bihar. This figure is much below the states such as Kerala, Maharashtra and even Orissa and Uttar Pradesh. The state is also manifested with a very high drop-out. Over 80 percent of students drop-out till they reach class X. This is an alarming situation for any state as it cannot catch the race of development in the absence of its weak human capital formation. Even the situation of other poorer states like Orissa and Uttar Pradesh is relatively better on this front. However, these states have yet to travel miles together to attain the level of school retention as prevalent in Kerala, Punjab and Maharashtra, etc.

In case of health indicators such as IMR, the situation of Bihar is abysmally low as compared to many developed states such as Kerala, Maharashtra and Punjab. It is, however, not so bad as in other states like Orissa and U.P. As high as 89% children are anemic in Bihar. The corresponding figure for India is marginally low at 81.2%. Only 31% of children in the age-group 12-23 months are fully immunized. In case of basic amenities relating to health, such as sanitation facility like access to latrines, about 13% rural households have such facility in Bihar (the corresponding figures for India is

22%). However, the position of the state in case of safe drinking water is much better than many sates. Yet another striking feature relates to very poor access of electricity to rural households in Bihar only 5% rural households are electrified as compared to over 43% in India and as high as 90% in Punjab.

In the wake of acute poverty, the state has been witnessing militant movements by the agricultural labourers and poor peasants. In many parts of the state, mobilization of poor peasants and agricultural labourers has taken place on a large scale. Earlier the mobilization was mainly in south Bihar but in recent times it has spread to several districts of north Bihar as well. Another response of the poor in the wake of impoverishment has been in the form of widespread migration to far-off places in search of work—both short-term and long-term. These migrants from Bihar, either as wage labourers or engaged in petty businesses, are common in many parts of the country. (Sharma, A.N., 2007)

Magnitude and Nature of Poverty

The NSSO data from the 61st round (2004-05) of the consumer expenditure survey shows that 41.4 per cent of the population of Bihar is below the poverty line, which is highest in India, next only to Orissa (Table 6). The incidence of rural poverty is 42.1 percent and that of urban one is 34.6 per cent. In fact, around 15 per cent of the total rural poor of India are in Bihar, whereas the share of state's rural population in the country is only 10 per cent. However, as can be seen from Table 7, the rate of reduction in poverty over time has been faster in rural Bihar as compared to rural India—during about two decades 1983 to 2004-05, while rural poverty in Bihar declined by about one-percentage-point annually, the decline was slower in India (0.83 per cent). The decline in poverty was particularly high in Bihar during 1993-94 and 2004-05.

The decline in poverty ratios is accompanied by the substantial rise in wages in rural labour, both for males and females, although in recent years the rate of growth has decelerated (Table 8). It is important to note that growth in wage rates is substantially higher in Bihar as compared to India. This is somewhat unusual given the relatively slower growth of the economy.

Along with total poverty, there has been substantial decline in the 'acutely poor' or 'very poor' category (defined as having 25 per cent less than average monthly per capita consumption expenditure, MPCE) (Table 9). This decline is not only much sharper than that of

TABLE 6

Percentage of Population below Poverty Line by Major States of India, 2004-05 (Basd on URP Consumption)

States	*Rural*	*Urban*	*Combined*
Andhra Pradesh	11.2	28.0	15.8
Assam	-22.3	3.3	19.7
Bihar	42.1	34.6	41.4
Chhattisgarh	40.8	41.2	40.9
Delhi	6.9	15.2	14.7
Gujarat	19.1	13.0	16.8
Haryana	13.6	15.1	14.0
Himachal Pradesh	10.7	3.4	10.0
Jammu & Kashmir	4.6	7.9	5.4
Jharkhand	46.3	2.0.2	40.3
Karnataka	20.8	32.6	25.0
Kerala	13.2	20.2	15.0
Madhya Pradesh	36.9	42.1	38.3
Maharashtra	29.6	32.2	30.7
Orissa	46.8	3.3	12.6
Puniab	9.1	44.3	19.0
Rajasthan	18.7	7.1	46.4
Tamil Nadu	22.8	32.9	8.4
Uttar Pradesh	33.4	30.6	22.1
Uttarakhand	40.8	36.5	22.5
West Bengal	28.6	14.8	32.8
All India	28.3	25.7	27.5

Note : URP Consumption = Uniform Recall Period consumption in which the consumer expenditure data for all the items are collected from 30 days recall period.

Source : Planning Commission, 2007.

India but the share of 'very poor' in Bihar which was higher than that of all-India in 1983, fell below the all-India share in 2004-05. This is reflective of a more equitable distribution among poor in Bihar than in all-India. The incidence of the nearly poor (having MPCE of 25 per cent more than the average) has also declined. However, this category is still prone to various shocks—such as small rise in the food prices,

TABLE 7
Head Count Measure of Poverty (%) and Annual Percentage Changes in Poverty for Rural Bihar and Rural India

Periods	*Rural*	
	Bihar	*India*
1983	64.7	46.5
1987-88	54.2	39.0
1993-94	56.6	37.2
2004-05	42.2	28.7
Annual % Change		
1983 to 1987-88	-2.38	-1.60
1983 to 1993-94	-0.77	-0.88
1993-94 to 2004-05	-1.30	-0.77
1983 to 2004-05	-1.04	-0.83

Source : Himanshu (2007).

TABLE 8
Average Daily-wage Rates of Rural Casual Labourers (at 1993-94 prices), Bihar and India

(*Fig. in Rs.*)

	Year (Growth Rate (% per annum))					
	1993-94	*1999-2000*	*2004-05*	*1993-94 to 1999-2000*	*1999-2000 to 2004-05*	*1993-04 to 2004-05*
Bihar						
Males	18.14	22.86	25.23	3.93	1.98	3.04
Females	15.38	20.28	21.77	4.72	1.43	3.21
Persons	17.46	22.25	24.60	4.12	2.03	3.17
India						
Males	22.41	25.85	28.02	2.40	1-.63	2.05
Females	15.32	17.94	19.15	2.67	1.32	2.05
Persons	19.96	22.99	24.80	2.38	1.53	1.99

Source : Calculated from the Various Rounds of NSSO.

small fall in food production, sudden illness in the family, etc. Such shocks are much probable in Bihar than most parts of India because of very high fluctuations in agricultural production coupled with recurring incidence of disasters (floods, droughts, etc.).

TABLE 9

Percentage Share of Population in Different Expenditure Categories in Rural Bihar and Rural India—1983, 1993-94 and 2004-05

Categories	*Rural Bihar*			*Rural India*		
	1983	*1993-94*	*2004-05*	*1983*	*1993-94*	*2004-05*
All Poor	100.0	100.0	100.0	100.0	100.0	100.0
Very poor	59.0	46.6	27.4	51.1	40.0	28.0
Moderately poor	41.0	53.4	72.6	48.9	60.0	72.0
All Non-Poor	100.0	100.0	100.0	100.0	100.0	100.0
Nearly poor	45.3	48.3	37.6	33.8	32.1	27.5
Not poor	54.7	51.7	62.4	66.2	67.9	72.5

Notes : 1. Very poor is defined as MPCE of a person 25% below the Official Poverty line.
2. Moderately poor is the rest of the BPL population estimated by using official poverty line.
3. Nearly poor is defined as the MPCE of a person 25% above the official poverty line.
4. Not poor is the rest of the APL population.

Source : As in Table 6.

The overall vulnerability in Bihar, more so of the poor, is also reflected in the consumption pattern. As can be seen from Table 11, the consumption pattern in Bihar is much more dominated by food and cereals than all other states of India (except Assam). Around 65 per cent of the total MPCE in rural Bihar is incurred on food as compared to only 55 per cent for India as a whole and as low as 45 percent in Kerala and 49 per cent in Punjab. Although the amount of average MPCE on food is lower in Bihar, the expenditure on cereals is higher than All-India average. It means that people in rural Bihar have much less diversification in their food baskets (and hence on quality food items). The share of expenditure on non-food items in rural Bihar is not only the lowest (except Assam), but also the amount spent is extremely low (Rs. 147 as against Rs. 252 for rural India). This also leads to lesser expenditure on health, education as well as on durable goods as compared to that in other states and India as a whole (Table 10).

TABLE 10

Share of Food and Non-food Expenditure in the Rural Areas of Some Major States, 2004-05

States	*Food*	*Non-food*	*Rank Food*	*Rank Non-food*
Andhra Pradesh	55.2	44.8	9	9
Assam	66	34	1	17
Bihar	64.8	35.2	2	16
Chhattisgarh	56.2	43.8	7	11
Gujarat	58	42	6	12
Haryana	48.6	51.4	16	2
Jharkhand	61.9	38.1	3	15
Karnataka	55.7	44.3	8	10
Kerala	45	55	17	1
Madhya Pradesh	52.9	47.1	12	6
Maharashtra	51.7	48.3	14	4
Orissa	61.6	38.4	4	14
Punjab	49.2	50.8	15	3
Rajasthan	54.8	45.2	10	8
Tamil Nadu	52.4	47.6	13	5
Uttar Pradesh	53.4	46.6	11	7
West Bengal	58.7	41.3	5	13

Source : Calculated from the item-wise average MPCE statistics for major states available from Report No. 508, NSSO 61st Round.

Another glaring fact is that health expenditure on institutional sources is almost negligible in Bihar, due to which poor spend much more on private health care. Out of Pocket (OOP) payments by households in rural areas in proportion to consumption expenditure is quite substantial in the absence of adequate primary health care services. It constitutes more than 5 per cent of total consumption expenditure of rural households. As distribution of health expenditure is often unequal, it leads to high number of rural populace being pushed below the poverty line. In rural Bihar, this number was close to 4.2 million in 1999-2000, which constitutes one-sixth of all India rural share. Together these have profound implications for the poor and also for the formulation of policy measures to alleviate this situation.

Changes in Poverty among Various Groups

The incidence of poverty is much higher among weaker groups—lower castes, landless, land poor groups and labour households. Scheduled castes (including scheduled tribes) who account for one-third of the total poor of the state, but less than one-fourth of the total population, have the highest incidence of poverty followed by other backward caste (OBC) people who either are landless or land poor (below 0.4 hectare of holding) (Table 13a). Lower backwards account for 37 per cent of the total poor, but their share in total population is only 29 per cent. The upper backwards (having more than 0.4 hectare of land-holding) and upper castes have almost half the incidence of poverty as compared to their population shares. The incidence of poverty, among Muslims as revealed from the NSSO 61st round, is higher than their population share, but only to a small extent. It is also important to note that poverty has become more concentrated among SCs over time in 1983, they constituted only about one-fourth of the poor; this increased to 30 per cent during 1993-94 and further to 33 per cent in 2004-05 (Table 12). Among Muslims, the concentration of poverty somewhat increased between 1983 and 1993-94 but shows a substantial fall in 2004-05 as compared to 1993-94.

TABLE 11

Average MPCE (in Rs.) on Various Items in Rural Bihar and Rural India, 2004-05

Items	*Rural-Bihar*	*Rural-India*
Cereals	112.98 (41.80)	100.65 (32.72)
Total food	270.26	307.60
Clothing	20.88 (14.2)	25.33 (10.0)
Footwear	2.21 (1.5)	4.24 (1.7)
Education	7.25 (4.9)	14.90 (5.9)
Medical: Institutional	1.76 (1.2)	10.03 (4.0)
Medical: Non-institutional	12.13 (8.3)	26.93 (10.7)
Durable goods	3.70 (2.5)	19.23 (7.6)
Total non-food	146.85	252.19
Total	417.11	558.78

Note : Figures in parenthesis for Cereals is the share in Total Food Expenditure. For the Non-food Items, figures in parenthesis indicate share in Total Non-food Expenditure.

TABLE 12
Percentage Share of Individuals from Different Household Types in BPL Population and Total Population in Rural Bihar, 1983, 1993-94 and 2004-05

(i) Social Groups

Social Groups	*% Share in BPL population*			*% Share in total population*		
	1983	*1993-94*	*2004-05*	*1983*	*1993-94*	*2004-05*
Hindu: SC/ST	24.6	30.0	33.0	19.3	24.2	24.1
OBC I	—	—	36.9	—	—	29.2
OBC II	—	—	12.0	—	—	22.3
Others	61.8	52.2	3.6	67.1	60.6	10.0
All Hindus	86.4	82.2	85.4	86.4	84.8	85.7
Muslim OBCs	—	—	9.9	—	—	8.4
Others			4.5			5.4
All Muslims	13.0	17.2	14.3	13.1	14.6	13.8
Others	0.6	0.6	0.2	0.5	0.6	0.6
Total	100.0	100.0	100.0	100.0	100.0	100.0
(ii) Household Employment Status						
Self-employed in agriculture	32.5	31.8	19.6	41.9	33.6	29.3
Self-employed in non-agriculture	12.5	10.9	17.6	12.5	11.3	14.0
Casual Labour in Agricultural	46.6	49.1	48.9	35.4	41.3	40.5
Casual labour in non-agricultural	1.2	2.3	3.6	1.0	7.8	11.3
Other households	7.1	5.8	10.3	9.2	6.0	4.9
Total	100.0	100.0	100.0'	100.0	100.0	100.0
(iii) Land Cultivated Groups (ha)						
Landless	37.8	45.0	56.6	30.7	36.5	41.4
Up to 0.40	28.0	25.9	25.3	25.0	23.3	21.8
0.41t-1.00	15.4	15.1	12.3	16.2	17.8	19.6
1.01t-2.00	11.5	10.8	5.5	15.2	14.4	11.4
2.01t-4.00	5.0	2.9	0.4	8.3	5.9	4.5
4.01 & Above	2.3	0.5	0.0	4.7	2.1	1.4
Total	100.0	100.0	100.0	100.0	100.0	100.0

Notes : (i) OBC I: Other backward castes having cultivated land up to 0.4 hectare; OBC II: having cultivated land more than 0.4 hectare.
(ii) For 1983 and 1993-94 OBC categorization was not available

Sources : 1. Calculated from the unit level data of EUS of 38th, 50th and 61st Round. 2. As in Table 9.

TABLE 13(a)

Percentage Shares of Various Social Groups by Land Cultivated and Household-Employment Status

Land cultivated (in ha.)	*Social Group*							
	Hindu				*Muslim*			
	SC/ST	*OBC I*	*OBC II*	*Other*	*OBC*	*Other*	*All Others*	*Total*
Landless	39.3	31.3	0.7	11.8	5.0	6.8	5.0	100.0
0.005-0.40	31.7	33.3	0.3	13.4	6.8	9.0	5.5	100.0
0.41-1.00	28.4	6.9	33.5	17.0	3.3	6.7	4.1	100.0
1.01-2.00	24.0	1.3	41.7	20.9	2.3	4.9	4.8	100.0
2.01-4.00	20.3	0.5	41.8	26.8	1.5	3.9	5.2	100.0
4.01 & Above	12.1	0.4	42.7	32.8	1.4	2.9	7.7	100.0
Total	28.8	18.8	18.6	17.2	4.5	7.0	5.2	100.0

TABLE 13(b)

Share of Different Types of Households by Social Groups (Row %)

Household type	*Social Group*							
	Hindu				*Muslim*			
	SC/ ST	*OBC I*	*OBC II*	*Other*	*OBC*	*Other*	*All Others*	*Total*
Self-employed in Agricultural	44.7	25.9	6.3	8.3	2.9	6.9	4.9	100.0
Self-employed in non-agriculture	21.2	29.3	7.8	17.1	9.3	10.6	4.7	100.0
Casual labour in Agriculture	39.6	28.1	4.3	10.3	5.1	6.3	6.4	100.0
Casual labour in non-agriculture	20.9	6.1	36.9	22.8	2.9	5.5	4.9	100.0
Others households	22.1	26.1	6.7	24.7	6.6	7.5	6.4	100.0
Total	28.8	18.8	18.6	17.2	4.5	7.0	5.2	100.0

Source : Calculated from the unit level data of EUS of 38th, 50th and 61st Round.

Coming to employment status categories, as expected poverty is much more concentrated among casual labourers in agriculture—they account for about half of the total poor during 2004-05 (Table 12). Self-employment in non-agriculture also has high a incidence of poverty—around 18 per cent of the total poor belong to this category although their share in population is only 14 per cent (a large proportion of artisan castes belong to this category). The incidence of poverty is relatively less among cultivators and labourers working in the non-agricultural sector. Quite expected, access to cultivated land is the most important factor in causing and perpetuating poverty. The landless, comprising of 41 per cent of the total population, account for nearly 57 per cent of the total poor. They are followed by the land poor households (having cultivated land up to 0.40 hectare) who account for one-fourth of the total poor households (but only 21.8 per cent of the total population). As the size of the land cultivated increases, the incidence and concentration of poverty decreases.

Thus, scheduled castes, agricultural labourers and landless households constitute the largest segment of poor in rural Bihar. They are followed by the lower backward castes (having land holding less than 0.4 hectare), self-employed in non-agriculture, and those cultivating very small holdings up to 0.4 hectare. Incidentally, in the context of rural Bihar, these three categories largely overlap. It is also very striking to note from Table 13 the decline of the economic status of the upper castes in rural Bihar. The upper strata of the OBC are ahead of them in terms of access to cultivated land. A large number of them have also jointed low-earning occupations (more than 8% of the agricultural labourers now belong to the upper castes). It is also observed that over time poverty is getting more concentrated among these vulnerable groups in 1983, landless accounted for only 38 per cent of the total poor which increased to 45% in 1993-94 and further to 56.6 per cent during 2004-05. However, the concentration has increased only slightly among agriculture labour households between 1983 and 2004-05 (Table 13).

IN MICRO LEVEL EVIDENCES OF POVERTY

Perceptions of Poverty

As per study by A.N. Sharma (1999) the poor use different criteria to assess their own situation and its change over time. An analysis of the criteria used by rural people in Bihar shows that they use a wide range of criteria in which, apart from ownership of assets and land, education, health status and physical ability feature prominently while ranking the state of their own well-being. Further, the poor attach considerable-importance to personal freedom and dignity.

It was further observed that villagers also identify the intensity and severity of poverty in terms of factors associated with their general livelihood pattern. For example, they identify those households as very poor or destitute where the head of the household is landless, a casual agricultural labour or jobless. Besides these, deserted women, widows, or women living alone without adult male are also categorized as very poor. According to the villagers they are at greater risks and have very little chance to recover because of a poor resource base, both material and human. In contrast, households with sizeable land possession, better jobs, capability of lending money, etc. are categorized as rich households. During the exercise of categorizing poor households, assetlessness, illiteracy, and physical inability also featured prominently. Based on the intensity of indicators arising out of the above criteria, households have been classified into four group *viz.* 'very poor', 'poor', 'middle', and 'rich'. However, these four classifications are relative categories as the villagers rank different families in relation to others in the village. Villagers' perception of poverty and ranking of families on the poverty ladder is based on a wide range of socio-economic indicators, which are associated with their day-to-day life cycle. Their perception gives a fairly good idea that the poor is not a homogenous group and there are lot of differences in terms of nature and intensity of poverty among different population groups. As such, there is also intra-group variation among the poor in terms of nature, extent, and intensity of poverty. However, the factors identified by the villagers are not mutually exclusive and these factors re-enforce one another to create a vicious circle. For example, in rural Bihar most of the landless agricultural labour comes from scheduled castes and they also represent one of the most vulnerable groups in terms of health outcome Indicators.

Consumption Expenditure

Household consumption expenditure is an important indicator of poverty. The Head Count Ratio (HCR) of poverty as revealed from these two surveys also give similar results as the NSSO surveys, showing a perceptible decline in rural poverty in Bihar during the 17 years between the two periods. Based on the survey data, it is estimated that the 17 years between the two periods proportion of poverty (in terms of consumption expenditure) has declined by approximately 25 percentage points between 1982 and 1999 (Table 14). Using the state specific poverty line of Rs. 333 for 1999 and Rs. 98.47 for 1983, it is estimated that not only is the poverty ratio significantly higher among many of the groups such as SC households, agricultural labour, landless, and poor farmers, but also the concentration in the 'very poor' category is substantially higher. If the household is characterised by SC, agricultural labour, and landless all together, the poverty ratio is as high as 80 per cent among them. While comparing the 1982 and 1999 data it becomes amply clear that it is this group which has registered the lowest poverty reduction between the two specified periods. However, there are some other households belonging to OBC I (lower backwards), Muslims, poor peasants and small farmers, who also suffer from high concentration of poverty and a substantial proportion of them are concentrated among the 'very poor' category. (For details of extent of poverty among other section of population, refer (Appendix Table 1).

The poverty ratio and also the concentration of people in the very poor category has declined significantly among other households who do not belong to SC, agricultural labour, poor peasant and small land holding groups. The poverty ratio among them was 59 per cent in 1982, which declined to 26 per cent in 1999. Besides this, their concentration in the very poor category also declined from 37 per cent in 1981-82 to merely 5 per cent in 1999-00. The comparison of the extent of poverty between 1982 and 1999 essentially shows that although poverty is widespread in rural Bihar, certain groups such as people belonging to SC households, agricultural labour, landless, non-agricultural class, etc. have not been able to improve their position significantly over the years and are suffering from 'acute poverty'.

What is more striking is that the SC, agricultural labour and landless households have increased concentration in the lowest quintile in 1999 in comparison to 1982 (Appendix Table 2). Another group facing increasing concentration in the lowest quintile group is lower OBC II. Besides these households, there are also some other households who fall within the lowest quintile group of consumption expenditure and consequently their average MPCE is considerably low. For example, a significant proportion of OBC I household, poor

TABLE 14
Proportion of Population below Poverty Line in 1999 and 1982 among Different Households

Household types	*1999*			*1982*		
	Moderate Poor	*Very Poor*	*All Poor*	*Moderate Poor*	*Very Poor*	*All Poor*
SC	38.39	28.16	66.55	14.11	68.81	82.92
Muslims	35.10	15.34	50.44	16.36	57.27	73.64
Agricultural labour	34.61	33.88	68.49	18.06	65.28	83.33
Non-agricultural	28.25	16.98	45.23	16.55	46.13	62.68
Landless	32.04	31.42	63.46	12.05	70.00	82.05
Land up to 1 acre	31.67	12.91	44.58	20.05	56.82	76.87
SC AL & Landless*	42.13	38.23	80.36	10.65	71.19	81.84
Others**	20.54	5.26	25.80	22.06	36.94	59.00
All	26.54	16.71	43-.25	17.91	51.48	69.39

Notes : Cut-off of poor and non-poor is based on the state specific poverty lines of respective years. 'Very poor' and 'Moderate poor' categories are defined as groups of households below 75 per cent of poverty line and between 75 per cent of the poverty line.

* The group is comprised of common households with overlapping characteristics of SC, agricultural labour and landlessness.

** Other are households rest of SC and Muslims by Caste, AL and Non-Ag. by class and landless and up to 1 acre of land, i.e. Others are better-off households in terms of their caste and class affiliation and have higher land holding size.

and poor middle peasants, small and marginal land holding class, etc. face severe poverty in terms of consumption expenditure. One of the most vulnerable groups of population in rural Bihar is non-agricultural class, which is largely comprised of rural artisan and landless (as in Appendix Table 2). In terms of social class, poverty is the severest among the non-agricultural class only next to the agricultural labourer class. However, these groups have not faced deteriorating conditions in terms of concentration in the lowest consumption expenditure quintile, i.e. their concentration in the lowest quintile group has declined over the years.

Composition of Total Consumption Expenditure

To reveal the inequality in consumption expenditure in all its components, we use graphical presentation for top 10 percent and bottom 10 percent of households based on the 1999 survey. The mean level of consumption of bottom 10 percent is Rs.189 and that of the top 10 percent is Rs. 1507. The breakdown of consumption basket shows that for the bottom 10 percent of the households more than half of their consumption expenditure is incurred on cereals and substitutes. For the top 10 percent this category constitutes only 15 percent. In contrast, more than half of the top 10 percent households' expenditure is accounted for by miscellaneous goods and services, constituting consumer and durable transport, court expenditure, taxes and cess, religious and marriage expenditure, and other items and services. In the case of bottom 20 percent, these constitute only 2.89 percent (Figure 1).

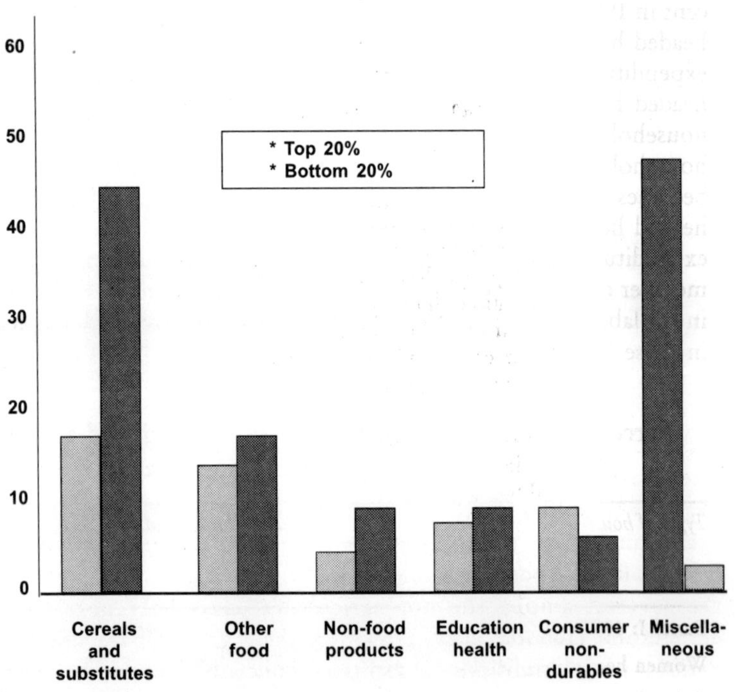

Figure 1 : Composition of Per Capita Monthly Consumption Expenditure of Households Belonging to Top and Bottom 20% of Consumption Class, 1999 Survey

Gender and Poverty

Though we do not have separate data for consumption expenditure of men and women across different households, some kind of variation in consumption expenditure can be seen in women headed households *vis-a-vis* other households. Table 15 presents the concentration of households with women as head of the households, and others households in different consumption classes.

There are approximately 7 per cent households, which have women as the head of their households. In these households the intensity of poverty is more acute and widespread as seen in 1999 where more than one-fourth of these households fall in the lowest consumption class category. In 1982 this proportion was as high as 40 per cent. Although there has been a decline in the proportion of women headed households falling in the lowest quintile (from 40 per cent in 1982 to 27 per cent in 1999), more than half of all the women headed households fall in the lowest two quintiles of consumption expenditure. One of the reasons of high poverty among women headed households is that in rural Bihar, women become heads of households mainly because of the death of the male head of the household. In such a situation, widow of the head of the household becomes the virtual head of the family. The first problem women headed households face, hence, is related to the daily consumption expenditure. Because of the loss of the main earning male family member of the household, and little access of women to employment in the labour markets, consumption expenditure levels fall drastically in these households.

TABLE 15

Percentage Distribution of Women Headed and Other Households by Consumption Class

Types of households	*Consumption expenditure class*				
	Lowest 20%	*20% to 40%*	*40% to 60%*	*60% to 80%*	*Highest 20%*
Panel I: 1982					
Women headed households	40.00	25.71	8.57	14.29	11.43
Other households	18.53	19.55	20.98	20.37	20.57
Panel II: 1999					
Women headed households	26.83	24.39	7.32	19.51	21.95
Other households	19.42	19.66	20.86	20.26	19.78

We can see in Figure 2 that the average annual consumption expenditure of women headed households is almost half that of the other households. Most of the fall is seen in respect of expenditure on quality food and non-food items. This means these households are just able to manage their minimum food requirements through food grains consumption.

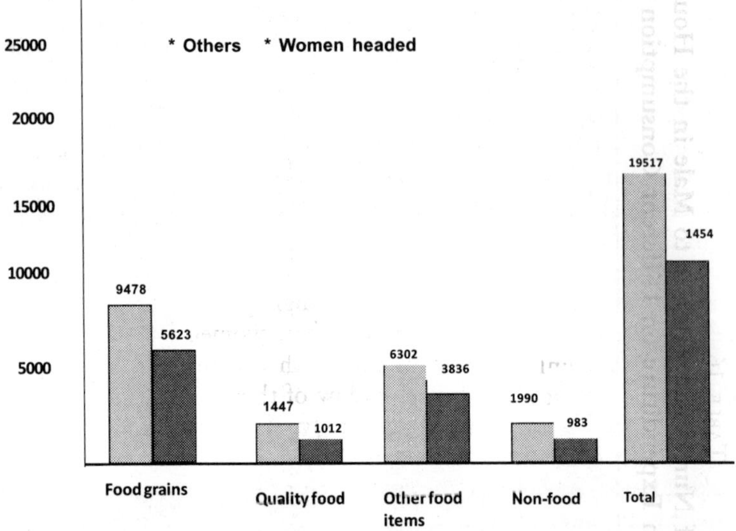

Figure 2 : Annual Average Consumption Expenditure (Rs.) on different Items among Women Headed and Other Households

In the absence of male and female consumption expenditure data separately, we can have yet another estimate to show the prevalence of poverty among women. Based on the consumption expenditure data of households, we can see a correlation between ratio of female to male members and level of consumption expenditure in the family. Table 16 suggests that the correlation between ratio of numbers of female to male and consumption expenditure on different food and non-food items is negative and significant. This means that as the ratio of female to male members increases in the family, the level of consumption expenditure goes down. This happens because of various reasons, such as women skip meals during times of shortages; they are the last to take quality food in the family; and they spend very less on the consumption of non-food items.

TABLE 16

Correlation between Ratio of Number of Females to Male in the Household the Household Consumption Expenditure on Different Consumption Items

	Ratio of female to male	*Total consumption expenditure*	*Expenditure on food grains*	*Expenditure on quality food*	*Expenditure on other food items*	*Expenditure on other items*
(1)	*(2)*	*(3)*	*(4)*	*(5)*	*(6)*	*(7)*
Ratio of female to male in family	1	—				
Total consumption expenditure	-0.09**	1				
Expenditure on foodgrains	-0.05*	0.83**	1			
Expenditure on quality food	-0.10**	0.75**	0.57**	.1		
Expenditure on other food items	-0.09**	0.90**	0.62**	0.63**	1	
Expenditure on other items	-0.08*	0.71**	0.33**	0.53**	0.56**	1

**Correlation is significant at the 0.01 level.
*Correlation is significant at the 0.05 level.

Gender bias in consumption expenditure within households also gets reflected in terms of expenditure on quality food items. In fact, the-correlation between ratio of females to males and expenditure on quality food is negative and significant at 99 per cent. This implies that consumption expenditure on quality food increases in households with the increase in male members in the family.

It can be seen from Table 16 that although a large proportion of women headed households is concentrated in the lowest quintile of consumption expenditure, over the years the proportion has declined suggesting that some sections of those households have been upwardly mobile and have shifted to higher consumption class. Again a caveat may be in order. If the women headed households belong to the lower castes and classes, they are more vulnerable in comparison to those who belong to the upper castes and classes. Apart from the total consumption expenditure, gender bias in consumption is also reflected within households across all sections of the society. One strong indicator of intra-household discrimination in consumption pattern is the skipping of meals at the time of some food crisis. During both the surveys a subjective question was asked from married women regarding their perception about "who skips meal first during the time of food shortage"? Their perception is presented in Table 17.

TABLE 17

Gender-wise Distribution of Persons Skipping Meal at the Time of Food Scarcity

Who skips meal	*1981-82*			*1999-2000*		
	SC	*Others*	*All*	*SC*	*Others*	*All*
Adult Females	68.79	72.35	70.66	59.78	67.44	62.41
Adult Males	17.89	5.37	9.85	2.23	1.16	2.33
All Females	12.54	13.35	12.95	7.26	11.63	10.07
Others	0.78	8.93	6.54	30.73	19.-77	25.18
Total	100	100	100	100	100	100

It can be seen from Table 17 that invariably adult women are the first in the family to skip meals at the time of food shortage. During both surveys—the proportion of adult males skipping meals are very low. Moreover, the proportion of adult males-skipping meals has gone down substantially over the years but in case of adult females it has increased. Similar discrimination is faced in terms of number of meals taken per day by each member of the family, particularly during food shortage periods. Other than consumption expenditure as an indicator of poverty, there are various other dimensions which show the total vulnerable position of women in the society. For example, women in rural Bihar face restricted physical mobility, less self-control over reproductive functions, and low representation in decision-making. Accordingly, their participation in social and political arena is at very low level.

On Food Security Front

Access to adequate and nutritious food by households has been one of the most important considerations in determining poverty levels. Although the overall food availability in rural Bihar has improved over the years, the per capita availability of food grains in Bihar is among the lowest in the country. The overall per capita availability of cereals has declined over the years. Approximately one-fourth of all the households face acute food crisis and do not get sufficient food round the year. This is reflected by the perception of none other than the villagers themselves. Table 18 presents the results of an analysis of answers to a question: "Do you get enough food round the year?"

TABLE 18

Percentage of Households Not Getting Enough Food in 1981-82 and 1999-2000

Type of Household	*Percentage of Households Not Getting Enough Food*	
	1981-82	*1999-2000*
SC	75.3	56.5
Agricultural Labour	88.5	66.8
Landless	88.6	45.0
SC, AL, landless	89.7	56.2
Women headed households	62.5	32.7
Others	56.5	19.3
Total	67.8	25.9

The percentage of households "not getting enough food" round the year has come down to 26 per cent in 1999 from 68 per cent in 1982. The situation of food availability for the landless and agricultural labour households, although considerably improved, is still grim. Almost two-thirds of agricultural labour households do not get enough food round the year (Table 18). More than half of the households belonging to one of the most vulnerable groups, having common characteristics of SC, agricultural labour, and landlessness, report that they do not get sufficient food round the year. Similarly, the proportion is also very high among the women headed households. It is important to note that, except for the landless as an independent category, for the other identified groups the food security situation has not improved significantly over the years.

Housing and Domestic Facilities

Housing and domestic facilities to households are among the most important indicators of levels of living of households. The types of housing and basic amenities facilities available to different types of households is presented in Table 19. It can be seen that in terms of any indicator of housing and other domestic facilities the conditions of SC and agricultural labour households has marginally improved between the two reference periods. In fact, in 1999 there is a higher proportion of households living in *kutcha* houses in comparison to that in 1982. Some improvement is, however, perceptible across all kinds of households in terms of lighting provision within the house (Table 19). We can see these related facts and figures in Appendix Table 4.

Presence of safe defecation is almost negligible in 1999 as it was in 1982. Only a few toilets can be found across villages largely belonging to upper castes and other well-off households. In the year some semi-pucca houses were found with SCs, agricultural labour and landless households mainly because these households were the beneficiary households under the government-run housing scheme (Indira Awas Yojna).

Domestic Consumer Durables

Possession of different types of domestic consumer durable is not only an indicator of quality of life but may also be taken as directly indicative of the level of poverty of a household. In fact, in the absence of proper income data, possession of domestic consumer durable gives an idea about the living standard of the households. In

TABLE 19

Percentage of Households with Different Housing and Basic Amenities Facilities

	1999					1982			
	Housing			Decent	Own	Housing		Decent	Own
	Kutcha	Semi-Pucca	Pucca	Lighting*	Toilet	Kutcha	Pucca	Lighting*	Toilet
(1)	(2)	(3)	(4)	(5)	(6)	(7)	(8)	(9)	(10)
SC	59.30	32.90	8.00	19 90	0.00	44.1	1.9	9.9	1.3
AL	75.60	22.10	2.4	0.19	0.00	62.0	0.0	9.7	1.3
Landless	52.53	37.62	9.85	25.35	3.52	53.0	3.1	15.8	2.8
SC, AL, landless	77.75	21.04	1.21	14.50	0.35	68.79		6.53	0.00
Others	35.39	37.89	45.63	62.53	15.89	38.35		65.32	9.75
All	45.1	32.1	22.5	42.65	9.65	43.0	13.5	37.9	6.4

* Includes lighting through electric, oil lamps, kerosene lamps.

Table 20 the percentage of households possessing different types of these consumers durable has been presented. The table show that apart from the ownernership of cot *(Charpoy and palang)*, the ownership of lantern/petromax, mosquito net, torch, and watch is widespread. Besides these, there is a substantial proportion of households who own some other consumer durables such as bicycle, chair/table, radio, etc. However, possession of these durables show a considerable variation across different sections of households. Almost all big farmers and upper class households possess items like cot, chair and table, torch, and watch, while only a small proportion of small farmers and lower class households possess these items.

TABLE 20

Percentage of Consumer Durables, 1999

	SC	*AL*	*Landless*	*SC, AL, landless*	*Others*	*All*
Bycycle	25.39	22.34	30.96	18.78	53.69	41.3
Chair/Table	7.89	4.26	20.18	0.7	42.24	29.85
Cot	65.34	58.51	66.74	54.95	89.72	77.33
Cooker	1.02	1.06	4.82	0	18.34	5.95
Fan/Stove	1.59	1.06	3.44	0	15.87	3.48
Lantern/ Petromax	38.59	35.11	52.98	31.55	71. 99	59.6
Mosquito net	32.35	29.26	48.85	25.7	68.84	56.45
Radio	13.24	9.57	18.35	6.01	37.31	24.92
TV	2.59	1.6	4.36	0	18.23	5.84
Sewing machine	2.35	1.6	5.5	0	19.35	6.96
Torch	46.75	40.43	50.92	36.87	74.01	61.62
Watch	32.65	22.34	38.3	18.78	60.76	48.37

There has also been a noticeable change in the ownership pattern of these items over the years. In 1982, only 15 per cent households owned mosquito nets, which increased to 56 per cent in 1999. In the same way percentage of households owning torches, bicycles, and radios in 1982 were 25, 15, and 8 respectively, which increased to approximately 62, 41, and 25 respectively in 1999. Accordingly, during 1982 there was no household owning a television, but in 1999 approximately 6 per cent of the households owned a television. In the same way today in almost all the villages, possession of motor cycle/scooter, sewing machine, watch, pressure cooker, etc. are more frequently visible. It is noteworthy that remittances from migration play major role in improving the consumer assets position of the households. In the case of lower caste and classes households in particular, migrant labour have been able to purchase consumer items such as watch, torch, radio, etc. more commonly.

There has been perceptible reduction in poverty in Bihar during 1980s and 1990s. The rate of reduction in rural poverty in Bihar has been higher than All-India. However, the level of poverty in the state remains to be very high.

The reduction in poverty has been very uneven among various groups. Some groups such as agricultural labourers, non-agriuclturists and with cultivating households small pieces of land (up to 0.4 hectares) have shown lower reduction in poverty as compared to other groups and as such over the years there has been increasing concentration of the poor among these groups. These groups overlap with scheduled castes, backward caste, households (both among Hindus and Muslims) cultivating very small pieces of land and women headed households.

Although there has been some improvement in terms of food security, access to domestic possession, literacy and health indicators, the level is still very low and most of them continue to be in the state of abject poverty. Women in general, disabled, and old people, face various kinds of intra-households discrimination.

A striking feature of the poor in Bihar is that they show high sensitivity towards the prevalence of relative poverty with regard to their economic conditions and access to basic amenities. They seem to particularly resent the indifference of the government for failing to provide adequate educational and health facility.

The skill development of the poorer workers, both migrants and non-migrants, will go a long way in increasing the productivity and earnings of the poor in Bihar, as low levels of education and skill development is the primary reason of their low earning.

The incidence of poverty is very high among Scheduled castes, Muslims and OBC I. Occupation and class-wise poverty was reported to be very high among agricultural labourers compared to non-agricultral labourers. (App. Table 1) Consumption expenditure is also, the lowest among agricultural labourers and landless persons compared to others. Housing and basic facilities are negligible among scheduled castes, Muslims and OBC I as the above tables indicate although percentage of house holds of such people has increased marginally in the year 1999 survey compared to 1982 with respect to enjoying the basic facilities.

References

Pal, P.K., 2003, "Poverty and Development in India : An Interstate Analysis paper presented at the National Seminar on current issues in the India Economy, Organized by the Department of Economics, Rabindra Bharti University, 21-22, March 2003.

Pal, P.K., Dimension of Poverty in India: Measurement and Determinates, Future in Iyenger, N.S. book Poverty and sustainable Development: Concepts and Measures, pp. 220-21, (2010).

Sharma, A.N., Political Economy of Poverty in Rural Bihar, Nature, Dimensions and Linkages, IHD, Delhi, 2007.

Deaton and Dreze (2002), "Poverty and Inequality in India: A Re-examination", *Economic and Political Weekly*, Vol. 37, No. 36.

Garg, Charu and Karan, A.K. (2004), *Catastrophic and Foverty Impact of Out-of Pocket Payment for Health Care in India: A State-Level Analysis*, Working Paper Series No. 23, Institute for Human Development, New Delhi.

Himanshu (2007), "Recent Trends in Poverty and Inequality: Some Preliminary Results", *Economic and Political Weekly*, February 10.

NSSO (2004-05), Level & Pattern of Consumer Expenditure, 2004-05, NSSO 61st Round, Report No. 508 (July 2004-June 2005), Government of India, December 2006.

Planning Commission (2007), "Poverty Estimates for 2004-05", Press Information Bureau, Government of India, March 21.

Prasad, Pradhan H., Gerry Rodgers, Shaibal Gupta and Alakh, N. Sharma (1986), *Dynamics of Poverty and Employment in Rural Bihar*, A.N. Sinha Institute of Social Studies, Patna.

Rogers, Gerry and Janine Rodgers (2000), "Semi-feudalism Meets the Market: A Report from Purnia", Working Paper 6, Institute for Human Development, New Delhi.

Sharma, Alakh N. (1999), *People on the Move: Nature and Pattern of Migration in Bihar*, Vikash Publishing House, New Delhi.

Sharma, Alakh N. (2001), "Agrarian Relations and Socio-Economic Change in Bihar", *Economic and Political Weekly*.

Sharma, Alakh N., Anup K. Karan and Sandip Sarkar (2001), *Dynamics of Employment, Poverty and Human Development in Rural Bihar*, Institute for Human Development, *(mimeo)*.

APPENDIX

TABLE 1
Incidence of Poverty, 1999 Survey

Caste Group	*Moderate Poor*	*Very Poor*	*All Poor*
Upper caste	20.29	6.02	26.32
Upper OBC II	18.48	9.89	28.37
Lower OBC II	17.97	26.43	44.40
OBC I	28.08	23.06	51.14
SC	38.39	28.16	66.55
Muslim	35.10	15.34	50.44
Class Group			
Agricultural labour	34.61	33.88	68.49
Poor middle peasants	22.06	7.84	29.90
Middle peasants	25.96	5.53	31.49
Big peasants	25.43	5.02	30.44
Landlords	12.85	5.84	18.70
Non-agricultural	28.25	16.98	15.23
Owned Land I (acre)			
Landless	32.04	31.42	63.46
0-1.0	31.67	12.91	44.58
1.0-2.5	17.65	4.94	22.59
2.5-5.0	19.97	3.05	23.01
5.0-10.0	7.65	0.00	7.65
10.0+	0.00	0.00	0.00
Total	26.54	16.71	43.25

TABLE 2

Quintile Group Distribution of Consumption Expenditure, 1999 Survey

Types of households	*Consumption expenditure class*				
	Lowest 20%	*20% to 40%*	*40% to 60%*	*60% to 80%*	*Highest 20%*
Caste Group					
Upper caste	8.66	14.17	20.87	27.17	29.13
Upper OBC II	10.91	12.73	31.82	24.55	20.00
Lower OBC II	25.00	18.06	13.89	22.22	20.83
OBC I	21.94	22.58	18.06	20.65	16.77
SC	37.31	25.87	17.41	9.45	9.95
Muslims	17.17	27.27	19.19	15.15	21.21
Class Group					
Agricultural labour	36.09	25.44	19.53	11.83	7.10
Poor middle peasant	11.11	14.81	22.22	25.93	25.93
Middle peasant	7.53	18.28	26.88	26.88	20.43
Big peasant	6.75	17.79	22.09	23.93	29.45
Landlord	7.45	10.56	14.91	27.95	39.13
Non-agricultural	21.10	22.02	21.10	20.18	15.60
Owned Land (acre)					
Landless	32.89	23.68	18.42	15.00	10.00
0-1.0	16.17	21.43	24.06	19.55	18.80
1.0-2.5	6.72	12.61	22.69	31.09	26.89
2.5-5.0	2.60	15.58	15.58	27.27	38.96
5.0-10.0		8.11	16.22	16.22	59.46
10.0-20.0			11.11	44.44	44.44
20+				33.33	66.67
Total	20.00	20.00	20.00	20.00	20.00

TABLE 3
Percentage of Households with Different Quintile Group Distribution of Consumption Expenditure, 1982 Survey

Caste					
Upper caste	10.53	12.78	19.55	22.56	34.59
Upper OBC II	12.50	12.50	31. 94	23.61	19.44
Lower OBC II	11.54	17.31	21.15	17.31	32.69
OBC I	32.22	24.44	17.78	15.56	10.00
SC	28.69	26.23	18.03	18.03	9.02
Muslim	21.05	28.07	14.04	22.81	14.04
Class					
Agricultural labour	28.38	28.83	17.57	16.67	8.56
Poor middle peasant	17.78	13.33	26.67	26.67	15.56
Middle peasant	13.33	3.33	40.00	30.00	13.33
Big peasant	10.38	11.32	20.75	28.30	29.25
Landlord	11.39	17.72	15.19	13.92	41.77
Non-agricultural	22.73	18.18	20.45	13.64	25.00
Land (in acre)					
Landless	30.84	26.17	14.95	16.82	11.21
0-1.0	19.55	21.80	24.06	17.29	17.29
1.0-2.5	13.64	12.12	27.27	28.79	18.18
2.5-5.0	6.38	12.77	25.53	23.40	31.91
5.0-10.0	3.03	12.12	15.15	24.24	45.45
10.0-20.0		7.14	25.00	21.43	46.43

(Sharma, A.N., 2001).

TABLE 4
Percentage of Households with different Housing and Basic Amenities Facilities

	1999					*1982*			
	Housing			*Decent*	*Own*	*Housing*		*Decent*	*Own*
	Kutcha	*Semi-Pucca*	*Pucca*	*Lighting**	*Toilet*	*Kutcha*	*Pucca*	*Lighting**	*Toilet*
(1)	*(2)*	*(3)*	*(4)*	*(5)*	*(6)*	*(7)*	*(8)*	*(9)*	*(10)*
Caste									
Brahmin	41.80	29.90	28.30	60.24	16.27	50.7	28.4	74.6	16.4
Bhumihar	17.30	44.90	37.80	62.50	28.41	21.1	39.2	71.8	18.8
Kurmi	9.80	27.30	62.90	38.46	3.85	3.2	55.1	70.2	22.6
Yadav	36.50	49.00	14.50	50.00	10.00	56.7	7.7	56.2	0.0
Koiri	18.10	51.50	30.40	57.14	28.57	3.0	17.4	65.3	1.8
Other OBC II	35.70	42.80	21.40	44.44	9.72	24.2	13.5	64.0	7.9
OBC I	66.40	24.10	9.80	36.77	2.58	54.7	1.2	15.0	0.9
SC	59.30	32.90	8.00	19.90	0.00	44.1	1.9	9.9	1.3
Muslim	82.20	14.60	3.30	45.45	10.10	74.6	11.1	31.9	5.5
Class									
ALNF	75.6	22.1	2.4	20.19	0.00	62.0	0.0	9.7	1.3
ALNA	70.7	24.6	4.7	11.11	5.56	27.0	0.0	11.1	0.5
ALLF	62.0	28.0	10.0	23.85	0.92	57.8	3.7	20.1	0.8

ALLA	69.1	17.6	13.5	33.33	0.00	42.8	0.0	8.6	6.0
POOMIDP	36.2	45.8	18.0	40.74	0.00	27.9	15.4	40.5	2.0
MIDP	26.6	46.2	27.3	51 61	5.38	31.4	20.2	67.4	1.0
BIGP	29.0	38.5	32.5	60.12	21.47	15.2	73.1	94.4	37.6
LANDLD	21.5	35.5	43.1	67.70	24.84	50.6	45.3	100.0	49.3
NAG	52.6	36.0	11.4	39.45	3.67	45.7	5.8	42.3	2.4
Total	45.1	32.1	22.5	42.65	9.65	43.0	13.5	37.9	6.4

* Includes lighting through electric, oil lamps, kerosine lamps.
(Sharma, A.N., Anup, K. Karan and Sandip Sarkar).

Chapter 4

Extent and Incidence of Poverty in India

The concept of poverty is multi-dimensional (viz. Income poverty and non-income poverty). It covers not only levels of income and consumption, but also health and education, vulnerability and risk; and marginalization and exclusion of the poor from mainstream society. The performance of India in terms of income and non-income indicators has not been satisfactory. When a substantial segment of a society is a deprived of the minimum level of living and continues at a bare substance level, that society is called to be plagued with mass poverty. A group of experts argues that poverty can be assessed on the ground when one fails to get certain minimum consumption standard. But others have asserted that it is difficult to agree on the amount of income that ensures the minimum consumption standard at one point of time. Poverty has been defined on the basis of minimum or good life obtained in the society. All the definitions of poverty approach to the average level of living in a society and reflect the existence of inequalities in a society. In India, the definition of poverty emphasise minimum level of living, rather than a reasonable level of living.

It means that for some decades it would not be possible to provide the masses even a minimum quantum of basic needs and therefore, to talk about a reasonable level of living or good life may appear to be wishful thinking at the present stage. Political considerations also enter the definitions of poverty because programmes of alleviating poverty may become prohibitive as the vision of a good life widens. The upshot of the entire argument is that the absolute standard of poverty expressed in terms of minimum requirements of cereals, pulses, milk, vegetables, butter, clothing or calorie intake is conditioned by the relative levels of living prevalent in the country. The deprivation of a significant section of the society of minimum basic needs in the face of a luxurious life for the elite class, makes poverty more glaring. Dandekar and Rath (1971) have defined poverty as "an inadequate level of employment in terms of its capacity to provide minimum living to the population."

Poverty has been an important issue in India since independence. The Planning Commission has been estimating the incidence of poverty at the national and the state level using the methodology contained in the report of Expert Groups on Estimation of Proportion and Number of Poor (Lakdawala Committee) and applying it to consumption data from the large sample surveys on consumer expenditure conducted by the National Sample Survey Organisation (NSSO) at an interval of approximately Five Years.

The latest large sample survey data on consumer expenditure are for the 55th Round covering the period of July 1999-June 2000. In the early surveys, the NSSO estimated monthly consumption expenditure on the basis of responses using a 30 days recall period for all food and non-food items. In the 55th round, consumption expenditure on clothing, footwear, medical, education and durable goods were collected using a 365 days recall period. For non-food items the 30 days recall period was used and the data on food consumption expenditure were collected using two reference periods of last 30 days and last 7 days from the same households. Poverty at the national level is estimated as the weighted average of state-wise poverty levels. Table 1 shows the poverty ratios estimated for the period of 30 days recall period for 1973-74 to 1999-2000 along with the poverty projection for 2007.

Table 1 shows that the combined poverty ratio has declined from 54.9 per cent in 1973-74 to 36.0 per cent in 1993-94. The poverty ratio declined by nearly 10 percentage points in the 5 years period between 1993-94 to reach 26.1 per cent in 1999-00. While the proportion of poor in the rural areas declined from 56.4 per cent in 1973-74 to 27.1 per cent in 1999-2000, the decline in urban areas has

TABLE 1
Estimates of Incidence of Poverty

Year	*Poverty Ratio (%)*			*Number of Poor (million)*		
	Rural	*Urban*	*Combined*	*Rural*	*Urban*	*Combined*
1973-74	56.4	49.0	59.9	261.3	60.0	321.3
1977-78	53.1	45.2	51.3	264.3	64.6	338.9
1983	45.7	40.8	44.5	252.0	70.9	322.9
1987-88	39.1	38.2	38.9	231.9	75.2	307.1
1993-94	37.3	32.4	36.0	244.0	76.3	320.3
1999-2000	27.1	23.6	26.1	193.2	67.1	260.3
2007 (Projections)	21.1	15.1	19.3	170.5	49.6	220.1

Source : Tenth Five Year Plan, Vol. 1, Planning Commission.

been from 49 per cent to 23.6 per cent during this period. In absolute terms, the number of poor declined to 260 million in 1999-2000 with about 75 per cent of these being in the rural areas. The poverty reduction target set by the Planning Commission for the Tenth Five Year Plan aims at achieving a poverty ratio of 19.3 per cent for the country as a whole by 2007, 21.1 per cent for the rural and 15.1 per cent for the urban areas.

Although various studies have been conducted for poverty estimation, the present chapter has taken the poverty estimation by Planning Commission.

Initially Economic Reforms were introduced by Mr. Rajiv Gandhi in 1985 with the aim of improvement in productivity, Absorption of modern technology and full utilization of capacity. In this regime private sector has to play grater roll. Since then the reform process continues. In 1991, a number of stabilization measures were adopted. Now the phase of second generation reforms has also been started. Elaborating on the philosophy of Second Generation Reforms, the then Finanee Minister Mr. Yashwant Sinha in his budget speech 2000-01 stated, "Growth is not just an end in itself. It is the critical vehicle for increasing employment and raising the living standards of our people, especially of the poorest. Sustained broad-based growth, combined with all our programmes for accelerating rural development, building roads, promoting housing, boosting knowledge-based industries and enhancing the quality of human resources, will impart a strong impetus to employment expansion. There can be no better cure for poverty than this in our country."

In this section of the chapter, efforts have been made to analysis the impact of economic reforms on poverty on the basis of GDP growth, employment growth and reduction of population living below poverty line.

GDP GROWTH AND REDUCTION OF POVERTY DURING REFORM

Planners assumed that a fast rate of growth of national income will by itself create more employment and produce higher income for the poor. But the theory of trickle down effect did not work and the benefits of high GDP growth could not reach to the poor. The Table 2 gives a glance of GDP growth and population below poverty line from 1983 to 1997.

TABLE 2

Percentage of People Below Poverty Line and GDP Growth Rate

Year	*NSS Round*	*GDP Growth rate at Factor cost (1993-94 Prices)*	*Percentage*			*Absolute Numbers (million)*
			Rural	*Urban*	*Com-bined*	
1983-84	(38th) LS	7.5	45.65	40.79	44.48	322.8
1987-88	(48th) LS	3.4	39.09	38.20	38.86	304.9
1989-90	(45th) TS	10.7	33.70	36.00	34.28	276.0
1990-91	(46th) TS	5.2	35.04	35.29	35.11	291.0
1992-93	(48th) TS	4.5	41.70	37.80	40.70	348.0
1993-94	(50th) LS	6.0	37.27	32.36	35.07	320.5
1994-95	(51st) TS	7.0	38.03	34.24	36.48	328.0
1995-96	(52nd) TS	7.3	38.29	30.05	36.08	328.0
1996-97	(53rd) TS	7.2	38.46	33.97	37.23	348.8

LS = Large Sample, TS = Thin Sample.

Source : Compiled from Household Consumption Survey, NSSO, Gal and Economic Survey, 2001-02.

Table 2 shows that economic reforms have been able to promote relatively higher growth during 1993-94 to 1996-97, i.e. growth rate averaged to more than 7 per cent per annum. During the same period the poverty percentage increased from 35.07 per cent to 37.23 per cent in aggregate. In this period, GDP growth rate increased to around 6.9 per cent per annum, the highest ever witnessed consecutively for four years in India. Thus, during 1993-94 to 1996-97, inverse relationship has been observed between poverty reduction and GDP growth.

Dr. S.P. Gupta, member Planning Commission, in his lecture on "Trickledown Theory Revisited: The Role of Employment and Poverty" brought out the fact that "In India the poverty reduction over 1983 to 1990-91 was around 3.1 per cent per annum, but it reversed to 1 per cent in the 1990s, i.e. between 1990-91 to 1997. In contrast to this, the GDP growth in India between 1983 to 1990-91 was around 5.6 per cent and between 1990-91 and 1997, this is expected to go beyond 5.7 per cent".

Dr. Gaurav Datt, of World Bank, has compared the decline in head-count index, poverty gap index and squared poverty gap index for rural and urban India in the pre-reform and post-reform period. In his study entitled "Has Poverty Declined Since Economic Reforms" Dr. Gaurav Datt has identified stagnation in rural growth as a basic cause of showdown in poverty reduction. Table 3 gives poverty profile of India from 1973-97 workout by Gaurav Dutt.

Table 3 shows that there was a marked decline in both rural and urban poverty between 1973-74 and 1986-87. For the rural sector, for the period 1973-74 and 1990-91, head count index of poverty declined at the annual rate of 2.7 per cent, but the rate of decline in post-reform period is not significantly different from zero. For the urban sector, the annual rate of decline in headcount ratio of poverty remained 2.2 per cent in pre and post-reform period. There is continuous reduction in poverty in urban areas in the process of growth but rural poverty reduction was choked-off by lack of rural growth. (Chawdhry 2010)

The harsh realities regarding the poverty in India are: the poverty ratio though, has declined over the years, yet the number of poor is still very high. Poverty ratio in 1973-74 was 54.9 per cent of the total population, it came down to 26.1 per cent in 1999-2000, yet the number of poor was 260 million in 1999-2000. The sorrow picture is continuing in 260 million inspite of the fact that there are a number of programs put forth and implemented by the government for the reduction of poverty in India. A high degree of poverty differential

TABLE 3
Poverty in India, 1973-97

NSS Round	*Survey Period*	*Head-count Index*		*Poverty Gap Index*		*Squared Poverty Gap Index*	
		Rural	*Urban*	*Rural*	*Urban*	*Rural*	*Urban*
(1)	*(2)*	*(3)*	*(4)*	*(5)*	*(6)*	*(7)*	*(8)*
Pre-reform							
28	Oct. 73-June 74	52.72	47.96	17.175	13.602	7.128	5.219
32	July 77-June 78	50.60	40.50	15.025	11.687	6.057	4.526
38	June 83-Dec. 83	45.31	35.65	12.649	9.517	4.841	3.557
42	July 86-June 87	38.81	34.29	10.013	9.100	3.700	3.395
43	July 87-June 88	39.23	36.20	9.275	9.121	2.982	3;056
44	July 88-June 89	39.06	36.60	9.504	9.537	3.291	3.293
45	July 89-June 90	34.30	33.40	7.799	8.505	2.575	3.038
46	July 90-June 91	36.43	32.76	8.644	8.509	2.926	3.121
	July 89-June 91	35.37	33.08	8.222	8.507	2.751	3.080
Post-reform							
47	July 91-Dec. 91	37.42	33.23	8.288	8.244	2.680	2.902
48	Jan. 92-Dec. 92	43.47	33.73	10.881	8.824	3.810	3.191
50	July 93-June 94	36.66	30.51	8.387	7.405	2.792	2.417
51	July 94-June 95	41.02	33.50	9.285	8.382	2.995	2.799
52	July 95-June 96	37.15	28.04	8.098	6.781	2.527	2.222
53	Jan. 97-Dec. 97	35.78	29.99	8.321	7.762	2.757	2.725
	July 95-Dec. 97	36.47	29.02	8.205	7,273	2.642	2.474

Source : Gaurav Datt, Has Poverty Declined since Economic Reforms?, *Economic and Political Weekly*, December, 11-17, 1999.

still persists among different states of the country. In the same way in spite of an good increase in the national income were on in the gross domestic savings (around 22 per cent of G.D.P.) and capital formation (around 23 per cent), but an increase in the unemployment rate (7.32 per cent in 1999-2000 from 5.99 in 1993-94) and number of unemployed (26.58 million in 1999-2000). How can we take pride of development when we still have extremely marathon challenge of eliminating over 27 per cent of rural poverty and around 23 per cent of urban poverty encompassing several crore of humanity in the coming years. Were five or is poverty invincible? If answer to both the questions is be, then one is compelled to doubt the efficiency of the successive governments and their line of thought. The following is a critical examination of the various poverty elimination programs and their contribution towards sustainable development. Let's see the idea of redistribution still have relevance in the present scenario. (*Swaminathan*, 2001)

"Food for all" was the primary focus of the poverty elevation. Program as food is a basic necessity of life. The result was a plethora of steps taken by the government through their policy aptly supplemented by the new technology. The success of green revolution can be proved easily by the fact that 4000 years of progress was repeated in just 41 years of production of wheat rose from 7 million tones in 1947 to 17 million tones in 1964-68. Total production of food grains too increased from 50 million tones in 1951 to 208.9 million tones in 1900-2000. Our population rose from 36 crore in 1951 to 103 crore, i.e. 3 times but food production increased by 4 times. (*Punchmukhi*, 2000)

Though not doubting the success of the green revolution, one would agree that green revolution fire reached a saturation point. It cannot feed the ever growing population of this country, unless technological development takes place. Again green revolution has encouraged uncontrolled use of chemical fertilizers, which has hampered soil fertility also adversely affecting its productivity. This goes the idea of sustainable development, marring future prospects for the fulfillment of present needs. Further, with the increase in the population, the per capita availability of the land is also going down, which will make India's food perspective more bleak in order to meet the challenge of making green revolution to evergreen revolution we will have to address all these challenges along with craving out for gene revolution, Eco-technology revolution and information and communication revolution, which will involve a lots of capital and at the time was to be an uphill task V.R. Panchamukh presented an international comparison of per capita food production and calorie consumption. According to him, India's historical growth of food production was 0.58 per cent. The required growth rate for India to catch up with China and Brazil in per capita production of food in 2020 is three and a half times and five and a half times the historical rate respectively. Secondly, the historical rate of growth of per capita calorie consumption of India for the period 1992 to 1994-96 was 0.56 per cent. If India has to catch up with per capita calorie consumption of China and USA by 2020, growth rate of India's per capita calorie consumption will. have to three times and four and a half times respectively. This analysis shows an uphill task before India to achieve food security (*Kurien*, 1990).

In agriculture and allied activism land is considered as one of the basic inputs of production. Land reform in India was introduced to alter the pattern of land ownership and to bring a systematic structural change in rural society for the attainment of the goal of production and justice. But close examination shows that the reforms actually did not evolve efficient production and egalitarian society. The first round of fragmentation was brought about by the land reforms itself. If the ceiling limit of the best category of land was 18 acres in July 1971 so that every land tiller is given justice, its level would certainly drop in 2001 when number of tillers have increased but not the land and would continue to come down with the increase in population. The marginal farmers of today would become big farmers for tomorrow and distributive justice will make them petty farmers of the yester year. Already in India the size of the agriculture holding is quite uneconomic, small and fragmented. The average size of holding in India is expected to decline from 1.5 hectares in 1990-91 to 1.3 hectares in 2000-01. The marginal holdings which were 59.7 per cent in 1990-91 are 62.1 per cent by 2000-01. N.J. Kurian observed that out of 97.8 million holdings in 1985-86, 58.1 per cent was of marginal category, and the remaining category of holding include small category 08.3%) @ semi and medium (8.1%) and large (2.0%) holdings can be considered as an economic Ionic and remaining 41.9 per cent as economic. The problem of increased sub-division actually finds its roots in the increasing pressure of population which has to be supported. This sub-division leads to further problems such as wastage of land, managerial problems, litigations, and low productivity and disguised unemployment. Thus, according to us the ceiling act of land reforms in no way holds relevance in the coming years and if followed would be a deterrent to development. To cover up the flaw of fragmentation of holdings, co-operative farm is suggested. A critical evaluation of co-operative farming too shows that it promotes inequality and unemployment. It also results in the loss of independence of farmers. With such marginal traits, co-operative farming can never encourage sustainable development. Moreover, in our view, co-operative farming on a large scale is also not feasible.

To cover up the flaw of fragmentation of holdings, co-operative farming is suggested. A critical evaluation of co-operative farming too shows that it promotes inequality and employment. It is also results in the loss of independence of farmers. With such marginal traits, co-operatives farming can never encourage sustainable development.

Further, there has always been a lot of hue and cry about prevention of immigration, which leads to the increase of liability of the, nation-state. But, influx of population from the neighboring countries continuously forming a significant portion of the nation's morning burden. This will have to be chacked if development is to be assured. Yet another point relating to poverty is human resource development. There is no doubt that human resource play a significant role in the development of any economy. We talk of providing education and employment to all. But, there is no thought given to from where the massive resource for this purpose will come and has the country capacity to absorb such a huge battalion of unskilled work force. Human resource can be greatest asset provided it is adequately equipped. India is a place where every 6th person of the world lives ranks 132nd in the group of 174 developing and developed countries. We are trying to feed all at the expense of a few in the name of social justice. Though, we do not doubt the pious intention behind this, but would the economy be able to sustain such a justice for a long time. Are not we on the path of ruin encouraging a jobless, futureless growth of population, which leave apart being an asset is a liability.

Finally, it is said that because of trickle down effect, the fruits of development can be reaped by the poorest of the poor also. But if the poor are in extremely bad condition and providing additional income to them enormously uplifts their welfare without diminishing the total out put and income of the society, the redistribution is definitely justified. But in reality it is found that transfer of income from the rich to the poor reduces the income and output of the society (*Gil*, 1976).

ANALYSIS OF ABSOLUTE AND RELATIVE POVERTY IN RURAL INDIA

The trend in absolute rural poverty and the extent of disparities in the food, non-food and overall consumption expenditure among different expenditure classes on the basis of our methodology are presented in Table 4.

TABLE 4

Absolute Poverty Ratios and Gini's Coefficient Representing Disparities in Food, Non-Food and Overall Consumption Expenditure in Rural India During the Last Six Quinquennial Rounds

(*in percentage terms*)

Quinquennial Rounds	*Absolute Food*	*Food Expenditure*	*Non-Food Expenditure*	*Total Consumption Expenditure*
1st Round 1972-73/1973-74	56.4	22.16	41.09	26.80
2nd Round 1977-78	53.1	25.86	51.29	31.32
3rd Round 1983	45.7	20.42	41.01	28.05
4th Round 1987-88	39.1	21.93	41.24	30.36
5th Round 1993-94	37.3	20.51	39.76	27.46
6th Round 1997-2000	27.1	20.58	32.83	25.50

Source : Estimated on the basis of last six Quinquennial rounds reports on Level and Pattern of Consumption Expenditure in India, NSSO, Dept. of Statistics, Government of India, New Delhi.

Following Table 5 reveals the growth rate of real per capita net domestic product in rural areas for different sub-periods.

Above tables show interesting facts. The real per capita NDP during 1970, increased at a rate of around 0.32% per annum while the rural poverty dipped marginally from approximately 56% to 53% only. During the same period, disparities in food, non-food and overall consumption expenditure increased significantly, especially the disparities in non-food expenditure.

TABLE 5

Growth Rate of Rural Per Capita Net Domestic Product in Real Terms

(*in Percentage terms*)

Period	*1970-71 to 1980-81*	*1980-81 to 1993-94*	*1993-94 to 1999-2000*
Growth Rate	0.32	2.98	3.36

Source : National Accounts Statistics of India, 1950-51 to 2000-01, EP1-Y, Research Foundation, Mumbai and Net Domestic Product by Economic Activity in Rural/Urban Areas, CSO, Government of India.

Obviously, the benefits of economic development has favoured the rural rich and the marginal decline in rural poverty, that has occurred, is owing to some possible drift of benefits of the increased per capita income to lower expenditure classes of society. Thus, on account of increased disparities in household consumption expenditure among different classes and that savings are largely constituted by the people in higher expenditure class, therefore, during 1970s, income disparities too have aggravated. Thus, our analysis fully corroborates the first part of Kuznets hypothesis that initially economic development will aggravate the inequalities in income distribution. Moreover, it also highlights the fact that initial decline in absolute poverty will only be marginal, especially in developing countries and which will possibly occur on account of insignificant drift of benefits of economic development towards the lower expenditure classes. The case of rural India is a testimony to it. Thus, mere rise in overall per capita income is not sufficient to reduce poverty. Rather, its distribution is more important for absolute poverty to decline.

The estimated growth rate of per capita rural NDP in real terms for the period 1980-81 to 1993-94 is approximately 3.0% per annum. It is in place to mention that this is a fairly long period, which we have to consider for estimating the growth rate of rural per capita NDP, as the data for rural and urban NDP was not available for other intervening years. The significant improvement in the per capita NDP growth rate from 0.3% per annum to around 3.0% per annum as well as considerable decline in disparities regarding food, non-food and overall consumption expenditure of different classes in rural areas has facilitated to reduce absolute rural poverty significantly. The absolute poverty which was 53% in 1977-78 has come down to 37% in 1993-94. There has been a gradual decline in absolute poverty between 1977-78 to 1993-94 but the decline in the disparities in consumption expenditure on food items of different classes is not so, during the same period (refer Table 4). In such a situation, one may argue as to how the redistribution of income had facilitated in reducing poverty when the consumption expenditure of different classes on the basic wage good (i.e. food) has not converged gradually. It has declined between 1977-78 and 1983, but thereafter, it has increased marginally. This is also contrary to Engel's law which suggests that with the rise in income, proportion of income spent on food declines, i.e. richer community tends to spend lesser proportion of income on food than the poor community. Since this did not happen, one may wonder whether redistribution has really helped in curtailing the absolute rural poverty. It is indeed noteworthy that between 1983 to 1987-88, there has been a major shift in consumption of food basket especially for rural rich. The shift is from the traditional items of cereals to more nutritious food items, such as milk, milk products, meat, etc. This shift is clearly evident from Table 6, which shows that although the MPCE (monthly per capita expenditure) on cereals has declined by 6 percentage points, but overall food expenditure has declined only marginally between 38th (1983) and 43rd (1987-88) NSS rounds. Prior to this, such a significant shift was not visible. It is in place to point out that though MPCE on cereals during the 27th (1972-73) and 32nd (1977-78) NSS rounds has declined by about 8 percentage points, but it has simultaneously led to a decline in overall food expenditure by about similar percentage points. This depicts absence of any compositional shift in the food expenditure of different classes, especially the rural rich during 1972-73 to 1977-78. However, such a change in food basket is clearly visible during 1983 to 1987-88. It is on account of this visible change in the food consumption basket which occurred during 1983 to 1987-88 that the distribution of increased per capita NDP even to the lowest classes is not at all evident in terms of decline in the disparities in consumption expenditure on food among different classes but its impact in curtailing absolute poverty from approximately 46% to 39% can well be explained in terms of the major shift occurring in the composition of food basket, especially for rural rich in India.

The shift in composition of food basket continued even thereafter, but the extent of change is not significant (refer Table 6).

As a consequence, there is a marginal decline in the disparities of food consumption expenditure among different classes during the period 1987-88 to 1993-94.

TABLE 6

Percentage Distribution of Monthly Per Capita Expenditure (MPCE) on Different Food Items over NSS Rounds in Rural India

Items	*Average MPCE as Percentage of Total MPCE*					
	27th	*32nd*	*38th*	*43rd*	*50th*	*55th*
Cereals	40.6	32.8	32.3	26.3	24.2	22.2
Gram	0.6	0.4	0.3	0.2	0.2	0.1
Cereal Substitutes	0.5	0.3	0.2	0.1	0.1	0.1
Pulses & Products	4.3	3.8	3.5	4.0	3.8	3.8
Milk & Milk Products	7.3	7.7	7.5	8.6	9.5	8.8
Edible Oils	3.5	3.6	4.0	5.0	4.4	3.7
Meat, Egg, Fish	2.5	2.7	3.0	3.3	3.3	3.3
Vegetables	3.6	3.8	4.7	5.2	6.0	6.2
Fruits & Nuts	1.1	1.1	1.4	1.6	1.7	1.7
Sugar	3.8	2.6	2.8	2.9	3.1	2.4
Salt & Spices	2.8	3.0	2.5	2.9	2.7	3.0
Beverages	2.4	2.5	3.3	3.9	4.2	4.2
Food	72.9	64.3	65.6	64.0	63.2	59.4

Source : Level and Pattern of Consumer Expenditure, 6th Quinquennial Survey, 1999-2000, NSSO, Dept. of Statistics, Government of India, New Delhi.

Further, it is also evident from our analysis that between 1977-78 to 1993-94, the disparities in the non-food consumption expenditure has declined from about 50% to 40%. The decline is fairly substantial but one should not interpret it as an indicator of declining income disparities too. There are three important reasons for it:

(i) Non-food expenditure in NSSO estimates represents a smaller fraction of total expenditure as compared to the food expenditure. Therefore, even smaller increases in non-food expenditure in money terms reflect large changes in percentage terms in it. On account of this, though the disparities in non-food expenditure has fallen from 51% to 40%, yet the overall disparities in consumption expenditure has declined from just about 31% to 27% during 1977-78 to 1993-94.

(ii) The household savings-income ratio has increased from 16.86% to 23.08% (refer Table 7), during 1977-78 to 1993-94. This increase in household savings appear to be far more than the decline experienced in disparities in consumption expenditure of different classes, a point which we have further discussed at a little later stage of our analysis in this section.

(iii) NSS estimates have been criticized for underestimation of consumption expenditure especially of the higher expenditure classes (Oandekar and Rath, 1971). Our analysis too has revealed (refer Table 7). This underestimation has been both in the food and non-food segments. The difference in the NSS and NAS estimates fairly low regarding food expenditure, while it is relatively high in case of non-food expenditure (refer Table 7), especially the expenditure on miscellaneous items. What is indeed noteworthy is that the underestimation with regard to non-food expenditure, especially the expenditure on miscellaneous category, as reported by NSS, has a tendency to increase. (*Awasthi*, 2010)

According to the 2008 World Bank Report the number of poor people increased by 39.8 million in absolute numbers during the 15 years (1991-2005) coinciding with the reform period. The increase is 9.6 per cent in relative terms, when we raise the level of income from US $ 1 per day to US $ 1.25 per day reality, 42.2 per cent or 4 out of 10 Indians, were poor in 2005 at an income about Rs. 50 per day. This is the most damaging observation on the quality of Indian governance. In fact, the number of poor in India, at 455.8 million in 2005, was strikingly higher than that in sub-Saharan Africa, where it was 384.2 million in the same year. The total lack of a humanistic social policy to improve lot of the poverty-stricken majority of this country, as seen from the *laissez-faire* attitude adopted towards them, is shocking. Therefore, in order to avoid such conflicting and misleading claims the poverty line must be redefined for realistic evaluation of the number of poor in our country.

The growth rate of real per capita income NDP in rural areas during 1993-94 to 1999-2000 has further gone up to 3.36% per annum

TABLE 7

A Comparative Estimates of NSSO and NAS Regarding Monthly Per Capita Consumption Expenditure (expressed in Rs.) of Different Items and Household Savings-Income Ratio (expressed in percentage terms)

	1972-73		*1977-78*		*1983*		*1987-88*		*1993-94*		*1999-2000*	
	NSS	*NAS*	*NSS*	*NAS*	*NSS*	*NA.S*	*NSS*	*NAS*	*NSS*	*NAS*	*NSS*	*NAS*
(1)	*(2)*	*(3)*	*(4)*	*(5)*	*(6)*	*(7)*	*(8)*	*(9)*	*(10)*	*(11)*	*(12)*	*(13)*
Food	33.90	38.67	47.40	59.60	79.39	99.30	110.55	139.06	273.0	2.71.0	323 12	496.27
Non-Food	14.11	28.78	27.83	48.20	45.53	85.78	70.50	132.33	131.21	259.20	266.03	542.70
Pan, Tobacco	1.44	2.23	3.00	2.80	3.52	6.50	5.40	8.25	9.44	14.12	14.01	38.48
Intoxicants	3.14	3.18	018	020	10.35	8.94	11.04	12.78	10.79	28.54	38.40	44 71
Clothing	0.24	38	0.53	0.02	1.28	1.22	1.84	2.00	2.93	3.75	0.07	6.11
Footwear	2.71	2.11	4.01	3.79	8.75	7.93	13.00	12.12	23.20	19.73	44.85	35.74
Miscellaneous	0.01	2088	14.25	34.78	21.63	61.13	38.09	97.18	78.84	193.00	161.43	41760
Total	48.00	67.45	75.29	107.87	124.92	185.08	181.06	271.39	404.21	530.21	589.17	1038.97
HH Saving Income Ratio	12.40		16.86		15.58		21.17		23.08		2433	

Sources : (i) Level and Pattern of Consumer Expenditure, 1 to 6 quinquennial Survey, 1972-73, 1977-78, 1983, 1987-88, 1993-94 and 1999-2000, NSSO, Dept. of Statistics, Government of India, New Delhi.

(ii) National Accounts Statistics of India, 1950-51 tc 2000-01, *EPW Research Foundation*, Mumbai.

but the disparities in consumption expenditure on food has not declined rather it has increased. There is no any further shift in the composition of food basket. It is evident in the table before.

All these observations clearly signify that absolute poverty has either declined marginally or has remained more or less stable during 1993-94 to 1999-2000. Further, the disparities in the non-food consumption expenditure has declined as revealed by Gini's coefficient, whose value has gone down from around 40% to 33%. This has resulted in the decline in disparities in the overall consumption expenditure of different classes. To some extent, decline in disparities in non-food consumption expenditure could be explained by the rise in the household-savings income ratio, whose increase has most likely occurred because of the further expansion of savings of the households belonging to the higher expenditure groups. Though we do not have any direct evidence to supplement our observation but whatever indirect evidences that are available, they reveal that in 1999-2000 the major recipients of interest and dividend are those households whose monthly per capita expenditure is highest, i.e. these households received enough amount of payment through interest and dividend that it constituted a good source of their income. This apart, to a great extent decline in disparities in non-food consumption expenditure has occurred on account of too much underreporting of non-food consumption expenditure by NSSO, especially of the households belonging to the middle and higher expenditure groups due to which discrepancy between NSS and NAS estimates regarding consumption expenditure in general and non-food expenditure in particular has substantially increased over time.

Analysis of Absolute and Relative Poverty in Urban India

During the process of development, there is substantial migration of workers from rural to urban areas in search of employment. Large scale migration of workers significantly influences urban population and which also affects absolute and relative poverty levels in the urban areas of the country. In such a situation, pattern of change in absolute and relative poverty in urban areas may not be same as in rural areas. Our detailed analysis on poverty for urban household sector in India will facilitate to throw light on it, as well as on Kuznets inverted-U hypothesis. Moreover, the analysis will also examine the behavior of absolute poverty to changes in per capita income, and trace the pattern of change regarding disparities in consumption expenditure on food, non-food and total expenditure components along with the overall distribution of income.

TABLE 8

Growth Rate of Urban Per Capita Net Domestic Product in Real Terms

(*in percentage terms*)

Period	*1970-71 to 1980-81*	*1980-81 to 1993-94*	*1993-94 to 1999-2000*
Growth Rate	-0.21	3.28	5.84

Source : Estimated from National Accounts Statistics of India, 1950-51 to 2000-01, *EPW Research Foundation*, Mumbai and Net Domestic Product by Economic Activity in Rural/Urban Areas, CSO, Government of India.

It is indeed noticeable that during 1970s, the real per capita NDP in urban areas has declined from Rs. 1294 to Rs. 1267. This is in contrast to what has been observed in the rural areas. One important reason for decline is that in the urban areas, population growth rate (3.75% per annum) was more than double the population growth rate in rural areas (1.46% per annum), which is possibly on account of large scale migration of workers to urban areas, as mentioned earlier. Moreover, an overall price increase of around 10% per annum in urban areas is also responsible for depressing the real per capita NDP in urban areas.

It is important to note that despite the decline in real per capita NDP during the period of 1970s (refer Table 8), absolute poverty in urban areas declined from 49% to 45.2%, while disparities in food, non-food and total consumption expenditure increased during the major period of 1970s (refer Table 8). The only plausible explanation for this contrasting pattern at the macro-level is the significant differential increase in the price of cereals, food and non-food items. For instance, price of cereals between 1972-73 to 1977-78 increased at a rate of just 5.6% per annum while the price of overall food items increased at around 8.4% per annum. A fairly higher increase of price of non-cereal food items forced people in the lower expenditure class to consume cereals rather than other food items, which are more nutritious and which are a part of the consumption basket of the rich people. This has caused disparities in the food expenditure to widen. Moreover, the disparities in the non-food consumption expenditure rose more sharply than the food consumption expenditure which is mainly on account of the fact that the price of non-food items showed an increase at a rate of 10.8% per annum between 1972-73 and 1977-78. It is owing to such a steep rise in the prices of non-food items that the overall prices index too displayed a rise at a rate of over 9% per annum. This, coupled with the fact that urban population increased at a rate of 3.75% per annum caused the real per capita NDP to decline. However, since the price of basic wage goods, like rice, wheat, etc. increased much slowly, therefore, consumption expenditure on cereals is not much affected as the consumption expenditure on other food and non-food items. Considering the fact that absolute poverty is mainly a function of the consumption expenditure on cereals in particular and food in general, its decline is not unusual despite the fall in real per capita NDP in urban areas during 1972-73 to 1977-78. Thus, the apparent contradiction between declining absolute poverty and real per capita NDP in urban areas is well explained by significant differential movements in the price indices of cereals, food, and non-food items. This differential movement is also responsible for escalating disparities in food, non-food and overall consumption expenditure. Our analysis thus, has clearly revealed that mere low per capita income is not the cause of high absolute poverty, rather it is influenced by other factors too. Moreover, rising disparities in consumption expenditure during the initial phase of economic development is at least an indicator of increasing income disparities or relative poverty too. Thus, the first part of Kuznets hypothesis is also corroborated by the available evidences from urban areas. This is in line with our findings for rural household sector of India.

The slow down in the urban population growth rate during the decade of 1980s and thereafter, along with a substantial acceleration in the net domestic product helped to make a marked improvement in the per capita NDP after 1981.

The improvement in nominal per capita net domestic product is so much significant that despite the prices of cereals, food and non-food items increased by over 12% between 1977-78 to 1983, the real per capita net domestic product increased on an average by about 3.28% after 1981 and until 1993-94. The benefits of economic development between 1977-78 to 1983 is certainly experienced by all sections of the society, but is definitely biased towards urban rich. Our observation is based on the fact that though absolute poverty declined from 45.2% to 40.8% during 1977-78 to 1983, but the relative poverty has increased further as is evident from the rising disparities in the food, non-food and overall consumption expenditure (refer Table 9).

TABLE 9

Absolute Poverty Ratios and Gini's Co-efficients Representing Disparities in Food, Non-Food and Overall Consumption Expenditure in Urban India During Last Six Quinquennial Rounds

(in percentage terms)

Quinquennial Rounds	*Absolute Poverty*	*Gini's Coefficient (p)*		
		Food Expenditure	*Non-Food Expenditure*	*Total Consumption*
1st Round (1972-73 to 1973-74)	49.0	16.70	28.17	25.84
2nd Round (1977-78)	45.2	20.55	40.05	31.86
3rd Round (1983)	40.8	24.08	48.24	33.96
4th Round (1987-88)	38.2	24.32	46.19	33.73
5th Round (1993-94)	32.4	23.56	46.13	33.55
6th Round (1999-2000)	23.6	23.76	43.69	33.91

Source : Estimated on the basis of past six quinquennial rounds reports on level and pattern of consumption expenditure in India, NSSO, Dept. of Statistics, Government of India, New Delhi.

Absolute poverty would have declined still further and disparities in consumption expenditure may not have increased, had the price of basic food items as well as of non-food items would not have been of a tall order.

The price of basic food items (cereals) increased at an average rate of about 13.6% per annum while that of non-food items increased at a rate of 12.6% per annum. Such a high rise in the prices of basic wage goods seems to have left little income in the hands of people in the lower expenditure group to spend on other food and non-food items, thereby enhancing the level of disparities in the food, non-food and overall consumption expenditure. Moreover, sharp increase in the price of basic wage goods has deprived many people in the lowest expenditure group to have enough quantities of these food items to be able to lift them above poverty line.

Therefore, it is sufficient to suggest that mere increase in per capita NDP is not enough to make a substantial dent on the absolute poverty. Rather, redistribution of income and the extent to which price of basic food items increases during the process of economic development are reasonably important variables governing the level of poverty in a country. Furthermore, the disparities in all types of food, non-food and overall consumption expenditure have increased between 1977-78 to 1983, therefore, it is quite reasonable to infer that relative poverty during this phase in urban areas has increased, i.e. the first part of Prof. Kuznets hypothesis, that rising disparities with increasing per capita incomes, continues to hold good. (*Awasthi*, 2010)

INCIDENCE OF POVERTY: PRESENT SCENARIO

The Planning Commission has been estimating the incidence of poverty at the national and state level using the methodology contained in the report of the Expert Group on Estimation of Promotion and Number of Poor (Lakdawala Committee) and applying it to consumption expenditure conducted by the National Sample Survey Organization (NSSO) at an interval of approximately five years. The latest available large sample survey data on consumer expenditure are for the 55th Round covering the period July 1999 to June 2000 (refer Table 10).

In the earlier Surveys, the NSSO estimated monthly consumption expenditure on the basis of responses using a 30 day recall period for all food and non-food items. In the 55th Round, the consumption expenditure on clothing, footwear, medical (institutional) and durable goods were collected using a 365 days recall period. In the case of all other non-food items, the 30 days recall period was used as earlier. The data on consumption expenditure on food items were collected using two different reference periods of last 30 days from the same households. The poverty ratios indicated in Table 3 are estimated on the basis of 30-days recall period for 1973-74 to 1999-2000. Poverty at the national level is estimated as the weighted average of state-wise poverty levels.

The success of the anti-poverty strategy is reflected in the decline in the combined poverty ratio from 54.9 per cent in 1973-74 to 36.0 per cent in 1993-94. The poverty ratio declined by nearly 10 percentage points in the 5 year period between 1993-94 to reach 26.1 per cent in 1999-2000. While the proportion of poor in the rural areas declined from 56.4 per cent in 1973-74 to 27.1 per cent in 1999-2000,

TABLE 10
Estimates of Incidence of Poverty in India

Year	*Poverty ratio (%)*			*Number of poor (million)*		
	Rural	*Urban*	*Combined*	*Rural*	*Urban*	*Combined*
1973-74	56.4	49.0	54.6	261.3	60.0	321.3
1977-78	53.1	45.2	51.3	264.3	64.6	328.9
1983	45.7	40.8	44.5	252.0	70.9	322.9
1987-88	39.1	38.2	38.9	231.9	75.2	307.1
1993-94	37.3	32.4	36.0	244.0	76.3	320.3
1999-2000	27.1	23.6	26.1	193.2	67.1	260.3
2007	21.1	15.1	19.3	170.5	49.6	220.1

*Poverty projection for 2007.
Source : Tenth Five Year Plan, Vol. 1, Planning Commission.

the decline in urban areas has been from 49 per cent to 23.6 per cent during this period. In absolute terms, the number of poor declined to 260 million in 1999-2000, with about 75 per cent of these, being in the rural areas.

Wide Inter-State disparities are visible in the poverty ratios between rural and urban areas as also in the rates of decline of poverty among major States, Orissa, Bihar, West Bengal and Tamil Nadu had more than 50 per cent of their population below the poverty line in 1983. By 1999-2000, while Tamil Nadu and West Bengal had reduced their poverty ratios by nearly half. Orissa and Bihar continued to be the two poorest States with poverty ratios of 47 and 43 per cent respectively. In 1999-2000, 20 States and Union Territories had poverty ratios, which were less than the national average. Among other States, Jammu and Kashmir, Haryana, Gujarat, Punjab, Andhra Pradesh, Maharashtra and Kamataka also succeeded in significantly reducing the incidence of poverty.

Apart from an indicative target of an 8 per cent average G.D.P. growth rate, specific monitorable targets for key indicators have been finalized for the Tenth Five Year Plan (2000-07) and beyond. One of these, pertains to the reduction in poverty ratio by five percentage points by 2007 and by 15 percentage points by 2012. The poverty reduction target set by the Planning Commission for the Tenth Five Year Plan aims at achieving a poverty ratio of 19.3 per cent for the country as a whole by 2007, 21.1 per cent for the rural, and 15.1 per cent for the urban areas (*Shandilya*, 2010). Poverty reduction target may be achieved through impressive growth in infrastructure, industry, agriculture and social sector.

References

Swaminathan, M.S., Food and Environment—Walking the Tightrope, published by Forum for Free Enterprise, Mumbai 2001, p. 5.

Panchamukhi, V.R., India Vision-2010, Presidential address, fourth annual conference of the Economic Association of Bihar, Patna, 27-29, May 2000, p. 11.

Kureen, N.J., Employment Potential in Rural India, *Economic and Political Weekly*, Dec. 29, 1990, p. 179.

Gil (1976), Quoted by Dhillon, S.S. and Raikhy, P.S., Social choice growth and income distribution: Theory and Evidence', *The India Economic Association.* Conference Volume, 1999, p. 453.

Dandekar, V.M. and Nilkan Jha Rath, "Poverty in India", *Indian School of Political Economy*, Bombay, 1971.

Choudhary Arun Prabha, Plan Strategy, Economic Reforms and Eradication, Poverty and Sustainable Development, Concept and Measure, N.S. Iyenger, Deep & Deep Pub., Delhi, pp. 230-34 (2010).

Awasthi, Arvind, Absolute and Relative Poverty in India, A new way to re-examine old Issues in Iyenger, N.S. book—Poverty and sustainable Development: Concepts and Measures, pp. 220-21 (2010).

Shandilya, T.K., Poverty a Danger to Prosperity in Iyenger, N.S. book—Poverty and Sustainable Development : Concepts and Measures, pp. 75-77, 2010.

Chapter 5

Major Factors Causing Poverty and its Eradication Strategies

Poverty is a multi-facet concept. It is a universal phenomenon. The phenomenon of poverty does not only affect the individual (poor) but is productive of danger to nations. The Philadelphia Chracter has postulated that "Poverty anywhere constitutes a danger to prosperity everywhere". Poverty is a relative term and it is understood in relation to prosperity. Poverty and prosperity are comparative concepts. Hence from time immemorial, the poor have co-existed with the rich in India as well as throughout the world. Adam Smith says, "Man is rich or poor according to the degree in which he can, which he can afford to enjoy the necessaries, the conveniences, and the amusements of life." The word degree is not equal in all periods and in all places.

Mahatma Gandhi considered poverty as a curse of God as well as a crime. He wrote: "Poverty was the curse of God. It deprived you of everything: food, clothing, shelter, your self-respect, your humanity, even your soul. In poverty, you suffered not only hunger, nakedness, the cruelty of cold and heat, the blind fury of Nature's wild elements: you also suffered from humiliation, loss of human dignity. You were driven to acknowledge defect and overwhelmed by distress and despair. You were compelled to take to crime or beggary for a morsel of bread, women having to sell their bodies and live in sin and shame, and men having to sell their own souls to keep their bodies or those of their wives and children, to keep the wolf from the door, to put an end to their pangs of hunger of thirst." Sri Aurobindo, however, looked at it from the point of view of an organized society. He said: "The acceptance of poverty is noble and beneficial in a class or an individual, but it becomes fatal and pauperizes the life of its richness and expansion if is perversely organized into a general or national ideal.

CAUSES OF RURAL POVERTY IN INDIA

Poverty has many faces, and its causes vary from one thinker to another and from one environment to another. Henary and George hold that the main cause of poverty is the personal ownership of large acres of land. Karl Marx is of the opinion that "Poverty is the exploitation of the labourers by the capitalist." Malthus, on the other hand, enunciated that the rapid growth of population was the main cause of poverty. He said: "Poverty increases because the food production increases in arithmetic progression, while population increases in geometric progression." However, poverty is the result of multiple causes. Economic, political, geographical, social and cultural factors, individually or collective, contribute to poverty.

Among the important economic factors, the steady growth of population and the prevalent inheritance laws have resulted in the fragmentation of land. Moreover, the economically non-viable farmers sell their land to big landlords and/or traders or urban dwellers and become agricultural labourers themselves, they have one partial employment. Low income, low productivity coupled with some ¥ices push a large number of people into poverty. The birth rate among the poor is also higher and ignorance is a contributory factor. For example, Family Planning workers in an Indian village demonstrated the use of condoms by unrolling them on a bamboo everyone; the workers left the village with enough stocks of condoms. But when they returned some months later, they were surprised to observe groups of pregnant women, who complained about the ineffectiveness of the new technology. The women, insisted that had followed the instructions to latter. And when the family planning workers visited their homes, they found gathering dust. The poor, because they are poor, often resort to robbery, etc. In short, there is a decline in the value system. Exploitation by the affluent also continues. In other words, poverty strikes the poor, physically, materially, socially and culturally.

In rural areas, land is the principal productive asset. But land is very unevenly distributed. The problem of poverty has been aggravated by the steady increase in population and the consequent rise in unemployment. By and large, the lower income groups tend to have large families. This fact, to some extent, accounts for the low consumption and high unemployment among the poor. Moreover, they suffer from social disabilities. Most of them belong to scheduled castes/tribes and other backward classes. They are illiterate and are engaged mostly in unskilled occupations, in which the wages are very low. (*Shandilya T.K.*, 2010)

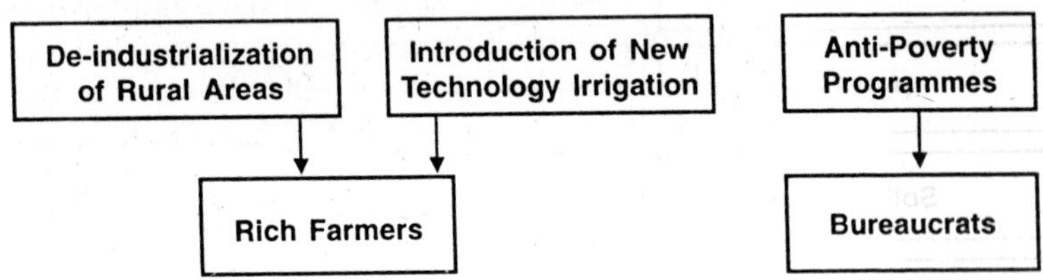

Rural Population Rising at 2.5%
Rural Employment at 0.5
Rural Real Income at 0.8

Most significantly, the perpetuation of rural poverty is ensured by the double strategy of de-industrializing the rural areas and pumping into agriculture resource, which fall into the hands of rich farmers. To make matters worse, the bureaucrats pocket a large proportion of the funds allocated under the so-called anti-poverty programme.

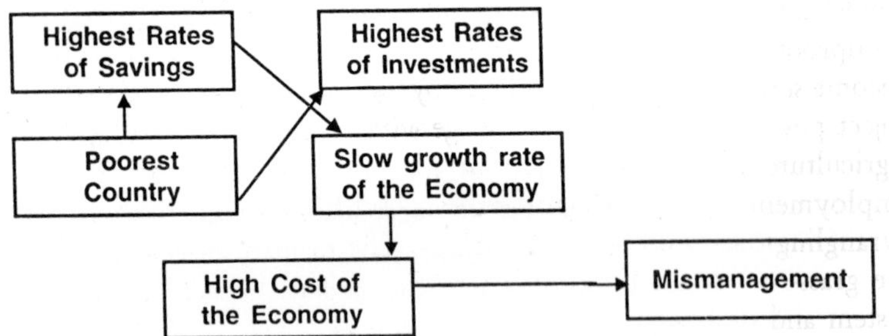

The rural poor are caught in another vicious circle. Whatever little improvement occurs in their incomes or assets in one year is washed away in the line except the incomes of those who have assured irrigation. Drought affects both the rich and the poor farmers. In fact, during the drought period, the crisis overtakes everyone, and ultimately affects industry. All these developments push the poor further down the line. They lose job, they lose incomes; and they cannot buy food.

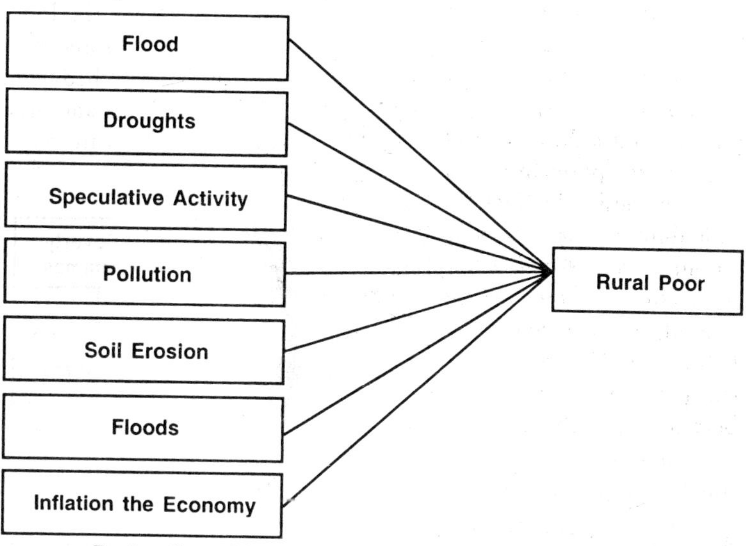

- **Destruction of Land**
- **Animals**
- **Desiltation**
- **Lose Jobs**
- **Health Hazards**

And when floods come, there is the destruction of other assets. Lands' are washed away, Cattle disappear, Houses collapse. The poor are uprooted in the process. They lose jobs, Health hazards for them become serious. According to a recent study, the cause of poverty are abject poverty (having meager means of livelihood), unemployment (agriculture provides about 175-190 days of work in a year), lack of employment opportunities outside agriculture, political disputes' (wrangling over land, women, family feuds or status), corruption at the grass-root level, dishonesty and bureaucratic inefficiency, caste system and illiteracy. The inadequacy of civic amenities, inefficient communication facilities, problems of transport and non-availability of safe drinking water accentuate poverty in rural areas.

The causes of poverty are multi-dimensional—they are social, economical, political, managerial, organizational, cultural, psychological, etc. Social inequality is linked to economic inequality-each being the cause and effect of the other. Socialist slogans, however meaningful, are only useful means of winning the votes of the ignorant, illiterate mass to be in power. Under the biggest democracy in the world, vast number of people continue to be born in poverty, live in poverty and die in poverty.

Widespread poverty in India is attributable to a host of factors, viz. population explosion, lack of industrialization, failures of land reforms and failures of fiscal policy to narrow the gap between the rich and the poor. Industrial development of the country has neither been on desirable lines nor at expected rate. Undue emphasis on capital-intensive industries has failed to generate sufficient jobs for the labour force. Land reforms programme was started with great fanfare soon after the independence. However, it has failed to achieve the desired, the incidence of poverty in rural areas is mainly due to the failure of land reforms. Similarly, taxation and expenditure policies of the government have not been used effectively to ridge the gap between the rich and the poor.

Summing up the whole issue we can say that the following are the important factors responsible for the problem of poverty in India.

(1) Rapid Growth of Population

The population of Indian during the decade 1981-91 has increased by 2.1 per cent per annum in a compound manner. This adversely affects the growth of per capita income and per capita consumption.

(2) Unemployment and Underemployment

The existence of mass unemployment and underemployment is an important cause of rampant poverty in the country. Most of the small and marginal farmers and landless agricultural labourers suffer from disguised unemployment in India. There are socio-economic factors responsible for poverty in India. Poverty in India is a deep-seated and long-term problem of our country.

(3) Low Agricultural Productivity

The level of productivity in agriculture in India is low due to sub-divided and fragmented holdings, lack of capital, use of traditional methods of cultivation, illiteracy, etc.

(4) Low Rate of Economic Development

The rate of economic development has been below the required level in India. Therefore, there persists a gap between levels of availability and requirements of goods and service. And the net result is poverty.

(5) Inequality

Inequality in the distribution of income and wealth has also been an important factor of mass poverty in India. As we know that production and distribution are inter-linked in a more fundamental sense, the pattern of income distribution determines the pattern of production. Unless the pattern of income distribution is altered, the objective of increasing the production of wage goods sufficiently to remove poverty will be distorted. And for this purpose an attack on the maldistribution of assets, both in the rural and urban sectors is a *sine qua non.*

(6) Price Rise

The continuous and steep price has added to the miseries of the poor. It has benefited a few people in the society and the persons in power income group find it difficult to get their minimum needs. (*Dhage, S.K.*, 2010)

Poverty Eradication Strategies

Efforts to reduce poverty have often focused on narrowly defined goals, such as implementing 'free market reforms' or spurring 'economic growth'. But as the World Bank's World Development Report, 2000/2001: Attacking Poverty argues, governments also need to ensure that the benefits of the growth reach the poor. Growth may not be enough. Almost half of the world's people (some 2.8 billion) live on less than $2 a day, and 5th (some 1.2 billion) live on less than $1 a day. This terrible level of poverty persists despite unprecedented—but unevenly distributed—raises in global wealth in the past century. Over the past 40 years the gap between rich and poor has doubled, with income in the richest 20 countries now averaging 37 times that in the poorest 20.

(A) Earlier Approaches to Reducing Poverty

The Bank's approach to reducing poverty has evolved over the years as new theoretical models have been developed and lessons have been learned from the experience.

(i) In the 1950s and 1960s the prevailing wisdom was that large investments, in physical capital and infrastructure would spur development, and the Bank financed large projects such as dams and power plants. The failure of those projects to significantly reduce poverty convinced Bank policy-makers that investing in physical capital was not enough.

(ii) World Development Report, 1980 captured the new thinking, arguing that investments in health and education were important not just in their own right but also as a way of increasing the incomes of poor people.

(iii) In the wake of the debt crisis and the global recession of the 1980s the Bank shifted emphasis once again, focusing on moving economic management and allowing market forces greater play.

(iv) Finally in the 1990s, governance and institutions moved to centre stage as development thinkers reached the conclusion that market reforms can't succeed unless the necessary institutions are in Place. (Thakur, R.N., 2010)

(B) New Strategy for Attacking Poverty

The Bank's new strategy builds on the experience of the past decade in proposing a broader approach to fighting poverty. The three-pronged approach focuses on increasing opportunities for poor people, facilitating their empowerment and enhancing their security.

(a) *Promoting Opportunities for Poor*—Poor people often leave without the opportunities that better-off people take for granted: jobs, credit, roads, electricity, market for their goods and access to the schools, water, and sanitation and health services that underpin the health and skills essential for work. This lack of opportunity locks poor people into a life of poverty.

To address the problem, the Bank's new strategy focuses on promoting opportunities for the poor by stimulating overall growth making markets work for poor people and building their assets by addressing in equalities in the distribution of such endowments as education for e.g. Specific recommendations include the following:

(i) Encourage effective private investment by reducing risks for private investors, ensuring the rule of law, and fighting corruption.

(ii) Expand into international markets.

(iii) Build the assets of the poor.
(iv) Address asset inequalities across gender, ethnic, racial, and social device.
(v) Improve infrastructure and increase knowledge in poor areas, etc.

(b) *Facilitating Empowerment*—State and social institutions can play a powerful role in promoting growth and reducing poverty if they function soundly and are responsive to the poor. Governments can act in a variety of ways to help create such institutions:
(i) Lay the political and legal basis for inclusive development.
(ii) Create public administrations that foster growth and equity.
(iii) Promote inclusive decentralization and community development.
(iv) Promote gender quality.
(v) Tackle social barriers.
(vi) Support poor people Social capital, etc.

(C) Enhancing Security

Vulnerability to illness, economic dislocation and natural disasters are much greater among poor people—the very people least equipped to deal with such setbacks. (*Thakur, R.N.*, 2010)

Economists from Adam Smith to Karl Marx, have emphasised the centrality of capital to enhancing incomes and wealth. The classical view about the role of capital in economic growth of nations is equally applicable to households. This is depicted below in diagram 1, which begins with low investment, leading to low income, which in turn leads to low or no savings and this leaves no scope for investment, completing the vicious cycle.

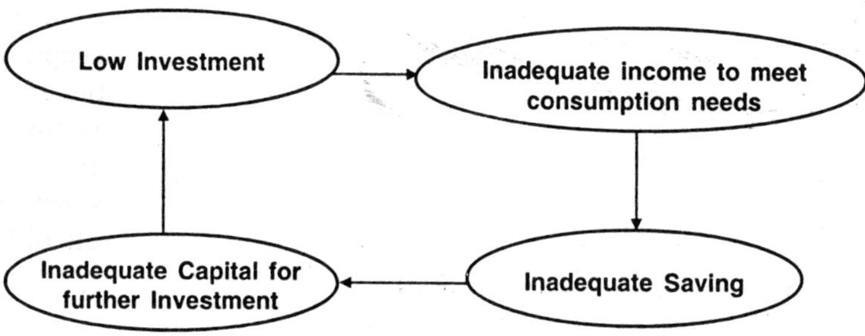

This situation is sought to be remedied by injection of a dose of capital (if possible by borrowing it from someone who has a surplus). Vicious cycle can be broken by increasing the level of investment, thereby enhancing productivity and eventually income. Additional income then leads to the possibility of enhanced savings, which then can be used to partly service the capital taken as a loan, still leaving a surplus for additional investments in the next cycle. This chain of "virtuous" events is depicted in diagram below, and as can be seen, it is based on several assumptions, including the absence of risk and the magnitude of surpluses generated.

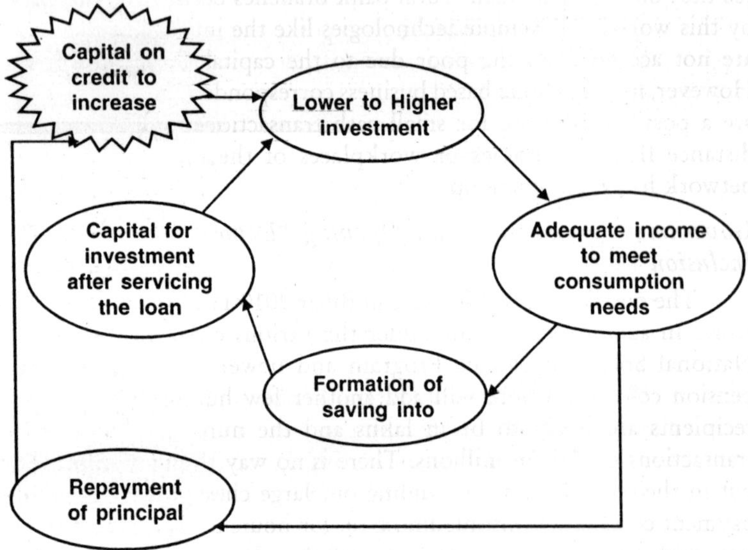

Financial Inclusion—not just Bank Accounts but a Transaction Network

The term financial inclusion began to be used in the India policy circles around 2005 and in 2006; a Committee on Financial Inclusion (CFI) was set-up under the Chairmanship of or Rangarajan, former Governor of the Reserve Bank of India. The report of the CFI (2008) recommended the opening of bank accounts for a large number of poor Indians, as a first step towards financial inclusion. Since then, India has made remarkable progress in the matter of bank accounts. In Bihar, too, a number of pilot projects for financial inclusion have been set-up by banks and these involve the opening of a large number of no-frills bank accounts.

Financial inclusion, however, is not just a matter of opening a large number of bank accounts, but also enabling poor people to use them for transactions, savings and eventually borrowing. That requires a high density of transaction outlets, since bank branches are not numerous enough for small transactions to be carried out conveniently. The Government must be credited with having seen this and enforcing the condition that NREGA payments must be made into bank (or post office) accounts.

But this solves only half the problem. To withdraw their money, if the beneficiaries turn up at the rural bank branches, one can clearly see the "one plus one man" rural bank branches being overwhelmed by this work load. Remote technologies like the internet and ATMs are not accessible to the poor due to the capital outlay required. However, mobile phone-based business correspondent outlets (BCOs) are a possible solution, for small cash transactions within walking distance from the homes or workplaces of the poor. This BCO network has yet to come up.

Government Payments as an Opening "Deposit" for Financial Inclusion

The outlay for just NREGA in Bihar 2010-11 is a few thousand crore. In addition, payments under the various components of the National Social Assistance Program and newer schemes like the pension co-contribution, will add another few hundred crore. The recipients are likely to be in lakhs and the number of payment transactions may be in millions. There is no way this can be carried out in the old style way of sending out large chest of cash to rural payment centers with people lining up for hours in front of a cubby hole with a grill, to receive their Rs. 1000 or less.

Lakhs of accounts have been opened for NREGA payments, and over half of these are in banks, the rest in post offices. However, there are also reports that a substantial proportion of these "no-frills" accounts are dormant. Many are not being used even to make the payments they were meant to channel and others are merely used as a one-way channel, with the balance being brought down to zero as the household withdraws the last Rupee it receives. In most cases, banks have not added any staff to manage these large number of accounts, and the existing branch staffs are reluctant to service customers. The occasional customer who does come to the branch finds it a discouraging experience.

SAVINGS—THE PRIMARY FINANCIAL SERVICE NEEDED THE POOR

Credit is the main financial service needed by the poor. Actually it is not. In Bank Rakyat Indonesia's village banking program, for example, there are six times as many savers as borrowers. The poor need and want to save much more than they want to borrow. The experience of SEWA Bank in India for example, shows that women value a safe place to keep their savings as an important service. The poor also want to cover themselves against risks. However, the microfinance field in general focuses on credit and does not adequately emphasize other financial services, such as savings and insurance. Savings are particularly important, as these act as self-insurance in case of smaller contingencies; meet sudden demands of cash such as due to illness in the family; act as "equity" for borrowing; and finally, to some extent, act as a collateral for repayment of loans.

Marginal Propensity to Save (MPS) rises as incomes rise, though at higher levels it may decline again. At low levels of income, the MPS is low, due to the necessity to maintain minimum levels of consumption. As the income rises, the MPS rises as people strive to save for their future and maintain a lifetime level of consumption. The issue is whether at income below the poverty line, MPS is positive or negative. In table ahead data from a survey in 2003 in Jharkhand was a poor state in India.

The lower the income level, the less the saving, with it becoming negative below a certain level. Thus the economists' view seems right. But does this mean that the poor do not save at all? In practice, we found they do. Dividing the year into just three seasons—summer, rainy and winter—we found that the poor were saving in the winter season, while during the rainy season they were breaking even, and in the summer they needed to borrow. In case they did not have adequate options of saving in the rainy and winter seasons, their distress in the summer became worse. Saving food grains at harvest could reduce their dependence on high interest consumption loans for buying food grains later at higher prices, and reduce annual expenditure for the same level of consumption. Thus, "grain banks" were tried by some NGOs.

Yet in an increasingly financialised world, it is not always possible to have such arrangements and saving in the form of money becomes necessary. Surveys done by BASIX have shown that the poor

TABLE 1

Saving as Percentage of Income among different Castes in Jharkhand

Community	*Annual income (Rs.)*	*Annual expenditure (Rs.)*	*Saving or deficit (as % of income)*
Bhuiya	10758	14496	-35
Chamar	14414	16754	- 16
Khairwar	22099	18728	15
Oraon	25582	23506	8
Koiri	34978	29755	15
Upper-Castes	53270	50422	5

Source : Household Survey by BASIX-JKLEAP Team, 2003.

are willing to save as long as they are reasonably sure of the safety of their savings and their ability to withdraw at a short notice. The rate of interest is not an important attribute compared to the safety and liquidity of deposits. Another important attribute was how small the amounts could be saved and how frequently.

INSURANCE—HOW IT PROTECTS ASSETS THAT HELP REDUCE POVERTY?

We spoke of the risk related to various economic activities—input prices (rising), output prices (falling). A hedging mechanism for inputs and output prices is commodity derivatives, but no MFI is yet working on this strategy. In addition to these risks, there are other risks that poor households face all the time. These include risks to their lives and their livelihoods the death of an earning member or illness in the family can cause a huge setback and the risks related to livelihoods—crop failure due to drought, floods or pest attacks; livestock death due to disease; theft or fire in case of a store or workshop, are all adverse events that do occur in the lives of the poor. The adverse event converts all further steps into uncertain dotted lines, including repayment of the loan. Thus, insurance is another important financial service for the poor, given their vulnerability to livelihood risks. Here one is talking of life insurance, health insurance as well as crop insurance and insurance for income earning assets such as livestock and irrigation pumps. Though insurance (except endowment life insurance) is by itself not an asset building strategy, it is fundamental to protecting whatever assets the poor may own. Recognizing the need for providing a comprehensive risk cover to its customers.

Credit—How and when it Converts an Opportunity into Income?

One of the points to be noted, though often forgotten, is that credit is a liability, not an asset. David Hulme appropriately calls it "micro-debt". Borrowing has been looked down upon in many cultures and borrowing beyond one's ability to repay has been reviled. The phenomenon of encouraging people to take loans to consume is relatively recent. Here the demand is sought be boosted by enhancing consumer spending based on borrowed money. This kind of credit liability can become indebtedness. However, credit which is used to enhance income, through an economic activity, is an example of a liability which can be converted into an asset, over a period of time and under certain conditions.

The favourable conditions are linked to input prices, output prices and conversion efficiency (output-input ratio). If the prices prevail in such a manner that with the achieved output-input ratio, there is a net profit, then the loan can be repaid over a period of time. The fact that these assumptions do not always hold true makes the credit based activity risky, both for the lender and the borrower. But there is enough of a subset of activities with fairly high rates of financial rates of return so that credit can indeed be serviced and over a period of time the liability can be retired and the asset becomes the borrower's property.

Two questions are often asked: how can micro-entrepreneurs pay high rates of interest and, if indeed, the rates of return are so high, why don't they become well-off after some time? The answer to these is to be found in the data above: the great paradox of micro-enterprise returns is "high percentages, but low absolute numbers". It is only by the stage that Rs. 25,000 of capital is employed that enough surplus can be generated for a poor household to break out of the vicious circle depicted in diagrams earlier. Thus, micro-credit at the lower end is not really an asset building strategy thought it enhances incomes. (*Mahajan, Vijay*, 2010).

PROMOTING SAVING THROUGH BANK BCOs AND COOPERATIVES

The poor want to save small amounts on a frequent basis and thus the transaction outlets have to be near their home or place of work. This is possible only if the network of business correspondent outlets (BCOs) reaches each and every village. Banks should take advantage of the recent RBI guidelines on BCOs and appoint a large number of kirana shops/STD PCOs and even SHGs as their BCOs. In Bihar, even the network of PACS is quite robust and suitable for becoming BCOs.

Insurance Services and the Poors

Health and life insurance can significantly reduce the financial impact of adverse events in the lives of poor households. There are a large number of group insurance products which are now available. The Rashtriya Swasthya Bima Yojana already is meant to cover all BPL households for health care expenses of up to Rs. 30,000 per annum.

Poverty, Micro Credit and Livelihood Promotion

Financial inclusion is a necessary but not sufficient condition for inclusive growth. In an impact assessment study BASIX in 2002 it was found that only 52% of our three-year plus microcredit customers reported an increase in income, 23% reported no change while another 25% actually reported a decline. The reason were un-managed risk, low productivity in crop cultivation and livestock rearing and inability to get good prices from the input and output markets.

Therefore, as revised study Microcrdit is a single intervention small loans, given for short durations, with repayments beginning as quickly and as frequently as possible. Moreover, whether given through groups, or directly to individuals, microcredit loans go to individuals, not to collectives. In contrast, Livelihood promotion will require large amounts: it may need more than just loans (it may need equity or risk funds and indeed some public subsidies); it will invariably be for long durations, at least five and may be 20 years, and its use will almost always be for collective purposes. Thus, microcredit and livelihood promotion are fundamentally two different schemes. Livelihood promotion would begin with organizing the poor, not just for disbursing credit but for encouraging savings (financial assets), but learning new skills (human capital) and building a sense of solidarity (social capital). Business development services—product design, market linkages, for example—will have to be integrated with financial services. Finally, to enable the rural poor to work together effectively, institutional development services would have to be provided. Only then would the poor be able to realize economic opportunity (or at least survive in face of adversity) in this globalizing world.

UPGRADING AGRICULTURAL EXTENSION AND LIVESTOCK SERVICES

The recent successes of agriculture in Bihar can be developed manifold, by upgrading the agricultural and livestock development services. Two outstanding initiatives in this connection are the work of PRADAN and IGS with WDC, related to System of Rice Intensification (SRI) for paddy cultivation, which dramatically enhances yields while reducing seed, fertilizer and water.

Ensuring Infrastructure in Small Towns to Promote the Non-farm Sector

Eventually, the non-farm sector has to take-off, to provide a fillip to the Bihar economy. This can be done by systematically encouraging agro-inputs, processing and services enterprises to come up in small towns. The pre-condition for this is the creation of infrastructure—reliable power supply, transport and telecom connectivity and warehouses/cold storages and industrial sheds. Specific processing units like sugarcane crushing or milk chilling plants can also be located at appropriate Places. (*Mahajan, Vijay,* 2010).

Building Institutions of the Poor-Strengthening SHGs and Coops in the State

One of the key. strategies that needs to be pursued vigorously is strengthening the SHG movement in the state. As indicated in the study, the SHG is lagging behind other Eastern India states, both in terms of quality and quantity. Some of the recommendations for promotion of SHGs in the state are:

- SHG promotion norms ought to be relaxed, given the cultural and socio-economic scenario. The concept of APL/BPL should not be strictly adhered as these often act as constraint in sustainability of SHGs.

- Promotion of SHG federation as a strong grass-root institution has to be initiated on a wider scale in the state as there are few examples. One of the key factors to SHG development in Southern states is building of these federations and creation of people's institution. The women have leverage their funds and collective strengths to reap greater economic and non-economic benefits.
- Bankers should undertake capacity building of Self Help Promoting Institutions (SHPIs) on group formation, lending process, micro enterprise development management (cost should be borne by bank). All programes related to it should be well implemented and properly monitored.

References

Shrivastva, Swami Prakash, Poverty, Inequality and Sustainable Development in India Ed. Future in Iyenger, N.S. book—Poverty and Sustainable Development: Concepts and Measures, pp. 220-21 (2010), pp. 212-13 (2010).

Shandilya, T.K., Poverty, A danger to Prosperity, pp. 79-81, 2010 in Iyenger, N.S. book—Poverty and Sustainable Development: Concepts and Measures, pp. 220-21 (2010).

Mahajan, Vijay, Financial Inclusion to Inclusive Growth International Seminar on Poverty in Bihar, 2010.

Thankur, R.N., Poverty—Progeny of Progress ed., book, pp. 110-12 in Iyenger, N.S. book—Poverty and Sustainable Development: Concepts and Measures, pp. 220-21 (2010).

Chapter 6

Micro Finance—An Effective Tool for Poverty Alleviation in India

Despite the focus of development planning in India on the alleviation of rural poverty since independence, rural India still continues to suffer from high incidence of poverty and unemployment both in percentage and absolute terms. Formation of self-help groups (SHGs) is very encouraging step in this direction. SHGs are voluntary organization associations of the poor who come together to improve their socio-economic conditions. SHGs are informal groups which operate on the principle of self-help mutual trust and co-operation. Usually 15-20 poor women or men living in the same area are in such groups who deposit small savings with the group. Initially financial and social requirements of the members are met through small savings therefore the groups collaborate with the local banks for satisfying the increasing credit needs of the members. As the groups mature they start taking part in meaningful community activities and sustainable income generation programmes. The groups are formed by NGOs, Government departments or any other project implementing agency. The need for making group is linked with our daily life and thus working together in group has been the old history of mankind. The formation of SHG has actually been inspired by Mairada, Bangalore and rural banks of Bangladesh. Some groups are functioning better and they are achieving the targets of self-employment and has played greater role in improving the lots of many poors. Among number of possible routes to the promotion of self-employment, promotion and strengthening of self-help groups is very significant, relevant, suitable and feasible of them. They provide the benefits of economics of scale, cost effective alternative for different financial services, collective learning, democratic and participatory culture, a firm base and platform for dialogue and cooperation and development mechanism.

This contributes to the emergence of production indivisibilities should be able to respond to these stimuli for poverty alleviation, the poor can internalize the production indivisibilities in groups only. Moreover, the participation of the poor in the planning and implementation of anti-poverty programmes is required to reduce the chain of implementation of anti-poverty programmes is required to reduce the chain of intermediaries between the government and actual beneficiaries and to improve their bargaining power. Further, the institution-joint-family system, patron-client relationships and traditional occupation-based institutions, that provide social security to the poor are breaking down at the grass-roots level. Thus, there is an institutional vacuum at the grass-roots level to safeguard the interests of the poor. There is substantial evidence that organizing women around thrift and credit services is one of the most effective methods, not only for empowering women (World Bank, 1995, 2000, 2001). As such the macro and micro concerns gave rise to the demand for women-based collectives centred around thrift and credit services. Such strategy based on the group concept and self help has provided larger space for poverty alleviation and women empowerment. (*Khan, S.A.*, 2003)

The socio-economic context, not only of India but the entire world has undergone tremendous changes since then. Access of finance at reasonable interest rates has become one of the essential pre-conditions, though not a sufficient condition, for successful entrepreneurship even among the poor successful experiments outside India such as the Grameen Bank of Bangladesh demonstrated how small groups of poor women could become successful entrepreneur through a combination of small savings and microfinance various NGOs and Self-Help Groups in different parts of the country have also demonstrated that microfinance could be a powerful tool for alleviating poverty. Micro finance has been recognized world over as one of the new development paradigms for alleviating poverty though social and economic empowerment of the poor particularly women.

Experiences of different anti-poverty and other welfare programmes worldwide have shown that the key to success lies in the evolution and participation and participation of community-based organization at the grass-roots level. Linking of formal credit institutions to borrowers through group approach have been recognized as supplementary mechanism for providing credit support to the rural poor. The term microfinance refers to a particular sub-set of financial services which provides small loans to very poor families most often without any collateral. The loan can be for consumption production activities or for small businesses. Of late, a range of financial services other than credit such as savings micro insurance, etc. are also included under microfinance. The characteristics of microfinance are that the financial services is small in magnitude and those who avail the services are poor or very poor. Microfinance refers to the provision of financial services on a small scale to the rural and urban poor, including the self-employed. Financial services generally include savings and credit; however some microfinance institutions also provide additional services like technical assistance. Microfinance activities usually involve small loans typically for working capital; informal appraisal of borrowers and investment; collateral substitutes such as group guarantees or compulsory saving; access to repeated and larger loans based on repayment performance; and securing savings products. Microfinance is not simply banking it is a development tool.

THE ORIGIN OF SHGs

The problem of timely repayments of loans and their best possible utilization has long plagued the planners in regard to the self-employment programmes in India. The paradigm of group base micro-finance which gained considerable currency during the concluding years of the last century was conceived to be an appropriate tool to handle this problem. It was now being argued that when finance was provided to a close-knit group, the internal group dynamics would ensure optimal utilization and better repayment of fund. This concept married with the neo-liberal approach of trimming down the state of some so called unnecessary responsibilities sought to open a different vista in poverty alleviation programmes. Consequently that idea of SHGs came into being. Certain developments within the country involving erstwhile failure of the individual micro-financing under the Integrated Rural

Development Programme (IRDP) coupled with moderately successful experience with the Development of Women and Children in Rural Area (DWCRA), group of nineties rendered it the status of 'magic potion' or panacea to all poverty-related problems. Eventually, Ministry of Rural Development Government of India embarked upon a scheme called Swarnajayanti Gram Swarojgar Yojna (SGSY), on 1/4/99 with an accent on group-based micro-finance. The basic accent of the scheme thus was to organize the rural poor into SHGs through a process of social mobilization, enhance their capacity in the socio-economic domain and encourage them to take up some economic activities so that these poor families scale the all decisive poverty line within three years of inception.

The Reserve Bank of India in its Master Circular on SGSy acknowledged the scheme as a 'holistic scheme covering all aspects of self-employment' where assistance to BPL families can be extended to initiate micro-enterprises in rural areas. Appropriate noise noise generated on the eve of Dr. Mohammad Younus winning the noble-prize in 2006 gave it further shot in the arm, the District Rural Development Cells (DRDC). Thus, with the active participation of the Panchayats leapt into the business of organizing groups of women and men from BPL dynamics as well some economic activities as per their inherent natural tendency or the demand of the market, evaluated their performance and linked them up with the nationalized and other banks so that they get the adequate funds as soft loan to persue their economic activities. The bank loan consisting of 'term loan' and 'working capital' was again backed up by a provision of back-ended subsidy from the government where normally 1.25 lakhs is the highest limit group can get. Thus, the bank loan was considered an imperative to start the sojourn of the SHGs.

CONCEPT AND RATIONALE

The process of SHGs is a methodology for making the poor contribute to economic growth. It provides a non-violent way out of the morass of deprivation, alienation, insecurity, political graft, and corruption experienced relentlessly over and finally the past fifty years of development and democracy. Social mobilisation takes vertical programmes, often 'owned' by particular departments of government, and makes a broad more horizontal. In other words, it is the process of change which happens to substantial parts of human population in countries which are moving from traditional to modern ways of life. This specific process of change, affects residence, occupation, social setting, associates, institutions, roles and ways of acting, demands and capabilities. The process in which major clusters of old social, economic and psychological commitments are eroded or broken and people become available for new pattern of socializations and behaviour.

The concept and practice of SHGs lies in the fact of pooling together, harnessing, actualizing and utilizing potential human resources for the purpose of development. It is a process whereby human beings are made aware of the resources at their disposal, and are also motivated and energized to collectively utilized such resources for the improvement of their spiritual and material conditions of living members of in the group. It enables the poor, marginalized and disenfranchised segments of society to build and manage their own organizations and thereby participate in decisions affecting their day-to-day lives through the use of their own creativity engaging a large number of people in joint action for achieving societal goals through self-reliant efforts. It organizes the target groups to take initiatives and assert themselves. It aims at making people more aware of the resources available to them, raise their consciousness and to give them the motivation to undertake development activities for their own betterment in the long-run empowering people to demand and generate the satisfaction of their needs.

SHGs as a tool enables people to organize for collective action by pooling resources and building solidarity required to resolve common problems and work towards community development. It is a process which empowers women and men to organize their own democratically self-governing groups or community organizations enabling them to initiate and control their own personal and communal development. It also promotes of marginalized people of the society making the poor historical actors for societal transformation as partners in development with the state private sector and civil society. Inview of present challeges in country and the state formation and promotion of SHGs for the better potential development of women to strengthen the women empowerment process by means of different economic activities is very significant from all angles under the income generating activities like rearing of cow, goat, bull, calf, chicken development of the wasteland creating the agriculture and irrigation potential petty business activities involvement in exposition of the existing skills like rope making, mat making, basket making, gain mills processing diary tailoring, transport, vehicles, tractors, jam, juice and pickle processing of tamarind and zinger, etc. are taken up and financially assisted. All these activities are based on locally available resources and needs of local people. There is provision of 50 per cent loan and 50 per cent as subsidy for women and SC/ST groups by the banks under the scheme for starting any enterprise/activity. SHGs activities helps to promote and establish entrepreneurship development for self-employment within the locality itself.

A part from all these the SHGs have been promoted to strengthen the rural credit system and smoothening the monetary transaction through the gentle tenor of the cooperative system further to develop the women potentiality through mutual trust and respect group cohesion and understanding to stand reciprocally as a supportive embodiments in times of emergency extending the helpful support and to act as the resurgent leaders to mobilize the Government Resources for the infrastructure development and rural reconstruction as well as social rehabilitation.

Not only this the members or the SHGs are also the forerunners in solving the problematic affairs of the village with mutual understanding and trust delivering the equitable social justice for the immediate solution of the arising problem in their todays lives. Their sharing with each other the space they for themselves for the first time the respect they received from the officials and public and they experienced changed them for the better perspective career in the spectrum of their life so much so that the needy women community also acknowledge the values of self-governance people rule in peoples hand and work with plan with mechanisms knowing the right to survive, right to live, right to enjoy and right to education well as the right to better health status with their own pace and domain, acting now as the torch bearing agents of the society a whole. Thus, the activities at a thematic level in a conglomeration on their own initiative in an attempt to meet as their individual and common needs with primary focus on self-reliance we brand them a Self-help group. Self-help implies a step further from the stage of passivity to activity and of making a creative contribution. The fundamental basis of the self-help group exists even prior to any external intervention and common bond like caste affiliation community or place of residence or activity links the individuals. The individuals functionary must have to identify these common bonds or bindings forces which are called natural affinities. The self-help group is not a static institution, it grows on the resources and management skill of its members and their increasing confidence to get involved in the issues and problems that require their involvement. The benefits of self-help groups are based on cooperation rather than competition. The real principle or formula of contribution according to ones to ability and extract according to ones need lies in promoting of SHGs.

IMPORTANCE OF MICRO FINANCE

Right from 1970s thanks to the initiatives of Bank Nationalistion the bank branches proliferated in India yet a large segment of the population remained outside the ambit of formal banking especially for its credit needs. A search for alternative notched up the concept of micro finance. The concept ensuring relatively paraphernalia and collateral free access to credit for the poor stole the show. Further bits ability to hinge on the traditional and collateral rural system immediate availability and a promise of financial stability and sustainability ensured greater comfort level to the rural masses. Gradually over time the SHGs-bank linkage programme emerged as the major microfinance programme in the country while it was implanted by Commercial Banks, RRBs and Co-operative Banks, Reserve Bank of India hence tried to precipitate an enabling atmosphere for the operation of micro finance in the country. Inspite of the success of microfinance in India not many Micro Finance Insituations (MFIs) have ventured into this market yet the lack of access to institutional credit for these farmers is a potential marker MFIs can make the informal sector more advantageous and welcoming for the average farmer.

Currently one of the most important factors preventing the emergence of MFIs into this sector is the risk involved with lending to this group. As mentioned earlier the prominent model of microfinance followed in India is to link self-help groups (SHGs) to commercial banks to help increase direct access to credit facilities for the poor while the savings first credit later model is successful, it appears impractical for these farmers presently most of the farmers are already in massive debt and their asset holding is minimal. Due to outstanding loan amounts many of them are highly unlikely to repay micro-loans offered let alone save however these risk factors can be mitigated by a more integrated approach of credit access and information, some components of the famous Grameens model which uses social pressure and collective responsibility may also help when lending to these farmers.

Based on a combination of the previously mentioned existing mechanisms our model strives to substantially reduce the risk associated with providing credit in this region primarily our model relies on a Microfinance Institution (MFI) can offer credit and technology to farming groups through partnerships. Thus, the MFI's emerge into this market will heavily depend upon relationship established within these communities, and tapping into sources, such as already existing grass-roots organizations that can create trust between the farmers and the MFI.

The microfinance institution will provide a loan to a registered group farmers who grow a variety of different crops. The farmers will have the freedom to choose their groups and each group will contain roughly 12-15 farmers with an average land holding of two acres per farmer. While the group have the freedom to decide the manner in which the loan is to be divided among its members, the MFI will provide advice and education on efficient ways of financing and allocating funds. Through a mutual agreement with the farmers, the MFI establishes its role as a sole buyer for the product. By promising to buy the product at the MSP the MFI provides a steady stream of each flow to the farmers. In turn, the MFI will sell the product in the open market for a profit. The farmers benefit as they are waived of the principal borrowed and are only charged a monthly interest that is payable once enough income is earned. Even after waiving the principal, the interest rate charged by the MFI will be lower than the existing informal interest rates. The loan amount disbursed should be used only to buy agricultural inputs and not for any other purpose. Due to high amount of corruption and fake input dealers in the region, the MFI will identify a set of authorized dealers who sell good quality inputs. The inputs may include seeds, fertilizers, pesticides and any other products that may help improve the productivity of the farmer. Similar to previous ICICI efforts with ITC, the MFI must strike a partnership with organizations that can successfully build rural technology. Rural information kiosks can help farmers obtain timely advice on external factors that may affect the productivity of their inputs. Thus, computer can also be used by the MFI to provide all necessary information to the groups and this will ultimate reduce costs involved with having frequent follow-up meetings (i.e., online consulting).

The farmers will be charged an interest on their loans. Nevertheless, they will not be required to service this interest until they obtain a sustainable level of cash flow over time, a saving requirement should be implemented in order to ensure the eventual repayment of the loan and mitigate risk. The group will be informed of the interest accrued every month. Since the principal is waived the interest rate will be based on the difference between the MSP and the market price received by the MFI.

By providing appropriate advice on crop growing techniques, our model attempts to keep the production cost below the MSP. Since most agriculture in this region is dependant on rainfall, it is important that the farmers have good information on the rainfall patterns and forecast to help them decide the exact timing to sow their seeds. The main idea is that at the end of the day the farmer will reap a profit by selling quality produce at the MSP and is able to repay the interest accrued the future. While waiving the principal for the farmers, the MA is able to make a profit by selling the product at market price, and receive interest from farmers savings which can be reinvested in global financial markets.

There are two main delivery channels for microfinance services. The first one is SHG (Self Help Group)—Bank Linkage Channel. This was developed from field experiments in the early 1990s by NABARD (National Bank for Agricultural and Rural Development). The second channel is the Micro Finance Institution (MFI). The first MFI in India was set-up in 1974, but the momentum was achieved only during the 1990s. Initially the formal financial institutions were reluctant to be involved with the MFIs. Increasing outreach has underlined the need for regulation to ensure further orderly growth. In response to certain undesirable practices with regard to interest rates and collection of some MFIs, Sadhan, the industry association of MFIs, evolved in 2006 a voluntary code of conduct for the sector. However the need for regulation for the sector remained intact.

The microfinance sector faces other challenges as well on its road to further growth. First, there is scope for substantially improving the quality and efficiency of service delivery by the organizations providing micro finance services. Second, the microfinance sector has begun to offer insurance pensions and remittance products. As more complex products also get added to the MFIs suite professional management becomes very important. Third, increasing urbanization poses new challenges and opportunities India is urbanizing at a rate higher than the world average a recent report by the United Nations population Fund on state of World Population 2007 says by 2030, 41% of India's population will be urban MFIs will hence need to gear up to cater to the needs of increasing number of urban poor. Fourth, there is disproportionate reliance on group lending MFIs need to offer individual-based lending options particularly to cater to the growing urban segment. This require focus on development of appraisal skills and more modern management information systems. The regulation of the sector should encourage MFIs to meet the challenges successfully. (*Shandilya & Prasad U.*, 2009).

IMPORTANT PROVISIONS UNDER MF BILL

The Bill seeks to promote and regulate MFOs microfinance (organizations) the definition of MFOs includes societies trusts and cooperatives. The Bill designates NABARD as the regulator for the sector Micro finance services are defined to include credit life insurance, general insurance and pension services while micro credit has been defined as loans not exceeding (Rs. 1,50,000 in case of housing) the other services have not been defined further. The Bill has at least four positive features. First, the Bill Permits MFOs to accept savings from members subject to their meeting certain conditions. As MFO which has been in existence for at least three years having net owned funds of at least Rs. 5 million and satisfactory management can obtain registration form, NSBARD and thereafter offer as savings services the non-availability of savings has been a major gap in the services provided by the sector. Financial inclusion should involve both savings and credit products. The provision of savings products will enable MFOs to offer a more complete suite of products to their customers. It will also enable MFOs to access an additional funding source.

Second, the Bill provides for mandatory Registration and periodic report submission by all MFOs seeking to accept deposits. These MFOs also need to submit annual audited financial statements. This has the potential to build a robust database of the sector over time and help institute greater professionalism in the functioning of MFOs. Third, it provides for inspection of MFOs by the regulatory authorities in case of complaints of harmful practices. There is also a mention that a dispute resolution mechanism may put in place. These steps can serve as important consumer protection steps in the microfinance sector

Fourth, contrary to the fears in some circles the Bill does not introduce interest rate caps which could have been damaging for the sector interest rates are a function of risk cost of funds and transaction costs. Transaction costs in micro finance typically include cost of group formation, group training and cost of weekly collections. The costs in these loans are higher than in the case of corporate and personal loan and because of the small value of the loan and weekly collection. Further, the services are provided at the customer's doorstep which again adds to cost.

Putting a cap on the rate of interest can lead to the exclusion of customers whose profiles call for interest rates in excess of the cap. In the context of microfinance a uniform interest rate would create incentives for MFOs to move away form difficult and new geographies where transaction costs are higher. There is also the possibility that as a result of the interest rate cap MFOs may be encouraged to repackage loan contracts by varying balances fees and other aspects in search way that effective interest rates remain the same, interest rate caps could also be detrimental in attracting capital to the sector. Attracting capital to the sector is critical so that the MFOs build scale and thereby reduce lending costs.

SHGs FORMATION AND FUNCTIONING

Self-help groups are not to be formed externally with the stakeholders/target group playing a passive role rather it is a participatory process of facilitating the target people/households to get organized into self help group interveners merely facilitate the entire process. It is important to note here that entire cycle of evolution/formation functioning and stabilization of SHG can be divided into three stages the interveners will have distinct roles to play in each of the three stages The sustainability will depend among others on the process of group formation in stage identification of natural affinities and formation of self-help group (about 4 to 6 months) is a very critical stage and the sustainability of groups will depend on how well the activities of this stage are performed. As first activity towards group formation process the intervener has to start awareness campaign in the area (a cluster of 2-4 villages) to sensitize the people/households about the concept and relevance of self-help group. Preparation of a detailed outline of the concept rationale and *modus operandi* of self-help groups is needed. Interveners or their representative (NGOs/block officials) should have adequate competence to explain and convince the individuals for group formation. Interveners should abstain themselves from making any kind of allurement to the people. After adequate sensitization of people towards the concept of self-help groups the next step should comprise sharpening the focus on disadvantaged sections such as households of scheduled and backward castes and women, it is but natural that after such an intense motivation drive villagers/people will automatically come forward to form groups for mutual cooperation with regard to their socio-economic problems. In the Stage II Stabilization of group (which takes 6 to 15 months saving becomes regular lending activities are strengthened repayment is timely in this stage group is linked with bank as per the guidelines issued by the National Bank for Agricultural and Rural Development (NABARD) the bank will fix cash credit limit for the group Entrepreneurial skill of group members and their interest areas for starting income generating self-employment programme is assessed by facilitator/intervener Group members are provided suitable training capacity buildings and skill development of the goup members should be stressed in the Stage III taking 15 to 24 months intervention is withdrawn and it becomes more clear and acceptable after sufficient intervention to build withdrawal becomes more clear and acceptable after sufficient intervention to build withdrawal becomes more visible and acceptable after the major interventions required to build up the groups taper-off-Management and productivity all round support for off-farm activities especially for design quality and marketing. Supportive role of intervener/facilitator should be substantially decrease but there will be continuous need to ensure that regular feedback and analysis of data is available in order to identify trends in financial management and group functioning. The time when group have stabilized; saving is regular and adequate capital built-up, individual group members can start individual micro enterprises or income generating activities by taking loan from their respective groups. Saving installment will also increase gradually which will financially enhance the common fund available with SHG group. But it is also a fact that group-saved amount will not be adequate for micro enterprises by all the group members. While on the other hand consists of consumption/unproductive loans meant mainly for addressing contingent needs. It has been seen that group saved money is sufficient only for small and short-term consumption loans.

It has also been in the observation that once consumption loan requirements of the group members are met from group-saved money/fund group capital can be enhanced through linking group with bank and fixation of cash credit limit. In order to streamline the working of SHGs and to achieve its objectives of self-reliance and sustainable income generating activities. The NABARD has launched pilot project for linking banks with self-help group. It has issued several guidelines to the banks. For the bank-SHG progrmme, certain criteria have been designed for eligibility of self-help groups to be linked with the bank. Important of them are the group should have been in active existence for at least a period of six months and the group should have successfully undertaken saving and credit operations from its own resources; democratic working of the group wherein all members feel that they have a say should be evident; the group is maintaining proper account/record; the banker should be convinced that the group has not come into existence only for the sake of participation in the programme and availing the benefits from SHGs activities. There should be a genuine need to help each other and work together among the members; the members of SHGs should preferably have homogeneous background and interest; and the interest of the NGO or self-help promoting institution concerned in the group should be evident and the agency is helping the SHG by way of training and other support for skill upgradation proper functioning and capacity building. If the group fulfill all these criteria, it gets linked with the bank which will fix cash credit limit for the group on the basis of its cumulative saving and monthly saving installment. Through this available fund the group may start micro enterprise on a large scale or some collective income generating activities according to the mutual understanding of all the members.

This stage is very crucial for the group therefore, the intervener provides complete guidance to the group members about selecting an activity, its managements, marketing, etc. The intervener has to assess to the interest and capability of group members about various possible income generating activities/enterprises. On the basis of such assessment the intervener compile and provide the relevant the information including marketing, etc. The most important task of the intervener/facilitator will consist of training, skill development and capacity building of the group members to manage the proposed enterprise and its processes. In this stage the intervener finances the training and skill and sometimes development programmes also for the group. The intervener should also help in establishing marketing linkages. All these activities save the way for group to prepare an enterprise/activity plan. With such activity plan the group should approach the bank for financing. The banks have no objection in providing finance as it has full confidence in the functioning and viability of groups. Group enterprise should be encouraged only in a case of perfectly homogeneous group.

Only those scoring fairly high on cohesiveness indices should be encouraged to go for joint enterprises. Otherwise individual enterprises would be better. Initially, the members will start income generating activities with the help of bank finance; however, gradually they will become self-reliant in financing and future growth. If every thing goes well the groups will have self-sustainable and self-employment opportunities with income generation. During the entire cycle of growth path, there is need of rigorous monitoring and evaluation of group functioning so that corrective measures could be taken in case of some gaps and constraints of group enterprise.

IMPACT OF SHGs ACTIVITIES ON WOMEN'S SOCIO-ECONOMIC STATUS IN BIHAR

Bihar which is lagging behind in all the indicators of development has very poor performance with regard to socio-economic development in general and for women in particular. The women constitutes about 50 percent of the total population of the state and this major segment has to play very important role in taking the state to the height of desired development in all spheres of lives. In the field of women SHGs progress in the state the picture is dismal so for as comprison to other states of the country. Although some districts in the state like Kishanganj, Dharbhanga, Katihar, Munger, Bhagalpur, Khagaria, Nawada, Begusarai, Samastipur, show different pictures. In these districts not only a good number of women SHGs have been formed but most of them have been financed through the different banks for starting income generating enterprises. As per recent study report the SHGs in these district are functioning well and it is only due to their better performance in the districts the repayment of loans has also been found very satisfactory. But at the same time some other districts like Araria, Bhojpur, Motihari, Siwan, Chapra and Gopalganj, etc. have not shown good performance even on the front of formation of group and income generating activities. This is mainly due to slow or least intervension by government agencies, NGOs and due partly to some socio-economic factors in the state.

As a result, of involvement in SHGs activities including planning, monitoring and cooperation the access and control over the natural resources in a best possible manner for the protection and management, has also been learnt by the women groups. Adopting the soil and water conservation measures, development of wasteland, watershed management programme like contour bunding and gully plugging, renovation of the old tanks and excavation of the new tanks; terracing measures, check dams, water harvesting structures, water diversifying channels and the pasteurisation measure involving the active participation of the SHG members, saddling the responsibility to look after the managements of natural resources in the area with decision-making approaches.

In order to strengthen the women empowerment process, priority on imparting the gender sensitisation training, imbibing the knowledge on gender equity and to maintain the scale up balance along with male in the society as well as to restore the dignity and respectability of women, which now widened the scope and the vast spectrum for the fullest involvement of the women community in the holistic development of villages. After group functioning the dependency on money lenders among members is declining due to the access to credit from SGHs. Nearly 61 percent of members reported that they would have gone to moneylenders had there been no SHGs. Of course, this percentage very across districts of Bihar. The access to credit has enabled the women to undertake economic activities. Around 8 percent of the members of SHGs reported that they might not have started the economic activity, had there been no SHGs. The incidence of such members also varied across the districts. The economic activities undertaken by the members of SHGs fall under three categories, agriculture, animal husbandry, and industry, service and business. The activities are dominantly production-oriented rather than service. They are largely continuous activities rather than seasonal. The ownership of bank sponsored enterprises (activities) is equally divided into individual and family ownership, which reveal that the enterprise is actually owned, assisted and managed by other members of the family also, though the financial assistance is provided to the women member of the family.

A large proportion of women, mostly from artisan families engaged in traditional occupations become members of the groups to strengthen and expand their ongoing economic activities. These women are continuing with their earlier occupations. Groups that formed with common interest in expanding for strengthening their existing traditional activities have been significantly successful. Although, a smaller proportion of them have taken up new occupations rather than remaining in traditional activities. These group women are not able to manage these activities due to lack of previous experience. Thus, most of the enterprises (activities), which are facilitated through group helped to utilize the existing skills by using the credit assistance provided. The attempts of the Government to impart new skills and upgrade existing skills have not reached a many areas of the state. As such, many women groups are not able to derive the benefits from the government. It has also been reported that some of the unemployed and wage employed have become self-employed. Many members who were housewife earlier became self-employed. The diversification of occupation to non-agriculture activities has enhanced the quality of income of the household as the dependency on risk-base agriculture has greatly reduced. The income accrued to the beneficiary women from the economic activities undertaken has contributed considerable proportion of beneficiary adult female family members has full employment under the scheme. A part of the income gained was spent, by some of the women member household, on nutritious food for family especially children. This has brought changes in the quality of consumption that might have led to the enhancement of the nutritional status of children, pregnant and lactating mothers. Majority of the children of the beneficiaries are going to school as the women had become aware of the need for basic education. But the group in the interior villages and scheduled caste have not been benefited to the extent of the extèrior villages and other caste beneficiaries in the different districts of the state.

As an impact of the SHGs activated some of group women are now able to mobilize the delivery of the health service mechanism and to access health facilities at the doorsteps of the community placing and urging the demands before the authorities, for regular immunization, regular visit of ANMs and health personnel for better sanitation and conducive environment in the village and around, with the fullest participation of the community with clean and green initiatives. Promotion of kitchen gardens in each target village for the development of nutritious food intake capacity, is one of the leading initiatives campaigned by the SHGs, which now target family which may ultimately reduce the long standing prevalence of malnutrition and anemia, specially in case of children and lactating mothers. Better care and management of the adolescent girl become possible while she is achieving the stage of puberty and maintained the balance of the equity in food distribution developing the intake capacity of the girl child. Due to the knowledge obtained, the prevalence of child marriage was also been reduced to an extent, through the attempts of the groups. The Traditional Birth Attendants (TBAs) of the villages became the dynamic promoter of health mechanism as better health and maternity services. As an impact of increase income due to SHG activities the gender poverty measured in terms of gender bias with respect to norms of feating, male preference in distribution of food and access to clothing has not declined significantly. Although gender poverty is lower among the dalits relatively higher levels of poverty among the dalits.

Gender disparities are much lower among the member households with respect to nutrition, child/adult premature death and ability of women to sign. Gender differences in children's Children using government child-care services have increased. Drainage facilities, toilet facilities and access to *pucca* houses, electricity and gas have improved. The improvements in the access to productive assets, improved livelihoods and control over all aspects of life of women have contributed to the decline of disparities among women. It has improved their control over their lives. More specifically, women have improved access and/or control over power to survive, their labour/family labour, resources, freedom to move and interact, leadership positions, reproduction, and body. Thus, there is all round improvement with regard to control over their lives. But there are variations with regard to improvement in access and/or control over the different aspects of this dimension of improvement. Highest achievements are made with respect to their mobility, breaking of gender division of productive labour, access to their own savings, access to friendship outside their family and access to leadership positions in gram panchayat; moderate achievements are made with respect to reproductive rights and body rights (freedom from violence); and lower achievements are made with respect to extent of access of women to husband's labour (productive and reproductive), rights of women to land and house. (*Khan, S.A.*, 2003)

Given the widespread gender bias against women in various fields, there are arguments that interventions like micro finance have the potential to enhance women's capabilities which can make a significant difference to overall development of women. Those who hold the above view argue for supporting micro finance interventions and tuning them to meet the needs of women specifically. On the other hand, there are arguments that microfinance interventions can at best have only a very limited impact in empowering women. Interventions like microfinance are constrained by the existing socio cultural structures like patriarchy in order for them to make a very a significant impact on women. Under such circumstances women hardly have any control in deciding or directing loan use for purposes, which can enhance their individual economic position over those dictated by familial requirements. Access to savings and credit can take care of mainly the practical needs of women instead of meeting their strategic needs.

A study which looked at the changes brought about by longer association of members with their SHGs concluded that: members of the old SHGs emerged as more confident, financially more secure, more in control of their lives, and in a stronger position *vis-a-vis* their family members. The personal abilities, ownership of economic assets, development of skills, ability to decide about self and extent of participation in political sphere are likely to improve for the better if the women members continue to participate in SHGs for a longer period.

A foremost impact discernible is the reduced dependence of SHG households on informal sources of credit The members of the SHGs have been able to reduce their dependence on moneylender very significantly. A study on SHGs reported a decline in the share of moneylender's loan from 66 to 15 per cent for the members. In another study, nearly 51 per cent of the members closed their old debt with the moneylenders using SHG loans. The members at the same time have been able to generate a substantial surplus for themselves due to cheaper interest paid on loans. Through credit obtained from SHGs, the members have made efforts both to protect their families from various vulnerabilities as well as build their economic base to escape from poverty. This is evident from the fact that members are making use of SHG loans for diverse purposes, while use of loan for consumption purpose still remains a major item of utilization, members are increasingly using the SHG loans for social and productive needs. Heal the education and housing are some of the areas members have begun to increasingly channelise their loans. In Tamil Nadu, it was found that nearly 14 per cent loan had been used for housing purpose. In Andhra Pradesh it was found that nearly 6 per cent of the members had utilized their loan for children's education, SHG members are also using quite significantly SHG loans for regular economic activities like animal husbandry, agriculture and petty business. This is evident from the fact that nearly 74 per cent of SHG members in Tamil Nadu have invested in creating various assets like land, livestock, and household durables after joining SHGs.

On the contrary, there are also studies which have found only a limited impact of SHGs, A study concluded that micro finance seems to have played a more critical role in facilitating clients to cope with situations rather than deal 'with life cycle events in a sustainable manner. The economic impact of SHGs has been more protectional rather than promotional in nature. This is attributed to exclusion of very poor and the general constraints faced by poor in making use of loan for productive investments. There are also some evidence to suggest that the participation in SHG has even led to change for worse on many counts.

Though SHGs have begun to contribute in improving the economic conditions of the poor households, the impact does not seem to be a uniform phenomenon. At the same time no evidence to establish the fact that the positive impact noticed in some instances are attributable to women's involvement. However, going by the evidence available from Bangladesh, it could be inferred that the involvement of women might have made a significant difference even in India wherever positive change have been noticed. The innovative efforts as micro financing is very encouraging in a developing country like India and providing penacia for poor entrepreneurs particularly women.

Today we see that there is increasing competitions in MFIs in providing micro finance services to the rural poors. It is time for micro finance practices to consider moving beyond group lending due to the increased competitions in MFI and the pressure to reduce interest rates. The Group Lending, i.e. Self-help Groups Linkage with banks is very popular and about 93% loans are available to group whereas only 71% loans are disbursed to individual borrowers. There are various alternative models of micro finance services and the group-lending has the preferred model, as that group emphasized on social collateral only. The adverse selection of the members of the group is another important problem in the group lending by MFIs. The selection is not sometimes objective and some undesirable member may come jeopardize its functioning which make repayment of loans difficult. The micro-financing lack collateral from the side of the borrowers. The integrity, responsibility and social obligation are considered as social collateral for lending money to the group. However, the credit risk is involved in different types of the projects which are subject to loan sanction. Now, the banks are required to monitor the credit risk of such loans in the market.

MICRO FINANCE MAJOR-HURDLES AHEAD

Despite the substantial increase in the number of SHGs and expansion of micro finance, there are certain issues to be addressed considering the future prospects of the programme in India:

(i) There is a skewed distribution of SHGs, in favour of southern region in the country. Nevertheless over 50% of the total SHGs credit linkage in the country are concentrated in the southern states.

(ii) The quality of a SHG is a big challenge. The quality of SHGs has come under stress owing to the fast growth of the SHG-Bank Linkage Programme. The target-oriented approach inadequate incentives to NGO and low level of skills of the SHG members are the factors affecting the quality of the SHGs.

(iii) It is desirable to provide proper training facilities to Self-Help Promoting Institutions (SHPI), bank officials and SHG members to cope with complex financial problems in the financial market.

(iv) The more critical challenge is to induce SHGs, to graduate into matured level of enterprise, livelihood diversifications, increase access to supplying chain linkage to the capital market and appropriate production and processing technologies.

(v) Of late, many SHGs have started promoting federation of SHGs, so that some of their functions can be performed by them in a cost effective and sustainable manner. However, no serious efforts have been made towards capacity building of the federation.

(vi) MFI model is comparatively costlier in terms of delivery of finance services due to low volume of loan and loan size and the cash of funds. A good number of MFI are subsidy dependent and only a few MFI are also to cover more than 80% of their cost. High rate of interest charged by them has become an area of concern

(vii) Successful delivery of flexible client driven and innovative micro finance services to the poor would not be possible without building up the capacities of MFIs. Innovation in various aspects such as social intermediation, strategic linkage and new approaches centered on the livelihood issues of the poor are the need of the hour. In spite of phenomenal growth of SHG-Bank Linkage Programme there is still a large segment of the society that is denied access to financial services. There is urgent need to widen the shape, outreach as also the scale of financial services to cover the unreached and neglected population of the country within a time frame.

Working of SHGs-Bank Linkages in Bihar

The recent data indicates that the performance of banks in linking self-help groups (SHGs) to the banking system scaled impressive heights during the year 2002-03 (197,653 SHGs during 2001-02). The cumulative number of SHGs credit linked with banks increased to 717,360 as on 31 March 2003 covering more than 11.6 million poor households as against 461,478 SHGs covering 7.8 million poor households as on 31 March 2002. Total bank loans disbursed to SHGs during the same year aggregated Rs. 10,223 million (including repeat loans of Rs. 3,318 million provided to 102,391 existing SHGs already financed in earlier years) as compared to Rs. 5,454 million disbursed during the previous year, registering a growth of 87% over the previous year. Though, full refinance from NABARD was available to all banks for SHG lending, some banks did not utilize the facility to the full extent. The refinance claimed by banks from NABARD stood at Rs. 6,223 million during 2002-03. Bank loans aggregating Rs. 20,487 million were disbursed to 717,360 SHGs with refinance support of Rs. 14,188 million from NABARD, up to 31 March 2003. The cumulative progress in financing SHGs up to the end of March 1992-99 was Rs. 32,995 with Rs. 571 million bank loan as against 114,775 SHGs and bank loan of Rs. 930 million in 1999-2000 and 263,825 SHGs and bank loan of Rs. 4,809 billion in 2000-01. Around 90 per cent of the SHGs linked were exclusive women SHGs. As revealed in the impact evaluation studies, the on-time repayment of SHG loans was around 95 per cent for each bank.

In Bihar the cumulative number of SHGs provided with bank loan upto March 2002 was 3,957, whereas, the number of SHGs provided with bank loan during April 2002 to March 2003 stood at 4,204. The cumulative number of SHGs provided with bank loan upto March 2003 was 8,161 with cumulative bank loan upto March 2002 was Rs. 38,155 million and the bank loan during April 2002 to March 2002 stood at Rs. 82.75 million. The cumulative bank loan by March 2003 was Rs. 120.90 million (NABARD, 2002-03).

A perceptible increase of SHG-Bank Linkage in states which had not shown significant progress in the past years is discernible. During the year 2002-03 alone, some states showed an increase in number of SHGs credit linked, which was equal to or even more than the cumulative number of SHGs credit linked in those states up to March 2002 (Orissa—21,719 SHGs; West Bengal—15,504; Rajasthan—10,178; Madhya Pradesh—7,290; and Bihar—4,204 SHGs). The states which already had a high growth record continued to maintain the trend during 2002-03 as well (Andhra Pradesh—79,037 SHGs; Tamil Nadu 35,701; Karnataka—25,146; Uttar Pradesh—20,582; Maharashtra—8,446; and Kerala—6,253 SHGs). All round growth was witnessed during the year in the states of Gujarat—4,379 SHGs; Himachal Pradesh—3,806; Jharkhand—3,567; and Chhattisgarh—3,000 SHGs.

The positive growth of SHG-Bank linkage in some of the regions and States was facilitated by the State and region-specific strategies developed by NABARD in consolation with its regional offices at the state level, banks, NGOs and the State governments. Promotional efforts were launched by NABARD through its Regional Offices in these States, participating agencies and other institutions including the government and non-governmental agencies, NABARD took specific steps to identify district-level bottlenecks in expansion of SHG-Bank linkage in the states of Bihar, Uttar Pradesh, Rajasthan, Assam, Madhya Pradesh, West Bengal and

TABLE 1
Positive Trends in Cumulative Growth in SHGs Linked to Banks

Region/State	*March 1999*	*March 2000*	*March 2001*	*March 2002*	*March 2003*
NE Region	93	196	477	1,490	4,069
KBK Region	526	1,425	4,192	9,869	18,934
Orissa	2,018	4,068	8,888	20,553	42,272
Bihar*	496	1,910	4,592	8,155	15,926
Uttar Pradesh*	2,812	12,953	23,152	36.437	59,549
Rajasthan	710	1,941	5,616	12,564	22,742
Madhya Pradesh	733	2,303	5,699	11,744	22.034
All India	32,995	114,775	263,825	461,478	717,360

* Undivided States.
Source : NABARD, Progress of SHG-Bank Linkages in India 2002-03.

Orissa, by conducting Goal Oriented Project Planning (GOPP) programme, for the district officers of NABARD in those states. This enabled NABARD to widen its network of partnership beyond the NGO sector in formation and nurturing of SHGs in these states. The partners included RRBs, farmers' clubs, government organizations and development departments which have effectively taken up the role of promoting and nurturing SHGs. Almost all commercial banks (48), RRBs (192) and co-operatives (264) participated in SHG-Bank linkage.

As indicated in the table above positive trends in cumulative growth in SHGs linked to banks are evident over the years. The member of SHGs linked to banks are growing in Bihar from a cumulative growth of SHGs 496 in March 1999 to 15,926 in March 2003. The all India trend is also in tune with this overall trend. The cumulative participation of commercial banks by March 2003 was with 2,979 SHGs with Rs. 43.99 million bank loan followed by RRBs with 5,197 SHGs and Rs. 72.96 million bank loan. The cumulative participation of cooperative banks was only with 91 SHGs with a bank loan of Rs. 3.95 million. The total number of SHGs cumulative participation by all agencies in 2003 was 8,161 SHGs with Rs. 120.90 million bank loan as per NABARD report 2003. (*Singh, L.S.*, 2003)

Bihar, till March 2003, the cumulative number of SHGs provided with bank loan was 5,195 with cumulative bank loan disbursed at Rs. 72.96 million. The Champaran KGB had highest number of SHGs provided with loan (2030 SHGs) with Rs. 28.28 million loan disbursed. The cumulative number of SHGs provided with bank loan in 2003 March end by Koshi KGB was 433, Vaishali KGB 340, Saran KGB 325 and Munger KGB 135. In case of the other RRB the cumulative number of SHGs at the end of March 2003 was nearly half of these RRBs and therefore, the loan amount disbursed was also very small (NABARD) as indicated in Table 2.

TABLE 2

SHG-Bank Linkage—Physical and Financial Progress of Participating RRBs up to 31 March 2003 in Bihar

Name of RRB		*Cumulative No. of SHGs provided with bank loan upto 31 March 2003*	*Cumulative bank loan disbursed upto 31 March 2003 (Rs. Million)*
1.	Bhagalpur-Bank KGB	121	1.42
2.	Vaishali KGB	340	6.4
3.	Samastipur KGB	146	2.13
4.	Mithile KGB	17	0.46
5.	Kosi KGB	433	11.54
6.	Begusarai KGB	37	0.76
7.	Champaran KGB	2,030	28.28
8.	Magadh KGB	1,271	13.38
9.	Madhubani KGB	131	1.59
10.	Nalanda KGB	115	1.28
11.	Bhojpur-Rohtas KGB	168	1.63
12.	Saran KGB	235	2.28
13.	Munger KGB	135	1.4
14.	Pataliputra KGB	16	0.37
	Total	5,197	72.96

Source : NABARD, 2003.

By the end of March 2003, 28 NGO's were given financial support. The number of SHGs promoted by these NGOs were 3,077 amount of Rs. 3,813 crores were sanctioned out of which the total

TABLE 3

Expendable Fund Support for Credit Delivery Innovations Details upto 31 March 2003 in Bihar

Sl. No.	Agency	District to be Covered SHGs	No. of Sanct.	Amount	Total Amount Released	Progress as 31 March 2003		
						No. of SHGs Pro-moted	No. of SHGs with SB Ales	No. of SHGs Credit Linked
(1)	(2)	(3)	(4)	(5)	(6)	(7)	(8)	(9)
1.	Avidya Vimukti Sansthan	Bodhgaya	67	72,000	72,000	88	82	68
2.	Samagra Sewa Kendra	Gaya	100	100,000	72,100	140	123	101
3.	Matadeen Mahila Manch	Muzaffarpur	100	100,000	47,000	171	155	61
4.	Gram Nirmal Mandal	Nawadah	100	100,000	20,000	58	37	
5.	Parivartan Vikas Rohtas	Rohtas	100	100,000	50,700	123	122	122
6.	Gramin Vikas Sansthan	Gaya	100	100.000	74,500	122	104	64
7.	Samajik Shodh Evam Vikas Kendra	East Champaran	200	200,000				
8.	Bhojpur Sampum Saksharta Abhiyan	Bhojpur	100	100,000	20,000	135	84	14
9.	Patna Notre Dame Sisters Society	East Champaran	140	210.000	50,100	62	43	13
10.	Gramin Samaj Kalyan Sansthan	Samastipur	60	60,000	35,800	77	50	12
11.	Mahila Silai Prashikshan Sah Utpadan Kendra	Samastipur	60	60,000	12,000	48	16	3

12.	Gramyasheel	Supaul	50	50,000	37,900	119	119	39
13.	Jan Jagaran Sansthan	Nalanda	100	100,00	20,000	31	9	
14.	Rachna	Madhubani	100	100,000	23,600	10]	101	
15.	Krishak Vikas Samiti	East Champaran	100	100,000	56,600	155	127	74
16.	Avidya Vimukti Sansthan	Gaya	200	200,000	152,300	236	235	205
17.	Darpan Sarvodaya Vikas Sansthan	Gaya	100	100,000	52,300	146	128	24
18.	Reshma Gramin Vikas Sangh	Jehanabad	100	101,000				
19.	Akhil Gramin Yuwa Vikas Samiti	Muzaffarpur	100	180,000	36,000	39	22	5
20.	Bihar Dalit Vikas Samiti	Jehanabad	100	172,000				
21.	Nidan	Patna	250	470,000	94,000	76	76	45
22.	Gramyasheel	Supaul	200	354,000				
23.	Nari Shishu Jagruti Kendra	Samastipur	100	163,000				
24.	Akhil Bharatiya Jan Kalyan Parishad	West Champaran	50	79,000				
25.	Nav Bharati Kala Manch	Saran	100	100,000				
26.	Kanchan Seva Ashram	Muzaffarpur	100	120,000				
27.	Jan Kalyan Vikas Sansthan	Saran	100	100,000				
28.	Samagra Vikas Sansthan	West Champaran	100	102,000				
	Total		3,077	3,813.000	9,27,200	1,927	1,633	850

Source : NABARD, Progress of SHG-Bank Linkage in India, 2002-03.

amount released was Rs. 9,27,200 crores and the number of SHGs, promoted by various NGOs was 1927 SHGs, out of which 850 SHGs were credit-linked as it has been clearly indicated in both the tables given ahead.

TABLE 4

SHG-Bank Linkages—District-wise Cumulative Physical and Financial Progress upto March 2003 in Bihar

(Rs. Million)

Sl. No.	*District*	*Cummulative No. of SHGs, Provided with Bank Loan Upto 31 March 2003*	*Cumulative Bank Loan Disbursed upto 31 March 2003*
1.	Banka	222	2.10
2.	Madhubani	564	8.00
3.	Muzaffarpur	438	4.02
4.	Vaishali	125	1.06
5.	Samastipur	193	2.33
6.	Katihar	60	1.72
7.	Darbhanga	29	0.67
8.	Araria	23	0.40
9.	West Champaran	1.713	27.95
10.	Begusarai	86	5.50
11.	Gaya	1.382	10.24
12.	Supaul	169	2.39
13.	Nalanda	151	8.18
14.	Sitamarhi	154	2.91
15.	Purnea	138	2.21
16.	Bhagalpur	308	5.88
17.	Gopalganj	09	0.04
18.	Bhojpur	90	1.69
19.	Kishanganj	32	2.10
20.	Nawadah	122	2.26
21.	Lakhisarai	08	0.01
22.	East Champaran	713	5.75
23.	Saran	361	2.43

24.	Jehanabad	84	1.74
25.	Rohtas	150	1.62
26.	Munger	60	2.99
27.	Patna	307	5.43
28.	Aurangabad	307	5.43
29.	Buxar	19	0.42
30.	Jamui	187	1.92
31.	Sheolar	70	1.63
32.	Arwal	10	0.23
33.	Kaimur	10	0.24
34.	Khagaria	9	0.71
35.	Madhepura	21	0.55
36.	Saharsa	64	2.36
37.	Sheikhpura	5	0.02
38.	Siwan	3	0.05
	Total	8.161	129.90

Source : NABARD (2003), Progress of SHG-Bank Linkages in India.

CONCLUDING OBSERVATION AND SUGGESTIONS

Evidently it can be said that participation in SHGs has improved the access of women to credit, which has helped women in reducing their dependence on moneylenders. The interest rates in informal credit sector have declined. The access to credit has helped women to meet their consumption as well as production needs. The non-farm activities undertaken by the women helped the households to obtain income from low risk activities and the quality of income of the households has increases. The incomes of the poor have increased and as a result the intensity of poverty (poverty gap) among the poor has been slashed. The women acquired some non-land assets; health, nutrition and education status of children has improved, which reveals that the intergenerational transmission of poverty has reduced. But at the same time a considerable proportion of the poorest of the poor are not included at all in the process of poverty alleviation under SHGs while on the other hand, it has been revealed that non-poor have entered this programme. Entry of non-poor itself might have hindered the entry of the poorest of the poor. The poorest of the poor, who are in the groups have absorbed relatively lower volume of credit among the poor due to low asset base including skills. Consequently, the activities undertaken with low level of credit and existing skills, given the demand, may not generate adequate surplus to repay the loans. This problem can be tackled to some extent by adopting repayment schedule suitable to the poorest of the poor. The improvement in skill base. given the other assets base, can also be a solution to tackle the problems of the poorest. Proper livelihood planning, bulk purchases of inputs and collective marketing of outputs help the poorest of the poor to organize their economic activity effectively. The welfare programmes by government for the aged and wage employment and land rights including usufruct rights on common property resources to arrest migration coupled with micro-credit for migrant agriculture labour may be the remedy. The skill base of women has not been broadened at all either through imparting new skills or upgrading existing skills to take up new activities or refining the quality of old product. Linking of SHGs with the corporate sector to capture the non-local markets beside local markets shows that the local markets are not adequate to absorb the products emanated as a result of widening the skill base of the poor. But the SCs and women headed households have not improved considerably compared to non-SCs and male-headed households In the state. Thus, it is clear that the poverty reduction is varying across different socio-economic classes given the low level of self-employment opportunities in the local economies.

Groups should be formed on the basis of inherent binding force already prevailing among the members. and should be as homogeneous as possible on the basis of caste, economic status, etc. The most important factor is commonness of issue/problem or interest. Groups should be formed around a common interest, which are called interest groups. As Interest groups tend to be more sustainable merely credit groups. There should be rotation of group leadership so that all members of the group get an opportunity to play managerial role. The SHGs should be cohesive i.e. all group members should have workable liking for each other. Group should have everlasting binding force for the group members. The government should recognize the groups as suitable platform for dissemination of knowledge/information and it will have to consider the groups as a two way link between people and it.

Thus self-help group programme for employment generation clearly seems to be a workable model. But utmost care in promotion of self help groups is required and the intervener should adopt absolutely participatory approach towards identification and strengthening of SHGs. It should simply facilitate the process and let the people evolve their own mechanism for formation of SHGs. The heterogeneous groups should be discouraged as there is remote chance of viability of such groups. Suitable monitoring and evaluation system should form part of the implementation plan of all the activities under SHG programme. Above all, following main key issues and thrust points have been identified as the causes for poor performance and functioning of SHGs in the state:

- Lack of entrepreneurial capacity among the members.
- Lack of coordinating tempo/attitude and leadership quality among the members.
- Unawareness, lack of skill in proper maintaining of the account of the groups.
- Inadequate Interventions by NGOs and lack of awareness on democratic values which is essential for a successful group.
- Irregular meeting *of* the SHGs due to lack of motivation by any competent NGO.
- Improper functioning *of* SHGs due to lack of adequate training to them.
- Poor participatory approach and conflict management.
- Poor and ineffective intervention of Government agencies.
- Lack of coordination and active interest by the banks.

Therefore, it is need of the hour to impart training to SHGs government agencies, bank officers which lack the qualities and skill on above important issues.

References

Khan, Shakeel Ahmad, Conceptual Framework of SHG and changes in Socio Economic Status of Women, BEA Conf., Vol. 2003, pp. 384-91.

Manimekalai and G. Rajeswari (2000), Empowerment of Women through Self-Help Groups, Margin, Vol. 32, No. 4, July-Sept.

Ojha, R.K. (2002), "Self-Help Groups and Rural Employment". *Yojana*, May.

Srivastava, A.K., Kushawaha, R.K. and Jain Rity (2003), "Socio-Economic Impact Through Self-Help Groups", *Yojana*, July.

Rao, Chandrasekhara N. and Galab, S., "Women's Self-Help Groups, Poverty Empowerment", *Economic and Political Weekly*, March 22-29, 2003, *Kurukshetra*, June 2003..

Singh, Lall Saheb, Working of SHG in Bihar : A Study of SHG Bank Linkages, BEA Conf., Vol. 2003, pp. 315-17.

Shandilya, Tapan Kumar and Prasad Umesh (2003), Agricultural Credit and NABARD, Deep & Deep Publication, New Delhi.
Desai, B.M. and Desai, K.K., Farm Production Credit in Changing Agriculture, Indian Institute of Management, Ahmedabad, 1971.
Venkatappiah, V., Role of RBI in the Development of Credit Institutions, Cokkale Institute of Politics and Economic, Poona, 1980.
NABARD Annual Reports, 2007-08.
Economic Survey, 2008-09, Govt. of India, New Delhi.

Chapter 7

Poverty Alleviation Programmes in India—A Critical Evaluation

Alleviation of rural poverty has been one of the primary objectives of planned development in India. Ever since the inception of planning, the policies and the programmes have been designed and redesigned with this aim. The problem of rural poverty was brought into a sharper focus during the Sixth Plan. The Seventh Plan too emphasized growth with social justice. It was realized that a sustainable strategy of poverty alleviation has to be based on increasing the productive employment opportunities in the process of growth itself. However, to the extent the process of growth bypasses some sections of the population, it is necessary to formulate specific poverty alleviation programmes for generation of a certain minimum level of income for the rural poor.

Rural development implies both the economic betterment of people of well as greater social transformation. Increased participation of people in the rural development process, decentralization of planning, better enforcement of land reforms and greater access to credit and inputs go a long way in providing the rural people with better prospects for economic development. Improvement in health, education, drinking water, energy supply, sanitation and housing coupled with attitudinal changes also facilitate their social development.

Rural poverty is inextricably linked with low rural productivity and unemployment, including underemployment. Hence, it is imperative to improve productivity and increase employment in rural areas. Moreover, more employment needs to be generated at higher levels of productivity in order to generate higher output. Employment at miserably low levels of productivity and income is already a problem of far greater magnitude than unemployment as such. It was estimated that in 1987-88 the rate of unemployment was only 3 per cent and inclusive of the underemployed, it was around 5 per cent. As per the currently used methodology in the Planning Commission, poverty for the same year was estimated to be 30 per cent. This demonstrates that even though a large proportion of the rural population was 'working', it was difficult for them to eke out a living even at subsistence levels from it. It is true that there has been a considerable decline in the incidence of rural poverty over time. In terms of absolute numbers of poor, the decline has been much less. While this can be attributed to the demographic factor, the fact remains that after 40 years of planned development about 200 million are still poor in rural India. In 1987-88, the rural poverty line in terms of per capita monthly expenditure was Rs. 131.80. The average incidence of rural poverty conceals wide interstate differences, which suggests that greater attention needs to be paid to the regions, which have a greater concentration of the rural poor. In recent years, several issues have been raised about the methodology of poverty estimation, both by professionals and State Government. An Expert Group appointed by the Planning Commission is looking into these issues relating to the definition and measurement of poverty.

The decline in rural poverty is attributable both to the growth factor and to the special employment programmes launched by the Government in order to generate more incomes in the rural area. Hence, in its more limited interpretation, rural development has been confined to a direct attack on poverty through special employment programmes, area development programmes and land reforms.

Experience of developing countries which adopted the IMF-guided reforms to globalize their economies indicates that poverty had increased since July 1991 when India also joined the race. Globalization of prices without significant expansion in employment and globalization of incomes and a cutback in public spending on various welfare programmes in order to reduce fiscal deficits, are common features of all present reforms. Public spending is a powerful instrument for fighting poverty, and certain categories of government expenditure which affect inequalities and poverty have been identified for decades: education and health, food subsidies, cash transfers, housing and public employment schemes. Any significant reduction in public spending on social welfare brings down the levels of consumption of the people who cannot afford to pay inflated prices without a commensurate rise in their capabilities, at least in the immediate short-run.

India has launched several such programmes, which focus the rural poor. They basically provide employment to targeted poor, enhance their income and generate assets to rural poor families, SGSY, SGRY, PMGY, PMGST, SJSRY, TRYSEM, IAY, MWS, EAS are the few among the series of such programmes. Some details of such programmes are given below.

THE SWARNAJAYANTI GRAM SWAROZGAR YOJANA (SGSY)[1]

SGSY was launched in April 1999 after restructuring IRDP and is the only self-employment programme currently being implemented. It aims at promoting microenterprises and to bring the assisted poor families (Swarozgaris) above the poverty line by organizing them into Self-Help Groups (SHGs) through the process of social mobilization, training and capacity building and provision of income generating assets through a mix of Bank credit and Government subsidy. The scheme is being implemented on a cost-sharing ratio of 75.25 between the Centre and the States. Since inception of the Scheme up to December 2002 a total allocation of Rs. 3496.66 crore, to benefit 32.48 lakh Swarozgaris.

NREGS was launched in February 2006 in 200 most backward districts in the first phase and was expanded to 330 districts during 2007-08. The coverage was extended to all rural districts of the country in 2008-09. At present, 619 districts are covered under the NREGS. During the year 2008-09, more than 4.51 crore households were provided employement under the scheme. As against the budgeted outlay of Rs. 39,100 crore for the year 2009-10, an amount of Rs. 24,758.50 crore has been released to the States/UTs till December 2009. During the year 2009-10, 4.34 crore households have been provided employement under scheme. Out of the 182.88 crore person days created under the scheme during this period, 29 percent and 22 percent were in favour of SC and ST population respecticvely and 50 percent in favour of women.

The Sampoorna Grammen Rozgar Yojana (SGRY) was launched in September 2001. The schemes of Jawahar Gram Samridhi Yojana (JGSY) and Employment Assurance Scheme (EAS) have been fully integrated with SGRY. The objective of the scheme is to provide additional wage employment alongwith food security, creation of durable community, social and economic assets and infrastructure development in the rural area. The scheme envisages generation of 100 crore mandays of employment in a year. The cost of the programme is to be shared between the Centre and the State on a cost-sharing ratio of 87.5 : 12.5 (including foodgrains component). During 2001-02, 22.00 lakh tonnes of rice and 12.49 lakh tonnes of wheat were allocated under the scheme. Off take upto April 2002 was 13.5 lakh tonnes of rice and 5.64 lakh tonnes of wheat. During the current year the total of foodgrains from the Central pool, under the scheme was 39.22 lakh tonnes upto December 2002. Under SGRY (Spi. Comp.) 47.63 lakh tonnes of foodgrains have separately been released until now, free of cost to the State Governments for facilitating employment generation programmes in drought prone areas.

PRADHAN MANTRI GRAMODAYA YOJANA (PMGY)

PMGY was launched in 2000-01 in all the States and the UTs (Union Territories) in order to achieve the objective of sustainable human development at the village level. The PMGY envisages allocation of Additional Central Assistance to the States and UTs for selected basic minimum services in order to focus on certain priority areas of the Government, PMGY initially had five components viz., Primary Health, Primary Education, Rural Shelter, Rural Drinking Water and Nutrition. Rural Electrification has been added as an additional component from 2001-02.

The allocation for PMGY in 2000-01 was Rs. 2500 crore. This has been enhanced to Rs. 2800 crore for 2001-02. For the year 2002-03, Rs. 2800 crore have been provided. During the last two annual plans, the six sectoral programmes of PMGY were managed by the concerned Central Administrative Departments. However, this programme, new guidelines on the implementation of the PMGY during Annual Plan 2002-03 have been issues to all the State Governments and UTs.

PRADHAN MANTRI GRAMODAYA YOJANA (GRAMIN AWAS)

The scheme seeks to achieve the objective of sustainable habitat development at the village level. Central allocation for rural shelter component between the Centre and the States. Since inception of the Scheme upto December 2002 a total allocation of Rs. 3,496.66 crore, to benefit 32.48 lakh Swarozgaris.

SAMPOORNA GRAMEEN ROZGAR YOJANA (SGRY)

The Sampoorna Grammen Rozgar Yojana (SGRY) was launched in September 2001. The schemes of Jawahar Gram Samridhi Yojana (JGSY) and Employment Assurance Scheme (EAS) have been fully integrated with SGRY. The objective of the scheme is to provide additional wage employment alongwith food security, creation of durable community, social and economic assets and infrastructure development in the rural area. The scheme envisages generation of 100 crore mandays of employment in a year. The cost of the programme is to be shared between the Centre and the State on a cost-sharing ratio of 87.5 : 12.5 (including foodgrains component). During 2001-02, 22.00 lakh tonnes of rice and 12.49 lakh tonnes of wheat were allocated under the scheme. Off take upto April 2002 was 13.5 lakh tonnes of rice and 5.64 lakh tonnes of wheat. During the current year the total of foodgrains from the Central pool, under the scheme was 39.22 lakh tonnes upto December 2002. Under SGRY (Spl. Comp.) 47.63 lakh tonnes of foodgrains have separately been released until now, free of cost, to the State Governments for facilitating employment generation programmes in drought prone areas.

PRADHAN MANTRI GRAMODAYA YOJANA—RURAL DRINKING WATER PROJECT

Under this programme, a minimum 25 per cent of the total allocation is to be utilized to be respective States/UTs on projects/schemes for water conservation, water harvesting, and sustainability of the drinking water sources in respect of areas under Desert Development Programme/Drought Prone Area Programme.

PRADHAN MANTRI GRAM SADAK YOJANA (PMGSY)

The PMGSY, which was launched on 25th December 2000, is a programme to provide road connectivity through good all-weather roads to 1.60 lakh Unconnected Habitations with a population of 500 persons or more in the rural areas by the end of the Tenth Plan period (2007) at an estimated cost of Rs. 60,000 crore. The programme is being executed in all the States and six Union Territories. While the focus of the programme is on providing road connectivity of Unconnected Habitations of stipulated population size, connectivity is being provided to all Panchayat Headquarters and places of tourist interest under the PMGSY irrespective of the population size. Since inception, project proposals for Rs. 7.553.26 crore have been cleared. About 56.200 kms. of rural roads have been taken up under the programme, benefiting about 37,225 habitations. The programme is being executed in all states and six Union Territories. Till December 2002, 10,882 road works have been completed providing connectivity to 12,508 Habitations with an expenditure of Rs. 3,321,059 crore.

The present source of funding for PMGSY is the diesel cess, 50 per cent of which is earmarked for PMGSY. Efforts are underway to raise additional resources for the programme with financial assistance from the World Bank and the Asian Development Bank.

ANTYODAYA ANNA YOJANA

The scheme was launched by the Prime Minister on 25th December 2001. Under the scheme 1 crore poorest families out of the BPL families covered under the Targetted Public Distribution System are identified. 25 kgs of foodgrains were made available to each eligible family at a highly subsidized rate of Rs. 2 per kg for wheat and Rs. 3 per kg for rice. This quantity has been enhanced from 25 to 35 kgs with effect from April, 2002 for a period of 1 year, i.e., upto March 31, 2003. Against an allocation of 19,060 lakh tonnes of food grains from the Central Pool, upto December 2002, was 24.08 lakh tonnes.

ANNAPURNA YOJANA

This scheme was launched on April 1, 2002 as a 100 per cent Centrally Sponsored scheme. It aims at providing food security to meet the requirement of those senior citizens who though eligible for pension under the National Old Age Pension Scheme, are not getting the same. 10 kgs of foodgrains per person per month are supplied free of cost. 1062 lakh tonnes of foodgrains (wheat and rice) at BPL rates was allotted to Ministry of Rural Development during 2001-02. Off-take were 0.37 lakh tonnes of wheat and 0.56 lakh tonnes of rice.

During 2002-03, 0.87 lakh tonnes of food grains have been lifted upto December 2002. The scheme has been transferred to the State Plan from 2002-03.

INDIRA AWAS YOJANA (IAY)

The Indira Awas Yojana (IAY) aims at providing dwelling units, free of cost, to the poor families of the Scheduled Caste, Scheduled Tribes, freed bonded labourers and also the Non-ST/ST persons below the poverty lines in rural areas. The scheme is funded on a cost-sharing basis of 75.25 between the Centre and States. The ceiling on construction assistance under the IAY is Rs. 20,000 per unit for the plain areas and Rs. 22,000 for the hilly difficult areas. Since inception, upto February 2003 about 94-lakh houses have been constructed by incurring an expenditure of Rs. 16,202.25 crore. A major scheme for construction of houses to be given to the poor, free of cost, it has an additional component, namely, conversion of unserviceable kutcha houses to semi-pucca houses. Further, a Credit-*cum*-Subsidy Scheme for rural housing was launched from 1.4.1999 targeting rural families having annual income up to Rs. 32,000. From the year 2002-03, this scheme has been merged with IAY.

JAI PRAKASH ROZGAR GUARANTEE YOJANA (JPRGY)

The scheme seeks to provide guaranteed employment to the employed in the most distressed districts of the country. Operational modalities for launching of the scheme are being worked out.

SWARNA JAYANTI SHAHRI ROZGAR YOJANA (SJSRY)

The Urban Self-employment Programme and the Urban Wage Employment Programme are two special schemes of the SJSRY initiated in December 1997, which replaced various programmes operated earlier for urban poverty alleviation. This is funded on a 75.25 basis between the Centre and States. During 2001-02 an allocation of Rs. 168 crore was provided for various components of this programme, which was reduced to Rs. 45.50 crore at RE stage. The expenditure was Rs. 39.21 crore during 2001-02. For 2002-03 an allocation of Rs. 105 crore has been provided for various components of this programme. The expenditure during the current financial year, upto January 31, 2003 is Rs. 73.61 crore.

VALMIKI AMBEDKAR AWAS YOJANA (VAMBAY)

This scheme was formally launched by the Prime Minister on the 2nd December 2001. The scheme seeks to ameliorate the conditions of the urban slum dwellers living the poverty line who do not possess adequate shelter. The scheme has the primary objective of facilitating the construction and upgradation of dwelling units for the slum dwellers and providing a healthy and enable urban environment through community toilets under Nirmal Bhanit Abhiyan, a component of the scheme. The Central government provides a subsidy of 50 per cent; the balance 50 per cent being arranged by the State Governments with ceiling prescribed both for dwelling units/ community toilets. During the current financial year, Central subsidy to the extent of Rs. 138.31 crore has already been released out of the budget provision of Rs. 2,53,085 crore. Till January 2003, a total sum of Rs. 211.87 crore has been released as Government of India Subsidy for the construction/upgradation of 1,06,038 dwelling units, 20,817 toilet seats under the scheme.

SCHEMES RELATED TO EMPLOYMENT CREATION

This is an established fact that the employment intensive acceleration of economic growth facilitates the reduction of poverty in the long-run. In a series of poverty alleviation programmes, employment generation has always been a focal point. But due to reduction in public sector expenditure on welfare programmes during post-reform and the weak implementation and execution of poverty alleviation programmes, as have been discussed in the earlier parts, employment generation targets could hardly be achieved. Wherever, our schemes fail to touch targets or prove to be weak to fulfill the goals, we in order to make them more effective, redesigned and restructured them. Various schemes have been merged and renamed. Various parts of schemes have been deleted. Various alterations have been made. But inspite of all such exercises, the review reports have always been disappointing. Our IRDP and JRY are the examples. More recently, Jawahar Gram Samridhi Yojana (JGSY) was introduced in April 1999 as a successor of JRY. Similarly, Swarna Jayanti Gram Swarozgar Yojana (SGSY) was also introduced in April 1999, which is the combined and restructured shape of IRDP and allied Programmes along with Million Well Schemes (MWS) into single Self-Employment programmes. Employment Assurance Schemes (EAS) has been extended to coverall 5449 rural blocks of the country situated in draught prone, desert, tribal and hill areas. The primary objective is the creation of additional wage employment opportunities during the period of acute shortage of wage employment through manual work for the rural poor living below the poverty line. But our past experience reveals that the ultimate results of such changes, alterations, deletions and mergers have been impressive. Such programming have been discussed as below.

FOOD FOR WORK PROGRAMME

The programme that laid emphasis on the generation of employment opportunities particularly for the weaker sections of the rural communities of creation of infrastructural facilities in the rural areas was the Government's Food for Work Programme (FWP). The programme was launched in 1977 to provide opportunities for work for the rural poor in the slack employment periods of the year which would, at the same time, create durable community assets. The Food for Work Programme (FWP) was conceived early in 1977 and formally launched in April 1977. The basic objectives of the programme were to generate additional employment in rural areas and create durable community assets which would strengthen the rural infrastructure. The workers were paid in food grains for the job done by them. At the time the programme was conceived, there was a huge stock of over 15 million tonnes of food grains. The FWP met with success in the first three years, though certain shortcomings in the programme had been pointed out by the Project Evaluation Organisation of the Planning Commission. There was, however, a certain slackness in its operation during 1980-81, when the generation of employment in terms of mandays recorded a steep decline over the two previous years. In view of the shortcoming of, and the need for, improving the system, the programme was launched in July 1980 as the National Rural Employment Programme, and made an integral part of the Sixth Plan.

Though the Food for Work Programme was launched for the first time, it was not unique in India, for it has been implemented in Egypt, Bangladesh, Pakistan, Peru, Indonesia, the Dominican Republic, Morocco, Kenya, Senegal and Sierra Leone. It has also been taken up in Sri Lanka and the Philippines, though on a smaller scale. However, it is only in India that the programme has been evaluated for the first time.

In the first year of the programme, i.e., 1977-78 a total quantity of 1.27 lakh metric tonnes of foodgrains was landed over as wages. The total employment generated during the period was 44.43 milllion mandays. During the Second Year (1978-79), the utilisation of foodgrains under the programme went upto 12.47 lakh metric tonnes, and the employment generated was nearly 356 million mandays. In 1979-80, most successful year so far, when the country experienced a severe drought, a much higher allocation of food grains at 28 lakh metric tonnes was made under the programme. The actual utilisation in that year was 23.74 lakh tonnes, and the employment generated was reported to be nearly 533.6 million mandays. It was anticipated that in 1979-80, 650 million mandays of employment would have been created. Despite the commendable objectives and the merits of the programme, during the period of three years in its operation a number of defects or shortcomings were also identified. The programme was, therefore, suitably modified and restructured. Accordingly, Food for Work Programme has been redesigned and called as the National Rural Employment Programme (NREP).[2]

INTEGRATED RURAL DEVELOPMENT PROGRAMME (IRDP)

This was launched in 1978-79 with its three clearly defined objectives, namely:

(i) Growth and production;
(ii) Benefits to the identified target group in the disadvantaged sections of the rural community; and
(iii) Full employment within a certain time frame. In fact, this has been a single most important programme for the improvement of the lot of the rural poor. The genesis of this programme was two-fold; first, the failure of beneficiary-oriented programme especially launched during the Fourth Five Year Plan to facilitate the rural poor to generate their income above the poverty line and second, there was large scale poverty in rural areas having at least 40 per cent of the rural households below the poverty line. This proportion has remained undiminished despite the inconsiderable growth in aggregate national income as well as in the rural sector.

As such, based on the past experiences of various beneficiary-oriented programmes particularly SFDA and MFAL the Planning Commission, in its Draft Sixth Plan, 1978-83 (revised), reviewed the approach to rural development, especially with reference to the poor. It visualised an integrated plan of development at the block level, within which a special beneficiary-oriented plan for the poor was to be appropriately fitted. In this context, the Draft Plan said: "The imperative laid for the plan for rural areas of the country is increasing productivity through a strategy of growth with social justice and providing full employment to the rural sector within a ten years time frame. As a comprehensive strategy and approach for translating these objectives into specific programmes the Integrated Rural Development now contemplated involves a multipronged attack on the problems of rural development. 'Integrated' here covers four principal dimensions: integration of sectoral programmes, spatial integration, integration of social and economic processes, and above all the policies with a view to achieving a better fit among growth, removal of poverty and employment generation. More specifically, it involves a sharp focus on target groups comprising small and marginal farmers, agricultural labourers and rural artisans and an extremely location specific planning in the rural areas. As spelt out in the manual on IRDP, the then Ministry of Rural Reconstruction, Government of India (January 1980), the broad components of the strategy envisaged are: the identification of the rural poor based on certain target group parameters; "selection of an annual target of about 600 families from these identified rural poor and provision of some suitable production assets to them through financial assistance (loan plus subsidy); comprehensive block level planning for agricultural, industrial, social and infrastructural development based on local needs and resources and minimum needs programme and integration of target groups programmes with the overall block development programmes".[3]

The Sixth Plan further stated that in these blocks the endeavour will be to secure full employment in the course of five years through a dearly designed plan of development of local resource potential and productivity, with special emphasis being given to specific beneficiary-oriented programmes. Antyodaya approach will be followed in the identification of beneficiaries starting from the weakest and the most needy among those below the poverty lines.[4]

The specific beneficiary-oriented schemes for the rural poor were to be set within the block plan, in the sense that these schemes had to be consistent with and form an integral part of the total plan for the block. As such, the block level plan was given the top priority while formulating and executing the IRDP. This conceived the concept of planning from below in which efforts were made to initiate a process of participative planning and implementation at the grass-root level. The planning phase was, thus, divided into three steps: (i) compilation of integrated resources inventory; (ii) preparation of draft action plans and undertaking amalady remedy analysis; and (iii) selecting appropriate programmes with the involvement of local community.[5]

According to the guidelines provided, IRD programme at the micro-levels should provide gainful employment, applied science and technology for optimum use of local resources and be simple enough to operate and economically viable. The pilot projects should aim at securing long-term benefits and that all the various programmes should be integrated. Keeping in view these rationales and approaches block plan for overall rural development the programme of Integrated Rural Development was started with effects from October 2, 1980 in all the 5011 blocks of the country. While formulating programme dichotomy between the small farmers agencies and the IRD agencies has also been done away with, as a result, there is now a single IRDP and this has taken over the beneficiary-oriented components even of DPAP.

In order to manage the programme effectively, a new district-level agency has come up in all districts in the country called as the District Rural Development Agency. It is to work under the guidance and supervision of a broad-based committee headed at some places by the Divisional Commissioner and at others, by the District Magistrate. All departments of the Government connected with rural development as well as co-operative societies, panchayat bodies and public men are represented in this committee.

The implementation of the programme was started with taking up 30 lakh families for the year 1981-82 to bring them above the poverty line. A sum of Rs. 125 crore was earmarked for the year, 1981-82 for this programme.[6]

Recently, an important appraisal of IRDP was undertaken by Rath-based on the long review of the IRDP experience the pointed out clearly on fact that the strategy of helping the poor in rural society to get over poverty with the help of assets given to them, is largely misconceived. Only a small proportion could be helped; what is equally true, is that only a very small proportion can be helped in this manner. Putting more burden on this approach will discredit the line of attack, generate wastage, corruption and ultimately cynicism. In a multipronged attack on rural poverty this approach surely has a legitimate place, but a programme.

Commenting Indira Hiraway in her discussion on the findings of Rath's study for owing major grounds on which Rath criticises IRDP: (i) IRDP is not an integrated programme in the real sense of the term. That is, it does not integrate resource-based or sectoral planning with household-based planning. IRDP is merely a household-based plan whose central attention is on the identification of the rural poor and preparing a plan for these individual beneficiaries. (ii) The Antyodaya approach of IRDP which aims at giving self-employment to the poorest households of the rural society is not a realistic approach as these households are the least capable of taking up self-employment. Most of these households are of the aged and the handicapped persons or the Boor who have little enterprise or risk bearing capacity. Studies on IROP also have shown that these households have framed the worst in various schemes. (iii) The subsidy element of IRDP has encouraged corruption in rural areas and has raised indebtedness of the poor in many cases. (iv) Gains of IRDP have not percolated to the lowest levels. Quoting from the NABARD study, Rath points out that hardly 18.7 per cent of the total beneficiaries have crossed the poverty line. (v) Our economy does not have enough productive assets for distribution to the poor under IRDP. Consequently, many times assets with very low productivity are given to the poor under the programme. This not only does help the proof, but it positively harms them. Rath, therefore, concludes that the IRDP strategy is largely misconceived. It is capable of helping only a very small number. He argues that putting more burden on this approach will discredit the line of attack, generate wastage, corruption and ultimately cynicism.[7]

Though in a multipronged attack on rural poverty this approach has a legitimate place, it cannot be the mainstay of such a programme. According to Rath, the strategy of massive wage employment generation alone can be the mainstay of the programme.

According to the 32nd round of the NSS, 62.52 per cent of the rural working force in India is self-employed in agricultural and non-agricultural sectors put together. This implies that self-employment is a major form of employment in rural India and the family unit is the most common production unit. Will it be realistic then, to base the rural development programmes on wage employment? It seems that even if one wants to change the form of production from family to non-family, it will not be desirable to ignore the needs of the self-employed or of the family units as such a process will take a long time. Self-employment is thus supposed to be a major form of employment in our economy for at least sometime to come.

In this context, it will be desirable to distinguish between two categories of poor: (i) those who have at least some asset or some skill, education or enterprise to take up self-employment, and (ii) those who neither possess any asset nor have any skill, enterprise, education, etc., to take up any activity independently. The former category is likely to get credit from banks while the latter category may not be considered credit worthy by them. It seems that the poor belonging to the former category should be given assets for self-employment and the latter should be offered wage employment. In other words, the two categories of poor should be treated separately by suitable policy measures.

Corruption on public works programmes has been observed by a number of studies. Misuse of materials, use of substandard materials, paying less than stipulated wages preparing wrong muster rolls, etc., and are reported frequently by these studies. It is also noticed that decisions about NREP works are taken by political leaders without giving any consideration to the extent of poverty and unemployment prevailing in various areas.

In many cases, there is a mis-match between the programmes that are sought to be implemented and the requirements to the region.

An Evaluation of the IRDP, made by Project Evaluation Organisation of the Planning Commission, gives a dismal picture of the ground level implementation of this programme. It has been found that the singular focus of IRDP/NREP/RLEGP has been on meeting targets in terms of financial allocations and the number of beneficiaries covered. The success in terms of job creation and income generation through sustained and durable asset formation has not been satisfactory, being less than 50 per cent.

Regarding the criticisms of IRDP, Mukul in his study, stressed the need to see the IRDP in the correct perspective so that we do not throw out the baby with the bath water.[8]

The current perspective is that the IRDP is an important policy innovation to provide productive assets to the poorest of the poor in order to generate sufficient incomes to raise them above the poverty line. An important ingredient of rural development is the active involvement of the rural poor in all development programmes. There is need for modernising the traditionally-oriented rural cultures through the application of the science and technology. Naturally, rural development requires a very wide ranging and comprehensive set of activities covering all aspects of rural economy and the entire rural population. The main focus is on generation of productive employment for weaker sections. The programme is centred to India's development strategy of growth with redistribution.

Not surprisingly, the major criticism of the programme is conceptual. The subsidy and differential rates of interest have been criticised and have been referred to as charity by those who argue that fundamental changes in the relations of production, that is land reforms are a pre-condition for poverty alleviation. However, some criticisms are also noted on the implementation part of the programme especially in the light of classification of the identification of the beneficiary group.[9] A study was based on both the old and new beneficiary pointed out that in the case of old beneficiary there was large evidence of misclassification whereas in the new beneficiary group the proportion of its classification has reduced to a large extent. So far impact of the programme is concerned it has shown potential for increasing employment and income of the beneficiaries. Despite these findings it is worth mentioning that of all the programmes for rural development, the programmes for poverty alleviation are the most difficult to design and implement programmes like the IRDP and the RLEGP seek to target benefits on the poorest, the 'Special publics', that is, groups in special need as well as generate incomes. They are the most complex because they depend on the tandem effects of reliance on infrastructural service facilities provided by the State, the motivation of village level implementers to ensure service delivery and access, as well as a positive response on the part of the 'special publics' to the assistance. The special public cannot be reached through institutional arrangements adopted for the welfare programmes. There are the organisational and administrative weaknesses, both in terms of lack of qualities and trained staff at various levels and organisations, as well as mechanisms to coordinate and integrate between these organisations so as to make the implementation effective. A look at the extent of activities involved in the IRDP would make this amply clear. These include identification of beneficiaries, selection of viable economic activities, procurement of suitable assets, obtaining of loans from banks, inculcating skills in the beneficiaries to operate these assets by training them, ensuring infrastructural support for the activity, marketing of the produce, etc., a whole range varied activities, and what is more important, their integration a very difficult process which is referred to as "backward and forward linkages" and is, if the guidelines are to be believed, to be achieved through exhortations.

An overall reading of the Seventh Plan document leads to summarise that the basic emphasis is on the generation of productive employment rather than the alleviation qf poverty, which was the primary objective of the Sixth Plan. The programme for poverty alleviation should be regarded as supplementing the basic plan for overall economic growth in terms of operating production assets and skills as well as incomes for the poor.[10]

There is no doubt, that the experience gained in the implementation of the programme can further crystallize the philosophy of the contents of the programme,·It can bring about pragmatism in the means adopted to achieve its objectives. It has to be understood, however, that there is no short cut to rural development and rural poverty cannot be washed away in a matter of two to three years. It would be worth while to quote here Kurin's views on IROP that there is nothing singularly bad about the IRDP. Also, it is not a Panacea for our ills. The truth is in between the extremes. In nutshell, the views of two experts regarding the strategy of the IRDP which is the most comprehensive of all the programmes are indicative of divergent ways looking of the same programme. For instance, Rath mentions that the problem of rural poverty is old and massive. The earlier hope of its improvement through percolation of the fruits of general economic growth failed. More land resources could not be made available to the poor. The IRDP experience of giving cattle and other assets has, as we have reviewed, come to little subsidy appears to be its centre of attraction. It could not be otherwise.

Eradication of poverty needs a multipronged strategy. But as things stand the most important indeed the central one, has to be the creation of massive wage employment opportunities for both on private, public account in rural areas then the other programmes will provide opportunities for the able and the enterprising among the poor. It is time resources organisation and skill are directed to this end, if poverty is to be tackled in the decade to come.

Commenting on these views Dantwala has expressed: "The point that if the test of coverage and quality deflections and distortions is adopted for judging the appropriateness of a programme for "Garibi Hatao", there is no firm basis for giving preference either to the benefitiary programmes or wage employment programme. Both are tarred with the same brush. Thus, if a choice is to be made, it should be on the basis of the conceptual content of the programme and its suitability and feasibility for poverty alleviation. More importantly, the choice should be governed by the type of society and social relations. We visualise toemerge as a consequence of the plans and programmes.[11]

In the Seventh Plan (1985:90), it is stated that "in formulating the employment strategy, a key role has to be assigned to the growth of the agricultural sector. A steady growth in agricultural production through the expansion of irrigation, increases in cropping intensity and the extension of new agricultural technologies to low productivity regions could create a large volume of additional employment because these means have a high potential for labour absorption".

"The growth rate of employment generating during the Sixth Plan period works out to be 4.32 per cent per annum. The employment programmes provide an interesting instance of a gradual erosion in the capacity of the ruling groups to keep the strategy for the poor pegged at the minimal level. The self-employment programmes, the need is felt to commission projects in public works as part of anti-poverty programmes to generate employment and thereby to provide supplementary incomes to the agricultural labour.

According to Dandekar and Rath, the generation of employment in public works programme is "the only feasible, and immediately available solution" for the removal of poverty.[12] Dantwala while recognising the importance of public works programmes for employment generation, emphasises that the aim of the programmes should be to develop the areas in such a way that in due course these areas would provide income and employment to all its labour force.[13]

Another major milestone in poverty eradication in the country was the massive programme launched under the central sector for guaranteed employment for the rural poor National Rural Employment Programme. National Rural Employment Programme (NREP)[14] was started in October 1980, replacing the Food for Work programme during the Sixth Five Year Plan. This was implemented as a central sponsored scheme and its actual commencement began from April 1, 1981. The pattern of financing NREP was on 50:50 sharing basis between the Central Government and the State Government.

The Programme had Three-fold Objectives

(a) Generation of additional gainful employment for the unemployed and underemployed persons, both men and women, in the rural areas; (b) Creation of productive community assets for direct and continuing benefits to the poor and for strengthening rural, economic and social infrastructure which will lead to rapid growth of rural economy and steady rise in the income level of the rural poor; and (c) Improvement in the overall quality of life in the rural areas.

Under the provisions of the programme it was made clear that amongst the beneficiaries landless labourers were supposed to get first preference for employment in all works. Amongst them the scheduled castes/scheduled tribes and women were to be given priority for employment. It was decided that works taken up under this programme could be executed during any part of the year but the labour-intensive operation may be concentrated during lean agricultural season.

In order to have an integrated approach at the district level, most of the responsibilities relating to planning, coordination, review, supervision, monitoring and implementation of the programme have been entrusted to District Rural Development Agencies (DRDA). The DRDA is the new implementing agency for execution of the works regarding the rural employment. It will be accountable to the returns/ reports in respect of the works taken up for execution in the district which are to be furnished in time.

The provisions for the implementation of the programme were also vested in the Panchayati Raj Institutions. This has been so because, these bodies have the capabilities of executing the works fulfilling the needs of the people on a decentralised basis and in turn ensure the involvement of the rural people. In the absence of the Panchayati Raj Institutions the village committees were given the task of implementing the programme. In case it is not possible, work should be executed through the block agency. In this collection it was laid down that some funds would be earmarked for implementation of the programme by NGO (non-Government Organisations) through People's Action for Development (India).

The priorities of works taken up under the programme has been provided in the guidelines. Accordingly, any rural work which results in creation of durable productive community assets can be taken up under this programme. Preference may be given to works having potential of maximum direct and continuing benefits to the weaker groups, which are or can be owned by or assigned to groups of beneficiaries either for direct use of assets to ensure continuing income to the groups. Also higher priority should be given to work which are acquired for infrastructure of poverty alleviation programmes like DPAP, IRDP and construction of primary school buildings particularly in those villages which have primary schools without buildings. Other works that can be taken up are; social without forestry works on government and community lands belonging to panchayats etc., soil and water conservation works, minor irrigation works, flood protection, drainage and waterlogging works, rural water supply works and construction/renovation of village tanks for providing water for human use for cattle or for irrigation or pisciculture; irrigation wells; sanitary latrines; houses for scheduled castes/scheduled tribes, rural link roads, etc. The outline of the projects was prepared for each district/block based on the needs of the rural people, so that village community should be involved in its preparation. It should be drawn up for the whole plan period. The preparation of the draft of the projects has to be a continuous process and these are to be reviewed every year. On the basis of the self, an annual plan for the district is to be prepared every year. The criterion for the allocation of resources for the states and union territories has been as follows: 75 per cent weightage is given to the incidence of poverty in states/union territories. In turn states/union territories are required to allocate resources to the districts on the same basis. In case the figures regarding the incidence of poverty are not available, 25 per cent weightage should be given to the number of persons belonging to the scheduled castes and, scheduled tribes in the districts. To improve the nutritional standards of the rural poor families, one kilogram of foodgrains per day is required to be given to workers as a part of their wages. For the convenience of the workers, payment of wages is to be made on a fixed day of the week which would preferably have the local market day. Payment is not to be delayed by more than a week except at the option of the workers and in latter case for not more than 15 days. In the areas where coarse grains like jowar, bajra are popular among the rural poor are permitted to be utilised under the programme, provided the state governments/union territories concerned procure the same at the local level. Other commodities such as cloth, edible oils, fuel may be given as a part of wage to the workers. In the draft 10 per cent of the resources of the programme are invariably earmarked for words of direct and exclusive benefits to the Scheduled Castes/Scheduled Tribes. The States/Union Territories, however, agree to utilise more resources than earmarked for this sector. But the earmarked allocation cannot be diverted to the other sectors.

The social forestry works have also been given due importance with rural employment programme. As such, 25 per cent of the resources are earmarked for utilisation on social forestry projects. The resources will be released so that 20 per cent of the allocations are in cash and 5 per cent in the form of food grains. The allocation to the extent of 5 per cent can be used for promoting decentralised nursery. Formulation of social forestry projects is to be done in consultation with Panchayati Raj Institutions such as gram panchayats. Selection and location of works are to be done after ascertaining the opinion of the local community through Gram Sabha meetings.

Under this programme the ratio between the material and the wage component of works taken up has been fixed at the 50:50 ratio respectively. This ratio is applicable both for individual works and district/State as a whole. Non-wage component comprises the cost of materials, administrative and supervisory expenses, cost of equipment, etc.

NREP fund cannot be taken as a substitute for departmental funds of different sectoral activities in the district. It can be linked up with other rural development programmes like IRDP, DPAP, TRYSEM, DIC, so that these programmes supplement and complement each other. For planning, implementation and monitoring of the programme at the state level, a state level co-ordination committee has been set-up. A representative of the Department of Rural Development, Government of India is invited to participate in the meetings of this committee. At the district level, DRDA is responsible for planning, coordinating, monitoring and reviewing the programme.

The assets created under the programme are taken over by the regular department/corporation/agency of the State Government and are also maintained out of the budgeted fund of these agencies.

Necessary allocation for this purpose is made in the state budget in different sectors. For maintenance of assets for which maintenance funds and systems are ordinarily not available, DRDA is responsible for 10 per cent of district allocation as being utilised for the maintenance of these assets. Contractor's are not permitted to be engaged for execution of works under this programme. No middlemen or any such intermediate agency is allowed for executing works under the programme so that the full benefits of wages do not go up on account of commission agency. An annual Action Plan for the district is prepared and approved by DRDA on the basis of the Projects before the start of the financial year. The district action plan is divided into blockwise and section-wise component. Each block and executing agency furnish their component plans to the DRDAs which facilitates in finalising the annual action plan for the district in the beginning of the year. In the preparation process, priority is given to completion of the incomplete works instead of taking up new works. It also indicates the department, agency/organisation responsible for the maintenance of the works and the financial arrangement made for this. Works approved by DRDA are taken up only after the notification which provides basic details of the works viz. cost, date of completion, employment generation, benefits likely to accrue, and groups to be benefited. Such information is furnished to the concerned gram panchayat, block, committee besides being displayed at the DRDA office.

As stated earlier, the programme was started functioning since the beginning of the Sixth Five Year Plan. During this plan period, an outlay of Rs. 1620 crores in both central and state sectors were provided. However, during the plan period the amount which was actually released was Rs. 1873 crores, while allocating the resources the important works for employment generation to be taken up were related to infrastructural facilities, construction works and social fores try.

Following the target of employment generation of 300 to 400 million mandays per almum, the achievement during the period from 1980-81 to 1985-86 was 413.58, 354.52, 302.76, 352.31 and 13 million mandays of employment each year. It can be observed from the achievement trend that there has been substantial reduction in employment generation in 1981-82 and marginal decline in 1982-83 and 1983-84. A study done on the performance and prospects of the National Rural Employment Programme has indicated the following factors for its partial achievement: (a) the quantitative and qualitative checks applied for proper implementation of the programme prevented the implementing agencies in taking up unplanned kutcha earth works as they were doing under Food for Work Programme; (b) with the diversification of work taken up under NREP, there is general declining trend in taking up kutcha earth work; (c) in material component of schemes, the States/Union Territories were allowed to utilise up to 40 per cent of the project cost to ensure the durability of assets created (later relaxed and made applicable to district as a whole). In mid-1983-84, the decision was taken to revive the earlier wage-material ratio from 60:40 to 50:50, so the availability of funds under wages component in the programme declined in percentage terms; (d) there was a rise in the wages payable to the workers in several states; and (e) cost of material inputs have increased over the years. These factors have limited the generation of additional employment opportunities to the expected desire under the programme.

The objectives of employment generation are further supplemented under the programme by strengthening the rural infrastructure creating durable community assets. As such, large number of assets have been created by the programme in different States/Union Territories. The allocation of 10 per cent is earmarked for works directly benefiting the scheduled castes/schedule tribes such as wells for drinking water and construction of group houses. Earth works are most popular under the programme. It comprises the construction of village tanks, minor irrigation works, soil and water conservation works and rural roads. The highest employment generation is found in this category of works. During the Sixth Plan period, the village tank construction was 0.54 lakh numbers, minor irrigation work on 9.32 lakh hectares, soil conservation, etc., for 5.14 lakh hectares, irrigation wells etc., 4.80 lakh numbers, rural roads 4.45 lakh kilometers. The earth works are well spread in the countryside right from the days of Food for Work Programme. However, the construction works like schools, balwadi buildings, panchayat ghars during the Sixth Plan period are made to the total number of 4.3 lakh. These works obviously involve heavy expenditure and take long duration for completion. Some problems creep in this type of work and violation of guidelines is also found occasionally. Besides the construction works another important component of the programme is social forestry. It start up with the outlay of 10 per cent of the allocation made under the programme which increased to 20 per cent in 1985-86 and 25 per cent in 1986-87. However, the afforestation and social forestry works suffered a setback due to widespread drought conditions in 1982-83 and increase in wage rates during 1984-85.

On the basis of the evaluation studies done by the Government as well as the non-government agencies it can be concluded that the programme has not succeeded in achieving its objectives of employment generation. Nevertheless, its importance in generating employment opportunities especially for the weaker sections of the society cannot be undermined. The need is, therefore, to implement the programme vigorously to make it all pervasive concerning all sectors and constituting important aspects of the rural economy and concerning all sections of the weaker people.

Rural Landless Employment Guarantee Programme during the Sixth Plan, it was visualised that the hardcore rural poverty, particularly that pertaining to the unemployment of the landless labourers during the lean agricultural season, had to be tackled in a more direct manner. Accordingly, new scheme called Rural Landless Employment Gurantee Programme (RLEGP) was introduced in 1983. The basic objectives of the programme are: (i) to improve and expand employment opportunities for rural landless with a view to providing guarantee of employment to at least one member every landless labour household up to 100 days in a year; and (ii) creation of durable assets for strengthening the rural infrastructure which will lead to rapid growth of the rural economy. The programme was fully funded by the Central Government while the overall responsibility of planning, and supervision, monitoring and implementation of the work projects under the programme rests with the State Governments. The criteria for allocation of funds to the State under the programme were based on the number of agricultural workers, marginal farmers and incidence of poverty. The programme had the stipulation that the wage component in the total cost of a project should not be less than 50 per cent and that the wage rate paid to the labourers has to be fixed at the statutory minimum level.

Though the programme is called employment guarantee programme, there is no provision for unemployment allowance either in kind or in cash for those landless agricultural labourers who fail to get the stipulated employment under the programme.

The obvious indications of the sidelining of the poor are: (i) contrary to the provisions of RLEGP, the works under the schemes are often assigned to contractors who choose their own labourers; (ii) the officials not check to find out how far the local target groups avail of the employment generated in the schemes; (iii) with numerous departments involved in the implementation of RLEGP, it is doubtful that any attempt is made in the programme to tailor the schemes according to the seasonal and spatial profile of the employment needs of the landless, and (iv) finally, RLEGP adopts a uniform wage rate rather than a wage rate decided in the light of the wage prevailing in different localities and the gap between the income of the landless and poverty line income.

Under the programme, the projects are formulated on works relevant to the 20-point programme and the Minimum Needs Programme. A central committee at the level of Union Government approved projects prepared by States/Union Territories. The approved projects are implemented through agencies of State/Union Territories governments including DRDA. The State government has the overall responsibility for planning, supervising, monitoring and implementation of the projects taken up under the programme. Even amongst 20-point programme and MNP activities the work projects would be restricted to the following important activities.

(i) Social forestry works; (ii) soil and water conservation works; (iii) minor irrigation works such as construction of irrigation wells, construction of intermediary and main drains and field channels etc.; (iv) food protection, drainage and water logging works; (v) rural water supply works and construction/renovation of village tanks for providing water for human use or for cattles or for irrigation, pisciculture; (vi) irrigation wells, fields, channels, land shaping and other land development works on individual holdings of members of SC/ST and allottees of ceiling surplus land, bhoodan land, provided they are below poverty line; (vii) construction of primary school buildings on high priority in those revenue villages which have primary school without buildings of their own; and (viii) land development and reclamation of waste lands or degraded land with special emphasis on ecological improvement in hill and desert areas.

It may be pointed out that though these programmes are at present largely weighed towards providing short-term employment to the rural unskilled labour they fall short even in this respect. The main reason for this is that the criteria, at present, which qualify a work/project for selection as a labour intensive project is that the wage and non-wage ratio should be 50:50. Thus, the wage component should be at least 50 per cent of the total cost. However, in the existing programme no distribution has been made between the wages of skilled labour that can be employed such as masons, carpenters and even road roller operators (provided that they are on daily wages and are not departmental employees) and the unskilled manual labour that the target group, i.e., the rural poor, particularly the agricultural labourers, can provide. As a result of this, the employment content of these programmes is reduced and it is possible to have projects works which require skilled workers and whose requirement of unskilled workers is negligible. In addition under the NREP this criterion is to be applied at the level of the district.[15] Thus, this requirement can be satisfied, for instance, by constructing a building with hardly any employment benefits for unskilled labour in one area of the district and compensating for this by taking up a totally employment-oriented work with hardly any expenditure on materials in another area. This can, therefore, result in distortions with hardly any employment given to one part of the district while the assets created in the other part of the district are not likely to be durable. In both these programmes the guidelines stipulate that the wages are to be paid partly in cash and partly in the form of foodgrains at the rate of 1 kg per manday of employment. The reason behind this is that the provision of wage goods is ensured and the inflationary effects of a public works programme reduced.

A few sample studies have been carried out by the Planning Commission on the working of the programme. The studies have noted that in addition to stabilising the wage rates, the programme has been able to create durable community assets and generate employment. However, some weaknesses too have been observed in the implementation of the programme.

The Department of Rural Development is restructuring the two programmes of wage employment viz., NREP/RLEGP in a manner that most of the weaknesses observed in the programme so far are eliminated. In order to bring about simultaneous instantaneous corrections a management information system, comprising closer supervision, better monitoring and quick feedback in the implementation of the programme has been attempted. Training of Youth for Self-Employment Part experience of the district level planning shows that in most cases the local people were almost completely excluded from the exercise. The reason lies in the old-dated and outdated attitude of officials and experts who consider the people as more beneficiaries rather than participants. It is well realised that upliftment of the poor is not an easy task. As already indicated; it not only involves provision of services from outside for fulfilling their needs but also the development of a feeling of self-reliance in them. One must have full knowledge of human resources and human problems, and village power structure, the exploitation of one class by another, the factional politics and also the value system of the people. The established relationship based on feudal, caste and class hierarchy may be too well entrenched for any plan to succeed. The development of special groups and minorities such as women, scheduled castes and tribes, the small and marginal farmers and the landless requires special attention and knowledge on the part of the planners. People's involvement in planning could complement the knowledge of the planners and, therefore, may be carefully promoted and maintained. The main vehicle of social action leading towards this goal will have to be based on specially motivated sections of the people such as youths and others. Liberal and enlightened elements of the population who would participate in these programmes even if they go against their class interests.

The then Ministry of Rural Reconstruction carried the responsibility of employment generation in the rural areas. For the purpose of evolving a suitable strategy to be followed to provide full employment in rural areas, the rural society could be broadly divided into three district segments: (i) the large unskilled manpower below the poverty line, (ii) semi-educated and educated persons below the poverty line, and (iii) educated unemployed youth of families above the poverty lines.[16]

For each category, a separate programme has been drawn up in order to generate employment opportunities in the rural areas. For the first category consisting of those who are capable of putting in manual labour only and urgently need two square meals, the erstwhile Food for Work Programme, now replaced by the National Rural Employment Programme is the ready answer. The programme has three objectives which are as follows: (i) generation of additional gainful employment for the unemployed and under-employed persons, both men and women in the rural areas; (ii) creation of durable community assets for strengthening the rural infrastructure, which will lead to rapid growth of rural economy and steady rise in the income levels of the rural poor, and (iii) improvement in the nutritional status and the living standards of the rural poor.

Following the objectives of the TRYSEM it appears that it should be treated as a part of IRDP especially meant for unemployed rural youths to embark upon a career of self-employment. Thus, the saliant features of the programme introduced on 15th August 1979, are: (i) Equipping the rural youth in the age group of 18-35 from families below the poverty line with technical and managerial skills to enable them to take up self-employment ventures in agriculture and allied activities, industries, services and business, (ii) Providing basic income generating investment to TRYSEM trainees.

Every TRYSEM trainee is thus a potential beneficiary of IRDP. The skill inputs provided under TRYSEM lead to higher productivity, (iii) Group production and service activities also stand to gain in productivity through TRYSEM inputs. The linkage between IRDP and TRYSEM ensures higher income per unit investment made under the programme. The distinct shift from primary to secondary sector under IRDP has further highlighted the importance of skill endowment and upgradation of TRYSEM; (iv) Priority is given to rural youth from scheduled castes/scheduled tribes. Their minimum coverage should be 30 per cent; (v) Coverage of women should be at least 33.33 per cent. The scope of TRYSEM is to train at least two lakh rural youths every year in the country and offer them facilities for self-employment during the Sixth-Plan. The scheme is to cover all the development blocks, 50 educated youth per year is to be selected in the age group 18-35 years from among those who have passed at least matriculation or an equivalent examination. The scheme has also a provision for a short-term training course not exceeding six months in technical skills relevant for rural areas, facilities of tools and equipments, finance, raw materials, and marketing of finished goods. A proper mechanism for vocational, guidance and counselling services to the students in the schools and colleges is also being developed under the scheme. On completion of the training, margin/seed money up to a maximum of Rs. 5000 would be advanced as loan from government to settle the trained youth in projects of self-employment. The difference between IRD and non-IRD blocks was removed from April 1, 1981. Therefore, TRYSEM has now been implemented as an integral part of the IRD programme and constitutes that part of which concerns the training of rural youth between ages 18-35 for self-employment avocations. The strategy for training of youth is that all modes of training are accepted. Apart from institutional training camp also be given through local servicing and industrial units, master craftsmen, artisans and skilled workers.[17]

During the course of training, the following financial is permissible: (a) a stipend up to Rs. 100 per trainee per month; (b) training expenses up to Rs. 50 per trainee per month to be given to the trainer; (c) a reward of Rs. 50 per trainee per course only in the case of individual master craftsmen/trainers; and (d) a sum of Rs. 100 for raw materials per trainee for the course. During the course of training, the trainees are helped to prepare project reports, which are converted into bankable schemes. They are helped to apply for bank loans and subsidies. Subsidies throughout the country are on the IRD pattern and have a maximum limit of Rs. 3,000 per trainee. The entire expenditure on the scheme is shared on 50:50 basis by the State and the Centre. A sum of Rs. 72.57 lakh was released to different States and Union Territories during 1979-80 and amount of Rs. 3.39 lakh has been released up to December 31, 1980, during 1980-81.[18]

Under TRYSEM, 16.40 lakh rural youth have been trained in the Sixth and Seventh Plan period upto September 1988. Out of these 5.92 lakh youth belong to scheduled castes/scheduled tribes. 6.17 lakh women were trained during the period, 7.78 lakh trained youth have been self-employed and 1.66 lakh youth employed on wages. Thus, a total number of 9.40 lakh trained youth have been employed since the inception of the scheme.[19]

However, training of rural women for productive vocations has not been given proper attention in the past. The most important part of the training programme is the identification of various fields and sectors of activity where there is considerable scope for gainful self-employment. This is best done at the district/block level, since any identification of the course of training would have to be related to the local needs and potentialities. State government may develop a suitable mechanism of: (a) identification of opportunities for gainful self-employment in different blocks, and (b) linking up the training programme with post-training services including credit and marketing.

Thus, in the detailed framework of the TRYSEM scheme the essential steps involved are: (i) careful identification of opportunities for gainful self-employment based on an economic analysis of the developmental assets and liabilities of each block; (ii) designing programmes which will help to impart the requisite skills, and identification of institutions which can impart; (iii) organisation of post-training services such as subsidy, credit and marketing arrangements; and (iv) organisation of training programmes in such a way that the training institution serves the need for continuing education of the trainee and acts like an umbilical cord between the training institution and the trainee.[20] Under this framework it was expected that the scheme would be able to train rural unemployment youth and thus prepare them for adopting successfully the self-employment schemes.[21]

NATIONAL RURAL EMPLOYMENT GUARANTEE ACT (NREGA)

NREGA now known as MNREGA is a great income security scheme for rural people. It came into force in 2006 in Indias 200 most backward districts in 2007 it was extended to another 130 districts and with effect from April 1, 2008 it is to cover all the districts Rs. 39,100 crores was provided for this scheme in 2009-10. It has been enhanced to Rs. 40,100 crores in the year 2010-11. At implementation level there are many weaknesses in this program like lack of professional staffs, project planning, transparency, social audit and other irregularities.

TABLE

District-wise Financial Allotment for NREGA in Bihar (in crores) for the year (2006-07)

Sl. No.	*District*	*Amount*	*Sl. No.*	*District*	*Amount*
1.	Arariya	11.62	13.	Munger	20.00
2.	Aurangabad	20.00	14.	Mujaffarpur	20.00
3.	Bhojpur	18.12	15.	Nalanda	20.00
4.	Darbhanga	20.00	16.	Nawada	16.92
5.	Gaya	20.00	17.	Patna	20.00
6.	Jamui	18.91	18.	Purniya	9.96
7.	Jahanabad	20.20	19.	Rohatas	19.92
8.	Kamoor	15.96	20.	Samastipur	20.00
9.	Katihar	20.00	21.	Shivahar	11.88
10.	Kishanganj	10.36	22.	Supaul	19.87
11.	Lakhisarai	11.47	23.	Vashali	20.00
12.	Madhubani	20.00		Total	405.00

Source : Millennium Development Goals and Bihar, published by VSSSSESS, Patna, p. 24 by Prakash Luice.

The table clearly indicates that Rs. 405 crores had been sent to Bihar in April 2006 for twenty-three districts in the first phase to implement this massive rural employment scheme.

Jawahar Rojgar Yojana

In the preceding part of the chapter several programmes for alleviation of the poverty through generating employment and income opportunities for the poor has been discussed. All these programmes were implemented in each and every block of the country. The scheme chosen reflected local aspirations and local needs. However, it is not necessary that a particular scheme should suit each and every block, district and the country. It has been observed that NREP, RLEGP schemes are not required every where, especially in areas where existing wages are much higher than the minimum wages. In many areas, like the green revolution belts of the country, the people are paid much higher wages on NREP/RLEGP and the records are manipulated to show that larger number of mandays have been generated. In such areas these schemes degenerate into target achieving exercises. So what is basically required is the choice of schemes. A district can be given funds on the basis of population; per capita income, poverty ratio, etc., and then the district should be left free to participate in those schemes which best meet its requirements.[22]

In order to make the employment-oriented programme more effective it was proposed to merge the two main existing programmes NREP and RLEGP into a single programme and to decentralise its implementation. The merged programme will operate throughout the country and will be funded 75 per cent by the centre.

However, it is conceded in the budget speech that the existing employment schemes fall short of the needs, especially because poverty and unemployment are intense in certain disadvantaged regions. A new intensive rural employment programme named after Pandit Jawaharlal Nehru has been proposed for 120 backward districts suffering from acute unemployment. The funds for this scheme will be besides those available in the district under NREP and RLEGP programmes. All these resources will be merged to take up locally useful schemes to maximize employment opportunities while creating productive assets.[23] Thus, a massive monolithic employment programme called "Jawahar Rojgar Yojana" was announced on 28th April, 1989. It was a comprehensive project in which the earlier "anti-poverty" measures, such as IRDP, NREP were proposed to be merged with, perhaps, a little more financial backing than the earlier measures enjoyed. It would undoubtedly benefit those who could avail themselves of it and, if programmes are wisely selected, it can benefit the community by augmenting facilities, such as tube-wells, roads, small irrigation schemes, etc., where they are most needed. The scheme was proposed to be implemented and administered by village Panchayats all over the country. It was also decided that 440 lakh families which are below the poverty line will be given benefits from this scheme. As a strategy, the scheme was expected to give employment to at least one member of each poor rural family for 50 to 100 days in a year in the vicinity of places of their residence. It was also expected that some integrated schemes will be introduced to provide employment among nomadic tribe. Provisions were made that 15 year of total resources transferred to village panchayats will be exclusively used for the benefit of the scheduled castes and scheduled tribes. The state governments will supply some model schemes to the village Pradhans for their guidance. Among the selected beneficiaries 30 per cent will be from women. In regard to the financial provisions 80 per cent and 20 per cent of total finances will be borne by the central and State Governments respectively. A sum of Rs. 2625 crores were earmarked for the total allocation.

The funds will be allotted to the state and union territories in proportion to the number of persons living below the poverty line. The allocation of funds to districts will be determined in terms of criteria of backwardness such as the share of scheduled castes and scheduled tribes in total population of the district, the share of agricultural labour to the total labour force and the level of agricultural productivity. It has also been decided to give specific consideration to such areas as the hills, deserts and the islands. The criteria for the distribution of resources to village Panchayats from the districts will be on the basis of population of each village panchayat. If the population is less than 1000, then it will be assumed 1000 for the allocation of 3000 to 4000 will be able to receive in grant between Rs. 80,000 to Rs. 1,00,000.

During 1989-90, central allocations/rebates of Rs. 2100 crores (including the value of foodgrains) were made to states/union territories for implementation of Jawahar Rojgar Yojna. The total allocation/released under JRY for the year 1989-90 was Rs. 2623.08 crores including state's share of 523.08 crores. Against this, the total utilization of resources up to December 1989 was Rs. 1195.77 crores, the percentage utilization being 52.28 per cent.

According to an estimation the employment generated under the scheme during 1989-90 (up to December, 1989) was 456;62 million mandays as against the assumed target of 873.41 million mandays. The employment generation for scheduled castes/scheduled tribes, landless and women was roughly 38 per cent, 15 per cent, 44.22 per cent and 23.15 percent respectively.[24]

"A new scheme of construction of irrigation wells for scheduled castes/scheduled tribes, called Million Well Schemes was introduced during 1988-89 for a period of 2 years as a sub-scheme of NREP/ RLEGP. The scheme seeks to provide open irrigation wells, free of cost, to small and marginal farmers belonging to scheduled castes and scheduled tribes who are below the poverty line and are listed in IRDP register of the target group. The scheme is confined to open wells only and does not cover boring and tube-wells. The unit cost of wells dug under this scheme is to be as per NABARD norms. The scheme has continued under JRY and its expenditure is met out per cent resources earmarked for scheduled castes/scheduled tribes. Twenty States and Union Territories in the country have failed to provide even 50 percent of the targeted employment under the JRY during 1989-90.[25]

The criteria of allocation of resources at village panchayat level should be the same as it is at the state level. On account of other factors the intensity of poverty differs from one villager to another. The population poverty of scheduled castes and scheduled tribes generally constituents the poorest section of the society but their condition is not uniform in every village. A list of households below the poverty line, describing their means of livelihood, income, etc., should be prepared at the village level and on the basis of this allocation of resources should be made.

PRIs are not competent to formulate the plans entirely by themselves and then to execute the same because expertise is not available to these institutions. It is therefore, suggested that expert body be constituted to assist them to formulate, execute and monitor the plans for the benefit of rural areas. It is feared that without this the huge resources may not be used optimally. As per provision of the scheme that blocks will provide the technical assistance to the village panchayats but the blocks themselves are not resources endowed to suggest plan for every village panchayat. The essential infrastructural excercise has to be done before releasing the funds to the village panchayat. Without an effective administrative control it is not possible to check on the funds given to the villages, consequently, as a result projects selected for the target groups may not give the desired benefits to them.

Despite all these weaknesses JRY is very important scheme in alleviating distress arising out of poverty, specially in the years of scarcity and drought, and not, as claimed, in eradicating poverty. It is a step in the right direction leading to decentralisation of planning and power. It is a pain-killer, not a cure for the disease of poverty. No doubt, it is a new experiment. Hence, some operational difficulties may crop up in its implementation.

The National Rural Employment Guarantee Scheme (NREGS), was launched in Feb. 2006 in 200 most backward districts in the first phase and later it was expanded to 330 districts during 2007-08. The coverage was extended to all rural districts of India in 2008-09. Currently, 690 districts are under this scheme during 2008-09 above 4.51 crore households were provided employement under this scheme. As against the budgeted outlay of Rs. 39,100 crore for the year 2009-10, an amount of Rs. 24,758.50 crore has been released to the States/ UTs till December 2009. During the year 2009-10, 4.34 crore households have been provided employment under the scheme. Out of the 182.88 crore person days created under the scheme during this period, 29 per cent and 22 per cent were in favour of SC and ST population respectively and 50 per cent in favour of women. Up to December 2009, 36.78 lakh self-help groups (SHGs) had been formed and 132.81 lakh swarozgaris have been assisted with a total investment of Rs. 30,896.08 crore.

SWARNA JAYANTI SHAHARI ROZGAR YOJANA

The Government has recently revamped the SJSRY with effect from April 1, 2009. The scheme provides gainful employment to the urban unemployed and underemployed; poor, by encouraging the setting up of self-employment ventures by the urban poor and also by providing wage employment and utilizing their labour for construction of socially and economically useful public assets. The revamped SJSRY has five components: (a) the Urban Self-Employment Programme (USEP) which targets individual urban poor for setting up of micro-enterprises; (b) the Urban Women Self-help Programme (UWSP) which targets urban poor women self-help groups for setting-up of group enterprises and providing them assistance through a revolving fund for thrift and credit activities; (c) Skill Training for Employment Promotion amongst Urban Poor (STEP-UP) which targets the urban poor for imparting quality training so as to enhance their employability for self-employment or better salaried employment; (d) the Urban Wage Employment Programme (UWEP) which seeks to assist the urban poor by utilizing their labour for the construction of socially and economically useful public assets, in towns having population less than 5 lakh as per the 1991 census; and (e) the Urban Community Development Network (UCDN) which seeks to assist the urban poor in organizing themselves into self-managed community structures so as to gain collective strength to address the issues of poverty facing them and participate in effective implementation of urban poverty-alleviation programmes. Budget allocation for the SJSRY scheme for 2009-10 is Rs. 515.00 crore of which Rs. 363.12 crore had been utilized till December 31, 2009. During 2009-10, as reported by States/UTs, 28,613 urban poor have been assisted to set-up individual enterprises, 13,453 urban poor women have been assisted in setting up group enterprises, 27,463 urban poor women have been assisted through a revolving fund for thrift and credit activities and 85,185 urban poor have been imparted skill training.

Social Protection Programmes

In view of the predominance of informal sector workers in the workforce, there is need for expansion in the scope and coverage of social security schemes for these unorganized workers so that they are assured of a minimum level of social protection. Many measures were taken by the Government of India along these lines.

Aam Admi Bima Yojana (AABY)

Under this scheme launched on October 2, 2007, insurance will be provided against natural as well as accidental death and partial/ permanent disability to the head of the family of rural landless households in the country. Up to September 30, 2009, the Scheme had covered 81.99 lakh lives.

Rashtriya Swasthya Bima Yojana (RSBY)

The RSBY was launched on October 1, 2007 for BPL families (a unit of no more than five) in the unorganized sector. The total sum insured is Rs. 30,000 per family per annum. The premium is shared on a 75:25 basis by the Centre and Hie State Government. In case of north-eastern States and Jammu & Kashmir, the premium is shared in a 90:10 ratio. The beneficiary is entitled to cashless transactions through a smart card. The RSBY became operational from April 1, 2008. Till January 12, 2010, 26 States/Union Territories have initiated the process implementing the scheme. Out of these, 22 States/UTs, namely, Assam, Rajasthan, Haryana, Punjab, New Delhi, Gujarat, Bihar, Andhra Pradesh, Kerala, Maharashtra, Tamil Nadu, Uttar Pradesh, Jharkhand, Uttarakhand, West Bengal, Goa, Nagaland, Chhattisgarh, Meghalaya, Tripura, Orissa and Chandigarh Administration, have started issuing smart cards and more than 97.19 lakh cards have been issued.

The Unorganized Workers' Social Security Act, 2008: The Act has the objective of providing social security to unorganized workers. The Unorganised Workers' Social Security Rules, 2009 have also been framed. The Act has come into force w.e.f. May 16, 2009. It provides for constitution of a National Social Security Board and State Social Security Boards which will recommend Social Security Schemes for these workers. The National Social Security Board has since been constituted and has met twice. The Board has made some recommendations regarding extension of social security schemes to certain additional segments of unorganized workers.

Bilateral Social Security Agreement

Bilateral social security agreements have been signed with Belgium, France, Germany, Switzerland, Luxemburg and Netherlands to protect the interests of expatriate workers and companies on a reciprocal basis. Negotiations for similar agreements with other countries like Check Republic, Norway, Hungary, Denmark, Canada and Republic of Korea have been completed. Negotiations are in progress with several other countries. These agreements help workers by providing exemption from social security contribution in case of posting, totalisation of contribution periods and exportability of pension in case of relocation to the home country or any third country. (*Economic Survey*, 2009-10)

Skill Development[26]

In the Eleventh Five Plan comprehensive skill development programme with Nide coverage throughout the country has been initiated by the Government. The Coordinated Action Plan for Skill Development has a target of 500 million skilled persons by the year 2022. In this regard, a three-tier institutional structure consisting of (i) the Prime Minister's National Council on Skill Development, (ii) the National Skill Development Coordination Board (NSDCB), and (iii) the National Skill Development Corporation (NSDC), has already been set-up to take forward the skill development mission. The NSDCB has addressed to five core areas of skill development, namely, (i) curriculum revision on a continuous basis, (ii) vocational education, (iii) apprenticeship training, (iv) accreditation and certification system, and (v) skill gap mapping. The NSDC has been set up to promote private-sector action for skill development, an institutional arrangement in the form of a non-profit corporation in the Ministry of Finance. The Corporation was registered on July 31, 2008 under Section 25 of the Companies Act, 1956. The National Skill Development Fund (NSDF) was incorporated as a Trust on January 7, 2009 as a receptacle for funds for the NSDC. A sum of Rs. 995.10 crore was subsequently transferred to the Trust. An Investment Management Agreement was concluded between the NSDC and NSDF on March 27, 2009, and a sum of Rs. 200 crore from the overall corpus of the Trust was transferred to the NSDC for implementation of its work programme. The NSDC has been mandated to train about 150 million persons by 2022 under the National Skill Development Policy which is now in place. The NSDC Board has received a large number of proposals for providing funding support for skill development and due diligence in respect of these proposals is under way.

Unique Identification Authority of India[27]

On June 25, 2009 the Cabinet approved the creation of the position of Chairperson, Unique Identification Authority of India (UIDAI). On July 30, 2009 the Prime Minister has also constituted a council under his chairmanship to advice the UIDAI and ensure coordination between the ministries, stakeholders and partners. The council will advice the UIDAI on programme, methodology and implementation to ensure coordination between ministries/ departments, stakeholders and partners. It will also identify specific milestones for early completion of the project. Initiatives like setting up of the UIDAI have been taken to bring in efficiency in the implementation of Government programmes. Once fully operational, the scheme will, besides facilitating financial inclusion, ensure better governance and improved service delivery so that the targeted group of people is actually benefited by the schemes implemented by the Centre and States. Subsequently, the Government constituted a Cabinet Committee on UIDAI on October 22, 2009. The Committee, *inter-alia*, will look into all issues relating to the UIDAI including its organisation, plans, policies, programmes, funding and methodology to be adopted for achieving the objectives of the Authority. The main features of the UIDAI model as per the strategy paper prepared by the UIDAI and broadly endorsed by the Prime Minister's council on the UIDAI are given below.

The UID number will only provide Identity

- The UIDAI's purview will be limited to the issue of unique identification numbers linked to a person's demographic and biometric information. The UID number will only guarantee identity, got rights, benefits or entitlements.
- *The UID will prove identity, not citizenship*: All residents in the country can be issued a unique ID. The UID is proof of identity and does not confer citizenship.
- *A pro-poor approach*: The UIDAI envisions full enrolment of residents, with a focus on enrolling India's poor and underprivileged communities. The Registrars that the Authority plans to partner with in its first phase—the NREGA, RSBYand PDS—will help bring large numbers of the poor and underprivileged into the UID system. The UID method of authentication will also improve service delivery for the poor.
- *Enrolment of residents with proper verification*: Existing identity databases in India are fraught with problems of fraud and duplicate/ghost beneficiaries. To prevent this from seeping into the UIDAI database, the Authority plans to enroll residents into its database with proper verification of their demographic and biometric information. This will ensure that the data collected is clean from the start of the programme. However, much of the poor and underserved population lacks identitj documents, and the UID may be the first form of identification it has access to. The Authority will ensure

that the Know Your Resident (KYR) standards don't become a barrier for enrolling the poor, and will devise suitable procedures to ensure their inclusion without compromising on the integrity of the data.

- *A partnership model*: The UIDAI approach leverages the existing infrastructure of Government and private agencies across India. The UIDAI will be the regulatory authority managing a Central ID Data Repository (CIDR), which will issue UID numbers, update resident information and authenticate the identity of residents as required.
- *Enrolment will not be mandated*: The UIDAI approach will be a demand-driven one, where the benefits and services that are linked to the UID will ensure demand for the number. This will not, however, preclude Governments or Registrars from mandating enrolment.
- *The UIDAI will issue a number, not a card*: The Authority's role is limited to issuing the number. This number may be printed on the document card that is issued by the Regist ar, Process to ensure no duplicates: Registrars will send the applicant's data to the CIDR for de-duplication. The CIDR will perform a search on key demographic fields and on the biometrics for each new enrolment, to ensure that no duplicates exist.
- *Timelines*: The UIDAI will start issuing UIDs in 12-18 months, and it plans to cover 600 million people within four years from the start of the project. This can be accelerated if more Registrars partner with the Authority for both enrolment and authentication. The adoption of UIDs is expected to gain momentum with time; as the UID number establishes itself as the most accepted identity proof in the country.

National Programme of Mid-day Meals in Schools

Under this programme, the Government has revised the food norm for upper primary children by increasing the quantity of pulses from 25 to 30 g, vegetables from 65 to 75 g and decreasing the quantity, of oil and fat from 10 to 7.5 g. Upward revision of the cooking cost (excluding labour and administrative charges) for primary to Rs. 2.0 and for upper primary to Rs. 3.75 has also been made. The cooking cost now includes the cost of pulses, vegetables, oil and fats, salt and condiments and fuel. A separate provision for payment of an honorarium to a cook-*cum*-helper @ Rs. 1000 per month has been made. Transportation assistance for 11 Special Category States Assam, Arunachal Pradesh, Himachal Pradesh, Jammu & Kashmir, Manipur, Meghalaya, Nagaland, Sikkim, Uttarakhand and Tripura has been revised to the rate prevalent under the Public Distribution System (PDS) in these States in place of the existing assistance at a flat rate of Rs. 125 per quintal. The new rates are effective from December 1, 2009. Besides the cost of construction of kitchen-cum-store has been revised. The cooking cost, honorarium and cost of construction of kitchen-*cum*-store will be shared between the Centre and the north-eastern State/UTs on a 75:25 basis.[28]

Women and Child Development[29]

The Integrated Child Development Services (ICDS) scheme, was launched in 1975 with 33 Projects and 489 Anganwadi Centres (AWCs). It has been continuously expanded to uncovered areas and has now been universalized with the Government of India approving 7,076 projects and 14 lakh AWCs including a provision for 20,000 AWCs on demand. The Scheme has also been revised with respect to cost norms, feeding norms and the sharing pattern between States and the Government of India. Alongside gradual expansion of the Scheme, its budgetary allocation has increased. The Annual Plan outlay for 2009-10 for the ICDS was Rs. 6,705 crore which was enhanced to Rs. 8,162 crore (RE). During 2009-10, an amount of Rs. 5,299.53 crore has been released under the ICDS to States/UTs up to January 14, 2010. Of the total number of 7,073 sanctioned ICDS projects, 6,196 were operational by September 30, 2009. Of 13,56,027 sanctioned AWCs/mini-AWCs, 10,78,973 were operational as on September 30, 2009.

Two schemes are being implemented for the development of adolescent girls, namely the Kishori Shakti Yojana (KSY) and the Nutrition Programme for Adolescent Girls (NPAG). The KSY is an intervention for adolescent girls and aims at addressing the self-development and nutrition and health status needs, literacy and numerical skills and vocational skills of adolescent girls in the age group 11-18 years. The scheme is currently operational in 6,118 ICDS projects. The NPAG is being implemented in 51 identified districts across the country to provide 6 kg. of free foodgrains per beneficiary per month to undernourished adolescent girls (11-19 years) irrespective of financial status of their families. Both the schemes are currently being implemented through the ICDS infrastructure. They will now be subsumed within a new scheme for adolescent girls, namely, the Rajiv Gandhi Scheme for Empowennent of Adolescent Girls also named in SABI. The new Scheme aims at empowering adolescent girls with an improvement in their nutritional and health status and upgrading of a various skills like home, life and vocational skills (for girls aged 16 and above).

The Rajiv Gandhi National Creche Scheme Children of Working Mothers provides for planetary nutrition, emergency medicines and contingencies to children in the age group 0-6 years. Up to March 31, 2009, 31,718 creches with proximately 7,92,950 beneficiaries had been sanctioned to the implementing agencies. The financial norms have been enhanced from Rs. 18,480), Rs. 42,384 per creche per annum. The honorarium to crèche workers has been enhanced on Rs. 800 to Rs. 2000 per month for two creche workers.

The Supplementary Nutrition Component

las been raised from Rs. 1.05 to Rs. 2.08 per childrens day for 25 children for 26 days in a month. The Integrated Child Protection Scheme (ICPS) launched in 2009-10 provides a safe and secure environment for comprehensive development of children in the country who are in need of care and protection as well as children in conflict with the law. The ICPS brings several existing child protozoon programmes under one umbrella with some new interventions. The scheme is now being implemented by the State Governments. The Central Government is providing funds in a pre-defined sharing ratio to the State Governments for setting up and running the various programme components. The budget allocation for the scheme during the Seventh Plan period is Rs. 1,073 aura. A number of States have so far agreed to implement the scheme by signing memorandums of understanding (MOUs) with the Government of India. The Scheme for the Welfare of Walking Children in Need of Care and Protection provides for non-formal education, vocational training, etc. to working children to facilitate their entry/re-entry into mainstream education. There are 121 projects currently being funded wider the Scheme, covering 12,100 children.

A conditional cash transfer scheme, Dhanlakshmi, for the girl child was launched as a pilot project in March 2008. The scheme provides for cash transfers to the family of a girl child on fulfilling certain specific conditionalities relating to birth and registration, immunization and enrolment and retention in schools up to Class

VIII. The scheme is being implemented in 11 blocks across seven States. An amount of Rs. 5.95 crore was released during 2008-09, which is expected to benefit 79,555 girl children in identified blocks of Andhra Pradesh, Chhattisgarh, Orissa, Jharkhand and Punjab. At present, 56 ministries/departments have set-up Gender Budget Cells and 28 ministries departments have reflected allocations for women in the Gender Budget Statement of the Union Budget in 2009-10. The Support to Training and Employment Programme for Women (STEP) seeks to provide, updated skills and new knowledge to poor women in 10 traditional sectors for enhancing their activity and income generation. During the year 1008-09, 31,865 women have benefited from the scheme. Up to December 31, 2009-11 new projects may been sanctioned and 12,866 beneficiaries covered under STEP in 2009-10. As of December 31, 2009, 318 Swadhar homes and 237 helplines are functioning across the country under the Swadhar Scheme which aims to provide the primary needs of shelter, food, clothing and care to marginalized women/girls who are without any social and economic support. The Scheme also seeks to provide them emotional support and counseling and to rehabilitate them socially and economically through education, awareness, skill upgradation and personality development through behavioral training. Ujjawala, a comprehensive scheme for prevention of trafficking and for rescue, rehabilitation, re-integration and repatriation of victims of trafficking for commercial sexual exploitation, was launched in December 2007. During the current year, up to December 31, 2009, financial assistance was provided for 17 new projects to NGOs, taking the total number of approved projects to 96. The total number of rehabilitation centres under these projects went up 1058 as compared to 48 in 2008-09, creating capacity for care and rehabilitation of 2,900 victims of trafficking).

Welfare and Development of SCs, STs, IOBCs and Other Weaker Sections[30]

Programmes for educational development, and economic and social empowerment of socially in advantaged groups and marginalized sections of society are implemented through State Governments, UT Administrations, and NGOs. Public-Private Partnership approach is also one of the strategies for attaining the objective of development of the targeted groups.

The Government is committed towards the educational development of SCs. A number of schemes are being implemented to encourage SC students to continue their studies from school to her education level. During the year 2009-10, the physical target under the Scheme of Pre-Matric Scholarships was about 6.60 lakh beneficiaries students. Against an allocation of Rs. 80 crore, an amount of Rs. 60.99 crore was released to State Governments/UT Administrations for providing scholarships to SC students during the year upto December 31, 2009. The rates of scholarship, annual *ad hoc* grant, pattern of funding and eligibility criteria have been revised with effect from April 1, 2008. Under the Scheme of Post Matric Scholarships the physical target was 38 lakh beneficiaries during 2009-10. Rs. 728.91 crore was released to State Governments/UT Administrations against a revised allocation of Rs. 830 crore up to December 2009 during the financial year. The earlier centrally sponsored scheme of hostels for SC boys and girls was revised and renamed Babu Jagjivan Ram Chhatravas Yojna with effect from January 1, 2008. As part of this revision, Central assistance for the construction of girls hostels was raised from 50 per cent to 100 per cent. During 2009-10, the physical target under the scheme was to construct 44 hostels for girls and 30 hostels for boys. Rs. 5.98 crore was released under the scheme against an allocation of Rs. 90 crore up to December 2009 during the financial year. During 2009-10, an amount of Rs. 80 crore was released by December 2009 as against the revised allocation of 105 crore under the Rajiv Gandhi National Fellowship for SC students for 1,333 new fellowships and 5,332 renewals for SC students pursuing M.Phil. and Ph.D. courses. Scheme of Top Class Education for Scheduled Castes (SCs) provides financial assistance for quality education to SC students up to degree/post-degree level without any burden on the pupil or his/her family. SC students who secure admission in the notified institutions are awarded scholarships. During 2009-10, the amount released up to December 2009 was Rs. 2.83 crore to assist about 1,520 SC students studying in institutions like the IITs and IIMs as against a revised allocation of Rs. 10 crore. The Scheme of National Overseas Scholarships for Scheduled Caste Candidates provides financial assistance to finally selected candidates pursuing master-level courses and Ph.Ds. in engineering, technology and sciences abroad. Thirty awards are given per year. During 2009-10, the amount released was Rs. 0.81 crore as against an allocation of Rs. 5 crore up to December 2009. Special Central assistance is given to the Scheduled Caste Sub-Plan, a major scheme for economic advancement of SCs. During 2009-10, the physical target was to cover 6 lakh beneficiaries. An amount of Rs. 381.60 crore was released to State

Governments/UT Administrations against a revised allocation of Rs. 480 crore up to December 2009. The National Scheduled Castes Finance & Development Corporation provides credit facilities to SC beneficiaries who are living below double the poverty line. During 2009-10, an amount of Rs. 44 crore was released to the Corporation upto December 31, 2009 to enhance its equity to Rs. 1,089 crore. The Corporation has the target of providing loans to about 29,453 beneficiaries during the year. The National Safai Karamcharis Finance & Development Corporation provides credit facilities to safai karamcharis, scavengers and their dependants for income-generating activities through State channelizing agencies. During 2009-10, Rs. 30 crore was provided to enhance the equity of the Corporation to Rs. 260 crore. The target of the Corporation is to benefit 23,270 persons during the year.

Scheduled Tribes (STs)

For the welfare and development of the STs, an outlay of Rs. 3,205 crore has been provided in the Annual Plan for 2009-10, which is 33.82 per cent higher than the outlay of Rs. 2,121 crore for 2008-09. The 2009-10 outlay has a Rs. 900.50 crore component provided as Special Central Assistance (SCA) to the Tribal Sub-Plan (TSP), which includes Rs. 100 crore for development of forest villages. An Additional Central Assistance (ACA) of Rs. 500 core was also provided during 2009-10 for a special initiative of providing residential education to tribal children in Schedule V and Naxal-affected areas. The SCA to the TSP is a 100 per cent grant extended to States as additional funding for family-oriented income-generating schemes, creation of incidental infrastructure, extending financial assistance to self-help groups for community-based activities, and development of forest villages. Grants-in-aid under Article 275 (1) are also being provided to States with an objective to promote the welfare of the STs and improve administration to bring them on par with the rest of the States, and to take up such special welfare and development programmes which are otherwise not included in the Plan programmes. Under the Scheme of Post-Matric Scholarships, 100 per cent financial assistance is provided to ST students whose family income is less than or equal to Rs 1.08 lakh per annum to pursue post-matric level education including professional and graduate and post-graduate courses in recognized institutions. The Scheme of Top Class Education for STs provides financial assistance for quality education to 625 ST students per annum to pursue studies at degree and post degree level in any of the 125 identified institutes. The family income of the beneficiary ST students from all sources should not exceed Rs. 2.00 lakh per annum. Financial assistance is also provided to 15 eligible ST students for pursuing higher studies abroad in specified fields at Masters and Ph.D. level under the National Overseas Scholarship Scheme.

Economic empowerment of the STs by means of extension of financial support through the National Scheduled Tribes Finance and Development Corporation (NSTFDC) continued. Financial support is being extended to ST beneficiaries/entrepreneurs in the form of loans and micro-credit at confessional rates of interest for income-generating activities. The Tribal Cooperative Marketing Development Federation of India Limited (TRIFED) is engaged in marketing development of tribal products and their retail marketing through its sales outlets. The responsibility for implementing the Scheduled Tribes and Other Traditional Forest Dwellers (Recognition of Forest Rights) Act vests with the State/UT Governments. As per information collected from the States till December 31, 2009, more than 26.63 lakh claims have been filed and more than 6.88 lakh titles have been distributed. Around 37,000 titles are ready for distribution. There is great emphasis on the education of ST girls, especially in the low literacy areas and a scheme for Strengthening of Education among ST girls in Low Literacy Districts to bridge the gap in literacy levels between the general female population and tribal women is being implemented.

Five communities, namely Muslims, Christians, Sikhs, Buddhists and Parsis, were notified by the Government as minority communities under section 2(c) of the National Commission for Minorities Act, 1992. As per the 2001 Census, minority communities constitute 18.42 per cent of the total population. For the development of minorities, the Plan outlay was raised from Rs. 100 crore in 2008-09 to Rs. 1,740 crore in 2009-10. Three scholarship schemes have been launched exclusively for the minorities with a total provision of Rs. 450 crore in 2009-10 as against Rs. 305 crore in 2008-09. A multi-sectoral development programme address the development deficits, especially in education. skill development, employment, situation, housing and drinking water, in 90 Monrity Concentration Districts (MCDs) has been launched from 2008-09. The outlay for this programme was Rs. 990 crore in 2009-10. The corpous of the Maulana Azad Education Foundation; (MAEF) has been enhanced from Rs. 100 crore in 2005-06 to Rs. 425 crore in 2009-10 to expand its activities for implementation of educational schemes/educationally backward minorities. The authorized share capital of the National Minorities development & Finance Corporation (NMDFC) has been raised from Rs. 650 crore in 2006-07 to Rs. 750 crore in 2009-10 for expanding its loan and micro finance operations to promote self-employment and other economic ventures among backward sections of the minority communities. Three new Plan schemes, namely, (i) the Maulana Azad National Fellowship for Minority Students, (ii) Computerization of records of State Wakf Boards, (iii) Leadership Development of Minority Women have been launched during 2009-10.

Other Backward Classes (OBCs)

The Government provides central assistance tc State Governments/UT Administrations for educational development of OBCs. During 2009-10, the Scheme of Pre-Matric Scholarships for, CBCs, it was proposed to provide scholarship to 10.80 lakh OBC students. An amount of Rs. 19.32 crore was released against an allocation of Rs. 30 crore to the State Governments/UT Administrations up to December 2009 during the financial year. In order to provide hostel facilities OBC students studying in middle and secondary schools, colleges and universities to enable them pursue higher studies, during 2009-10 an amount Rs. 8.58 crore was released against a revised allocation of Rs. 30 crore for construction of 160 schools out of which 53 are for girls. The National backward Classes Finance & Development corporation extends credit facilities to persons belonging to backward classes for undertaking various income-generating activities including agricultural and allied activities, artisan and additional occupations, technical trades, self-employment, small-scale and tiny industry, small businesses and transport services. During 2009-10, Rs. 35 crore was provided as equity support to the Corporation enhancing its equity to Rs. 765 crore. During the year, the Corporation aims to assist about 1.06 lakh persons.

Persons with Disabilities

A large number of programmes are implemented through national and apex institutes dealing with various categories of disabilities. These institutes conduct short-term and long-term courses for various categories of personnel for providing rehabilitation services to those needing them. Under the scheme of Assistance to the Disabled for Purchase/Fitting of Aids and Appliances (ADIP), approximately 2 lakh persons with disabilities are provided assistive devices every year. During 2009-10, an amount of Rs. 23.02 crore was released to implementing agencies up to December 2009 against a revised allocation of Rs. 70 crore for providing assistive devices to persons with disabilities. The target is to cover 2 lakh persons with disabilities. Rs. 6.79 crore has been released up to December 2009 against a revised allocation of Rs. 92.99 crore during 2009-10 under the Deen Dayal Disabled Rehabilitation Scheme to voluntary organizations for running special schools for children with hearing, visual and mental disability, vocational rehabilitation centres for persons with various disabilities and manpower development in the field of mental retardation and cerebral palsy.

The Scheme of Incentives to Employers in the Private Sector for Providing Employment to Persons with Disabilities was launched with effect from April 1, 2008. Under the Scheme, the Government will have to make payment of the employer's contribution to the Employees Provident Fund and Employees State Insurance for the first three years as an incentive for every employee with disabilities appointed on or after April 1, 2008 with monthly emoluments up to Rs. 25,000. During 2009-10, an amount of Rs. 1 crore was released up to December 2009 against a revised allocation of Rs. 3 crore under the scheme.

The National Handicapped Finance and Development Corporation provides credit facilities for economic empowerment of persons with disabilities with family income not exceeding Rs. 2 lakh in urban areas and Rs. 1.6 lakh in rural areas. The Corporation provides loans at confessional rates of interest to about 5,000 persons with disabilities annually. During 2009-10, an amount of Rs. 9 crore was released as equity support to the Corporation. The target of the Corporation is to provide loans to 7,000 persons with disabilities and training to 555 persons with disabilities during the financial years.[30] (*Economic Survey*, 2009-10)

Thus we find that all the schemes are based on poverty elimination, such programmes also provided welfare and employment to the weaker section including minorities. But there are some flaws and weaknesses at executive level of these welfare and development orientated schemes and against this backdrop the implementing agencies need to rectify it for ensuring better results.

Notes and References

1. Shandilya, T.K., Poverty—A Danger to Prosperity, pp. 82-83. Poverty and Sustainable Development : Concepts and Measures, Iyenger, N.S., Deep & Deep Publications (P) Ltd., New Delhi, p. 290.
2. *Ibid.*, pp. 85-86.